Cornerstone Investors

Books by Philippe Espinasse

Non-fiction
IPO: A Global Guide
IPO Banks: Pitch, Selection and Mandate

As joint author:
Study Manual for the IPO Sponsor Examinations in Hong Kong

As co-author:
The IPO Guide 2012
The Hong Kong IPO Guide 2013

Fiction
Hard Underwriting
The Traveler

Cornerstone Investors

A Practice Guide for Asian IPOs

Philippe Espinasse

HKU PRESS
香港大學出版社

Hong Kong University Press
The University of Hong Kong
Pokfulam Road
Hong Kong
www.hkupress.hku.hk

ISBN 978-988-8455-84-3 (*Hardback*)

British Library Cataloguing-in-Publication Data
A catalogue record for this book is available from the British Library.

10 9 8 7 6 5 4 3 2 1

Printed and bound by Paramount Printing Co. Ltd., Hong Kong, China

Contents

Introduction

Cornerstone investors have now been around for at least 15 years, yet very little has been written about them over that time span, bar the odd academic study or short, factual articles on individual transactions published in the media.

Despite a few attempts to introduce the concept to European markets, cornerstone investors are still essentially a phenomenon limited to three jurisdictions within Asia: Hong Kong, Malaysia, and Singapore. However, they have become so essential to the success of initial public offerings (IPOs) that I thought now was perhaps an opportune time to explain in some detail who they are, as well as the process that is used to gather from them the equity bids that make or break new listings in these marketplaces.

Even though the geographical footprint of cornerstone investors remains limited, the influence they have today on global capital markets activity cannot be ignored, not least because Hong Kong has once again become the world's most active exchange for new equity listings, and cornerstone investors now increasingly dominate demand for IPOs there.

According to InvestHK, a government organization whose remit is to attract and retain foreign direct investment of strategic importance to the economic development of Hong Kong, in 2015, total equity funds raised through IPOs in this special administrative region (SAR) of China amounted to the equivalent of US$33.6 billion. The Stock Exchange of Hong Kong was not only the top stock exchange for IPOs for three consecutive years from 2009 to 2011, but also maintained a top five ranking in the global IPO market for the past decade, thanks almost exclusively to Chinese issuers.[1] According to Reuters, between mid-2015 and mid-2016, cornerstones accounted for about

1. http://www.investhk.gov.hk, accessed 31 August 2016.

50 per cent or more of the deal proceeds for nine out of the top ten IPOs in the territory, underscoring the growing influence of share sales to cornerstone investors in Hong Kong IPOs.[2]

The institutions and corporates who act as cornerstone investors come from a wide range of jurisdictions, from the United States to the United Kingdom, continental Europe, the Middle East, and Australasia, which makes them a truly global phenomenon, well beyond the limited scope of the three markets they have now pervaded. However, cornerstone investors now increasingly come from mainland China, which is fast becoming unavoidable in the commercial and financial sphere, as China slowly, but surely, opens up to the wider world.

In a nutshell, cornerstone investors serve two functions: they de-risk equity transactions for both issuers and the underwriters and, because they are generally well-known stockholders, also encourage a wider pool of market participants to invest in new issues. In many instances, their presence (or, conversely, absence) can actually dictate the success or demise of IPOs.

As with many aspects of new listings, there is often a lot of confusion about cornerstone investors, not just in the media, but also on the part of market participants, be they issuers, investment bankers, or stock pickers. In this guide—the first of its kind—I have sought to clarify the role of cornerstone investors and how they come to subscribe in what are often (but not always) visible and prestigious equity offerings.

Just like my other non-fiction books, this guide is purely a practical one. In these pages, the reader will not find any mathematical formulae, theoretical research, or lengthy legal considerations, but instead clear explanations about the various types of cornerstones and the marketing and documentation processes that are used by investment banks and issuers to secure the commitments made by cornerstone investors, across each of the markets in which they are found.

Accordingly, I have included a wide variety of real-life examples, sample documents (such as a script for the initial approach to potential cornerstone investors, a non-disclosure agreement, and a subscription agreement, all of which were actually used in past IPOs) as well as selected profiles for some 145 institutions and corporates, most of which have already subscribed for

2. Elzio Barreto, 'Hong Kong's cornerstone investors dominate but drain IPOs of vitality', Reuters, 26 June 2016.

equity securities (shares, or units in real estate investment or business trusts), in a cornerstone investor capacity. Readers will also find an investor target list, a comprehensive glossary, and an index to more easily navigate what can be a complex—and even at times daunting—subject.

With any topic related to capital markets, rules and regulations—not to mention market practice—often change. So I would caution readers to seek legal or financial advice, where appropriate, having regard to their specific circumstances. Information included in this book, while generally based on actual transactions, does not in any way convey investment, investment banking, corporate finance, legal, accounting, tax, or other regulatory advice of any kind, and no responsibility whatsoever will be accepted by the author or the publisher in this regard. It should not be relied upon, or used as a substitute for consultation with professional advisers.

As ever, whether you are a prospective IPO candidate, an equity issuer, a capital markets professional, an investment banker, a private equity practitioner, an investor, or a journalist, I am always keen to hear from you. Please do not hesitate to reach out to me through one of my websites.

I hope you will enjoy this new book and that it will contribute to better understanding of the somewhat opaque, and certainly misunderstood, world of equity issuance in Asia—and beyond.

Part 1

Key parameters

1.1

What are cornerstone investors?

Simply put, cornerstone investors are investors who subscribe for shares (or units, in the case of real estate investment trusts—REITs—or business trusts) in an IPO or follow-on equity offering, and who benefit from an allocation of stock that is pre-agreed in advance, both with the lead banks (that is, the global coordinators and bookrunners) and the issuer.

In new issues, it is well known among market participants how difficult it often is to secure a sizeable allocation in a transaction that is well oversubscribed, and therefore likely to be successful in the aftermarket (also assuming that the securities have not been overpriced, and that the book of demand includes a good proportion of 'quality' names, with a long-term investment horizon).

Conversely, investors often receive more than they bargained for (even when their allocation has been scaled back, as compared to their actual order) in offerings that receive poor subscription demand, and that are accordingly likely to experience a fall in the price of the securities after the start of trading.

Cornerstone investors get around the first issue by securing an allocation that is, subject to certain requirements (for example, in Hong Kong, a lock-up restricting them from selling the shares for a period of six months after an IPO), agreed at the outset, and even before the marketing process has started in earnest, so that they know exactly how much stock they will receive, irrespective of the level of subscription of a transaction.

If the bet they make is successful, this means that they will have managed to buy a large chunk of a deal that trades up after listing, potentially generating a substantial capital gain for them, or for the other investors on whose behalf they acquired the shares (as a fiduciary or agent). On the other hand, if they did not read the outcome of the transaction correctly, they could find themselves sitting on a substantial amount of securities while the price of the latter 'tanks' in the aftermarket, selling at a loss, often over, or after a period of time has elapsed. In that sense, the risk they take is similar to that of other IPO investors, although it is perhaps magnified on account of the scale of the investment they make. By contrast, they often stand to make a fair bit more money than other investors in offerings that do well.

It can probably be argued that cornerstone investors generally derive proportionately more benefits than drawbacks from the practice. In 2009, Mr Low Chee Keong, an associate professor in corporate law at the Chinese University of Hong Kong and a former member of the Listing Committee of the Stock Exchange of Hong Kong, published an empirical study on cornerstone investors, in which he concluded that 'despite the supposed risks that are assumed by cornerstone investors, the evidence suggests that these are more perceived than actual'.[1]

1. Low Chee Keong, 'Cornerstone investors and initial public offerings on the Stock Exchange of Hong Kong', *Fordham Journal of Corporate and Financial Law*, Vol. XIV, No. 3, 2009.

1.2

From early beginnings in Europe to three key Asian jurisdictions today

Even though it can now essentially be found in Asia, the concept of cornerstone investor perhaps actually originated in Europe in the 1980s, when the so-called *noyaux durs* (which translates as 'hard cores'), or reference shareholders, were first introduced in French privatizations (starting in 1986, under the then prime minister Édouard Balladur), to ensure that a significant proportion of IPOs—of businesses often essential to the French economy—went to friendly, stable or long-term investors (that is, generally, French corporates and financial institutions), often with no underlying strategic or industrial considerations. According to a French report written in the late 1980s, a minimum of 20 per cent and, often, about 50 per cent of the capital of most French privatized firms of that era was held by a group of 15 to 20 friendly hands.[1] This was, for example, the case for banks Paribas and Société Générale, advertising agency Havas, and engineering company Compagnie Générale d'Électricité (CGE).[2]

Since then, there have been a few additional attempts to introduce cornerstone investors in European transactions, although these have overall remained limited, in comparison with the magnitude of the practice in Asia.

For example, there were three cornerstone investors in the IPO of Aena, the Spanish airport operator, in 2014:

- Corporación Financiera Alba, a holding that owns interests in companies in the retail, media and new technologies, fixed-line and mobile telephone, Internet access, construction, and banking and financial services sectors in Spain;

---

1. *Rapport sur les Opérations de Privatisation* 1989, Vol. 2, 858–863.
2. http://www.ina.fr, 'Exemple: Noyaux durs des privatisées', Institut National de l'Audiovisuel (INA), accessed 23 February 2017.

- Ferrovial, a Spanish multinational company involved in the design, construction, financing, operation, and maintenance of transport, urban, and services infrastructure; and
- The Children's Investment Trust (or TCI), a London-based hedge fund management firm that makes long-term investments in companies globally, founded by Chris Hohn in 2003, and which manages The Children's Investment Master Fund.

These investors had committed to investing subject to different price caps but, ultimately, the IPO, which was initially pulled due to unfavourable market conditions, was priced above the maximum price conditions imposed by two of them.[3]

Other IPOs in Europe in which cornerstone investors have featured have included, among others, those of:

- Kennedy Wilson Europe Real Estate, a property company that invests in real estate across the UK, Ireland, Spain, and Italy, on the London Stock Exchange—the LSE—in 2014;
- Hispania Activos Inmobiliarios and Merlin Properties, both also real estate businesses—on the Madrid Stock Exchange—both in 2014;
- Pershing Square, a closed-end hedge fund—on Euronext Amsterdam—in 2014;
- Lifco, a conglomerate with a diverse universe of businesses, ranging from dental equipment to nuclear power plant machinery, also in 2014; Eltel, a supplier of technical services for infrastructure networks; and Dustin Group, one of the leading Nordic resellers of IT products and additional services to companies, the public sector and private individuals, the latter two in 2015—all on Nasdaq Stockholm; and
- Malin Corporation, a global life sciences company focused on the therapeutics, devices, and diagnostics industries—on the Irish Stock Exchange—in 2015.[4]

---

3. Ross McNaughton and James Cole (Paul Hastings) and David Gossen (Deutsche Bank), 'Cornerstone investments in IPOs. The new normal for European markets?', *PLC Magazine*, September 2015.
4. Ross McNaughton and James Cole (Paul Hastings) and David Gossen (Deutsche Bank), 'Cornerstone investments in IPOs. The new normal for European markets?', *PLC Magazine*, September 2015.

In 2011, cornerstone investors also featured in the US$10 billion equivalent IPO of Swiss commodities trader Glencore, with a dual listing on both the LSE and the Stock Exchange of Hong Kong—or HKEx, but largely on account of the presence of a Hong Kong tranche in the transaction. They included, in particular, the investment arm of the Abu Dhabi government, Aabar Investments, US asset manager BlackRock, and the Singaporean sovereign wealth fund Government of Singapore Investment Corporation (better known as GIC), all of which, together with other funds, subscribed for just under a third of the transaction.[5]

Similar cornerstone activity in Europe could be found more recently, in December 2016, when J.P. Morgan and Italian investment bank Mediobanca attempted to secure cornerstone investor demand to help refinance the ailing Italian bank Monte dei Paschi di Siena. The lead banks next unsuccessfully launched a €5 billion equity capital raising (without the underwriting back-up of cornerstones), before a state bailout and recapitalization of what is Italy's oldest lender finally brought some measure of relief to the country's financial system.[6]

In Europe, and in the UK in particular, the process through which the bookrunner banks target certain leadership investors at an early stage in an IPO is sometimes referred to as 'pilot fishing'.

Despite these few examples, cornerstone investors remain a phenomenon that essentially exists only across three jurisdictions in Asia: Hong Kong, Malaysia, and Singapore. Indeed, as market commentators speculated on the possible listing location(s) for the multibillion dollar IPO of oil giant Saudi Aramco in 2016[7] and early 2017, one of the advantages in favour of Asian exchanges was the possibility of securing demand from cornerstone investors.[8] Accordingly, for the purpose of this book, we will essentially focus on cornerstone allocations in these three markets, since this is where they can, first and foremost, be found.

---

5. John West and Anjali Piramal, 'Cornerstone IPO structure may be Asia's latest export', *Financial Times*, 15 March 2013.
6. Tyler Davies, 'Monte places €7bn of bonds in drive to improve liquidity', *GlobalCapital*, 26 January 2017.
7. Dinesh Nair, Ruth David, Andrea Tan and Joyce Koh, 'Singapore said to plan slew of incentives to lure Aramco listing', Bloomberg, 6 February 2017.
8. Philippe Espinasse, 'From the Kingdom to the Middle Kingdom', *GlobalCapital*, 10 May 2016.

There have been countless IPOs on HKEx, *Bursa Malaysia* (that is, the Kuala Lumpur Stock Exchange), and the SGX (the Singapore Exchange) in which cornerstones have appeared. In Asia, cornerstone investors were first introduced in the late 1990s and early 2000s, following the Asian financial crisis of 1997, and essentially to provide impetus with brand-name investors to what was then a moribund primary equity market. Examples of such cornerstone tranches can be found in Appendices 1, 2, 3, and 4 herein.

Unlike now, however, not all large IPOs in these markets at that time included cornerstones. For example, there were no cornerstones in the US$4.3 billion IPO of the Tracker Fund of Hong Kong, the first ever privatization in the territory—and an open-end passive exchange-traded fund (ETF). Similarly, cornerstones did not feature in the US$1.4 billion privatization IPO of MTR Corporation, the operator of the mass transit railway (and a major property developer) in Hong Kong, which was also one of the largest new offerings of that era in the city. Nowadays, however, it would be pretty much unthinkable to launch a sizeable IPO without at least trying to secure cornerstone investor demand.

1.3

Cornerstone tranches or corporate placings?

IPOs in Hong Kong, Malaysia, and Singapore feature offers to both institutional investors (also known as placings, placements, and international offerings or tranches) and domestic retail investors (which are also called public offers).

For example, in Hong Kong, it is a requirement under the Listing Rules that the offer structure of an IPO on the Main Board of the exchange includes a public offer if it is likely that there will be significant public demand for the securities. In practice, IPOs in each of the three markets that we will look at always include public offers, since this is the only practical way to achieve the minimum number of shareholders necessary to satisfy the listing criteria laid out by their respective stock exchanges. And, in all these three markets, the public offer usually takes place concurrently with, and in the last few days of the institutional offer.

The only exception to the rule is in Singapore, where issuers and their lead banks have the alternative option of structuring IPOs with sequential retail offers, that is, when the public offer follows the institutional offering and determination of the IPO price. In other words, in such cases (which are, in any event, rare nowadays), the retail portion of the IPO is conducted at a fixed price, and after such price has been determined based on institutional demand only. The reason why this is possible is that retail tranches in Singapore are usually small, and only account for around 5 to 10 per cent at most of the overall IPO size, so a transaction there can more easily be priced based on institutional investor demand only. On 8 March 2017, the SGX actually mandated a minimum allocation of 5 per cent of the offer size (or S$50 million, whichever is lower) of Main Board IPOs to retail investors, to encourage members of the public to consider equity investing.[1] By contrast,

1. http://www.sgx.com, accessed 8 March 2017.

in Hong Kong, except in the case of very large IPOs, the minimum allocation to retail investors is 10 per cent, but this can increase to up to 50 per cent of the entire deal, thanks to automatic clawback triggers (which I will explain in detail later).

For a listing on the Main Board of HKEx, the equity securities in the hands of the public must be held among at least 300 holders.[2] For a listing on the Main Market of Bursa Malaysia, 25 per cent of the shares sought for listing must be owned by at least 1,000 public shareholders, holding not less than 100 shares each.[3] And to secure a listing on the Main Board of the SGX, a minimum spread of 500 shareholders is required.[4] In all three cases, it would be wholly impractical to achieve such numbers by allocating stock to institutional investors only, even in the case of a billion (US-dollar) IPO.

In Hong Kong and Malaysia, securities allocated to cornerstone investors explicitly form part of the institutional tranche of IPOs, even if the treatment of cornerstones by the underwriters is somewhat different from that of other institutional investors, as we will see later. Conversely, in Singapore, cornerstone investors are technically considered to be outside the scope of the IPO offering itself (with the cornerstone tranche being treated as a separate, but concurrent offering).[5] However, this is for technical, legal, and regulatory reasons only. To all intents and purposes, in all three markets, cornerstone investors typically fall within the ambit of professional, institutional, or accredited investors (including high and ultra-high net worth individuals).

Cornerstone tranches have not always been known by that name: as we have already seen, they were at one point called *noyaux durs* in France (although that practice has now subsided). In both the Hong Kong IPOs of Industrial and Commercial Bank of China (ICBC) in 2006 and Agricultural Bank of China (ABC) in 2010, the IPO prospectuses referred to a 'corporate placing' instead, even if the cornerstone investors in these transactions actually included a majority of banks, insurance companies, sovereign wealth funds, and high net worth individuals, or tycoons, rather than *bona fide* industrial corporations.

---

2. http://www.hkex.com.hk, accessed 1 September 2016.
3. Baker & McKenzie, Cross-Border Listings Handbook 2013.
4. http://www.sgx.com, accessed 1 September 2016.
5. Tze-Gay Tan and Jeanne Ong, 'Cornerstone investors in IPOs—an Asian perspective', *Capital Markets Law Journal*, Vol. 8, No. 4, August 2013.

In the past, a distinction was also sometimes made between cornerstone and other investors that were seen as 'strategic'. For example, in connection with its IPO, ICBC had established non-exclusive 'strategic' cooperations with Goldman Sachs, Allianz, and American Express, as part of its efforts to accelerate its corporate governance reform and business development.[6] These were separate from the agreements entered into with cornerstone investors.

On occasion, however, the distinction was rather tenuous: in the IPO of ABC, the issuer had actually entered into such cooperation agreements with several of the cornerstone investors themselves. For example, it had entered into a non-binding memorandum of understanding (MoU) with Archer-Daniels-Midland, an American processor of feedstuffs, food, feed ingredients, and agricultural commodities, which 'set out the parties' mutual intentions with respect to the establishment of a long-term and mutually beneficial cooperation relationship'. It had also entered into such a non-binding MoU with Qatar Investment Authority, which 'set out the principles upon which the parties wished to develop and strengthen their strategic economic cooperation'. Further MoUs or 'sets of key principles relating to cooperation' were entered into at the same time between ABC and Rabobank Nederland, Standard Chartered Bank, and Seven Group (an Australian media corporation controlled by local tycoon Kerry Stokes), all of which were cornerstone investors in ABC's IPO.[7]

In practice, cornerstone tranches and corporate placings are effectively the same thing, and the investments made by cornerstones are usually (although, as we have just seen, not exclusively) made with financial interests and/or speculative objectives in mind.

6. Prospectus for the Hong Kong IPO of Industrial and Commercial Bank of China Limited, 16 October 2006.
7. Prospectus for the Hong Kong IPO of Agricultural Bank of China Limited, 30 June 2010.

1.4

Differences with pre-IPO investors

Cornerstone investors, however, differ from what are known as pre-IPO investors in several ways.

First, cornerstones always commit to buying shares (or units) *in* an IPO or follow-on equity offering. By contrast, investments made by pre-IPO investors—which are often private equity firms or the principal investment arms of investment banks—usually (although not always) take the form of debt securities, which are in turn convertible into shares or other equity securities upon the later listing of the company on a stock exchange.

That way, if for some reason the IPO does not happen, the pre-IPO investors can get their money back upon maturity of the debt (plus interest, together with, possibly, a penalty amount). They will also rank higher than shareholders in the event of a liquidation of the business. This is obviously a mechanism designed to protect their investment in a company that is still at a relatively early stage of development.

Second, the price paid by pre-IPO investors and cornerstone investors is also different. Cornerstone investors subscribing in an IPO actually pay the same price as any other institutional investors (and also, in most cases, retail investors, although in some rare transactions, investors subscribing under the public offer tranche benefit from a discount, as compared to the price paid by institutions). So the price paid by cornerstones is actually the IPO price (also known as the offer price).

Therefore, the only advantage that cornerstone investors have is a guaranteed allocation which, as we have already seen, can actually turn out to be a pretty good deal for them in a transaction that performs well after listing.

Conversely, pre-IPO investors normally buy securities at a discount to the IPO price. For example, this would be the so-called 'conversion premium' to which they are entitled, in the case of a pre-IPO investment made through a convertible bond. However, in Hong Kong (only), any price adjustment provisions (for example a guaranteed discount to the IPO price, perhaps by way of an adjustment linked to the market capitalization of the shares, such as a re-set provision in a convertible bond) are no longer allowed under the Listing Rules for pre-IPO investments.

This is because it would effectively create two different prices for the same securities for pre-IPO investors and other shareholders at the time of the new listing, and is accordingly seen as potentially disruptive for the IPO. As we have seen, this is obviously debatable since retail investors can, on occasion, benefit from such a discount to the offer price when applying for shares in an IPO—although this is increasingly no longer the case.

The main reason why pre-IPO investors buy at a discount to the IPO price is by way of compensation, because their investment is usually made at a much earlier stage. By contrast, while cornerstone investors subscribe for securities before an IPO is marketed to the wider universe of investors and the management roadshow starts, their subscription agreements are usually signed in a relatively short space of time—a couple of weeks at most, and often only a few days—beforehand, and their shares are actually delivered at the same time as those of all the other participants in the IPO.

In turn, pre-IPO investments are usually made months (and sometimes even years, in the case of private equity shareholders) before the actual launch of an IPO. For example, in Hong Kong, under the Listing Rules, pre-IPO investments must be completed either by no later than 28 days before the first submission of the listing application to the exchange (which, under the new IPO sponsor regime, would be at least a month, and in most cases probably two or more months, before the start of the marketing phase for the offering), or 180 clear days before the expected first day of trading in the securities on offer. Such pre-IPO investments are considered completed when the funds are irrevocably settled and received by the issuer.[1]

Any investment made closer to an IPO would not therefore be considered as a pre-IPO investment, and would need to be made under the IPO itself, either by way of an order placed in the book of demand, or through a cornerstone investor subscription.

Finally, pre-IPO investors, in contrast to cornerstone investors who are only entitled to a guaranteed allocation, may also be offered special rights.

---

1. HKEx guidance letter HKEX-GL43-12, October 2012, updated in July 2013.

Such rights, usually granted on account of the early nature of their investment, effectively represent an unequal treatment of shareholders, and are therefore generally not allowed to survive the listing—with a few exceptions.

Examples of special rights that may be granted to pre-IPO investors, although, again, not to cornerstone investors,[2] may include some or all of the following:

- **Put or exit options**: These are granted to pre-IPO investors to put back their investments to the issuer or its controlling shareholder. They are generally only allowed when the terms of a pre-IPO investment clearly state that such put or exit option can only be exercised when the proposed listing does not take place.
- **Director nomination rights**: Any directors that may be nominated under such rights are normally subject to retirement and reappointment requirements under the company's articles of association after listing.
- **Veto rights**: These may include, for example, contractual rights to exercise veto power over some of the major corporate actions to be made by the company, such as the making of a petition or passing of a resolution for winding-up; the carrying on of businesses other than the business being carried on by the company; or the amalgamation or merger by any member of the group with any other company or legal entity, etc. Such rights must usually be terminated upon listing.
- **Anti-dilution rights**: These would include, for example, preferential rights to purchase additional securities to be issued by the company in the IPO, so as to maintain a certain percentage of shareholding in the company. Such rights must be terminated upon listing.
- **Profit guarantees**: Under such guarantees, pre-IPO investors may be entitled to compensation if a company's profit does not meet a certain threshold in the future, except where such compensation is linked to the market price or market capitalization of the shares (as already mentioned above).
- **Negative pledges**: These would include, for example, provisions not to create or effect any mortgage, charge, pledge, lien, or other security interest on a company's assets and revenues, or not to dispose of any interest in the economic rights or entitlements of a share the controlling

2. HKEx guidance letter HKEX-GL43-12, October 2012, updated in July 2013.

shareholder owns or controls. Any pledges that remain after listing must usually be in line with normal terms of debt issues.

- **Prior consent for certain corporate actions or changes in articles**: This may include, for example, a declaration of dividend by any member of the group; the sale, lease, or transfer of a substantial part of the company's business or assets; any amendments to constitutional documents; or any change in executive directors. Such terms must normally be removed before listing unless the issuer can demonstrate that the relevant terms do not disadvantage other shareholders.
- **Exclusivity rights (and no more favourable terms)**: These may include rights to the effect that the company is not allowed to issue or offer any shares, options, warrants, and rights to any direct competitor of the pre-IPO investor, or to other investors on terms more favourable than the terms on which the securities are issued to the pre-IPO investor. Such rights are usually only allowed where the investment agreement includes an explicit 'fiduciary out' clause—so that directors are allowed to ignore the terms if complying with them would constitute a breach of their fiduciary duties (that is, the directors must not be prevented from exercising their judgement to ascertain whether certain corporate actions are in the best interest of the company).
- **Information rights**: These are usually only allowed when the pre-IPO investor receives published information or information that is at the same time made available to the general public, with a view to avoiding unequal dissemination of information—unless safe harbours apply.
- **Representation and attendance rights**: These may include rights to nominate senior management and committee representatives and these are contractually granted to pre-IPO investors. Because such appointments are subject to the decision of the board of the company, the directors are not contractually obligated to approve pre-IPO investor nominations without further review, since they owe fiduciary duties to all shareholders.
- **Rights of first refusal or tag-along rights**: Under this category would be rights whereby the controlling shareholder of a company may grant a right of first refusal to a pre-IPO investor, so that the controlling shareholder must first offer to sell shares to the pre-IPO investor at the same price and on the same terms and conditions as a proposed sale of shares to a third party purchaser. If the pre-IPO investor does not exercise its right of first

refusal, it is then permitted to include its shares for sale together—that is, to tag along—with the shares of the controlling shareholder as part of the sale to the third party purchaser. Such rights can normally survive the listing since they are purely contractual rights between two shareholders.

- **Compensation provisions in the event that the company does not get admitted to listing within a specified period of time**: Such rights are generally allowed if the amount to be compensated is set out in the investment agreement or can be derived from the compensation provisions under the agreement.

The above rules addressing special rights surviving an IPO (or not, as the case may be) are specific to the Asian jurisdictions in which cornerstones can be found (and to Hong Kong in particular, for some of them). However, since there are no specific regulations in Europe covering cornerstone investments, there have been examples where cornerstone investors there have benefitted from advantages beyond and above a simple guaranteed allocation.

For example, in the IPO of Merlin Properties in Spain, which we have already briefly mentioned, two cornerstone investors were each entitled to nominate a board member, so long as they owned at least 3 per cent of the issuer's share capital for one year after the IPO. Similarly, the largest cornerstone in the IPO of Eltel in Sweden in 2015 was entitled to nominate a board member at the first AGM following the listing of the company.[3] Finally, in the IPO of Aena, also in Spain, two of the cornerstones had placed orders subject to different price caps, which is clearly different from market practice in Asia.

In Asia, the general rule remains that cornerstone investors should not have any special rights or advantages, other than the guaranteed allocations which they receive. Where such advantages exist, these investors are instead normally reclassified as pre-IPO investors (provided that the investment is being made early enough) and, as mentioned, any special advantages or privileges normally terminate upon listing and the start of trading.[4]

---

3. Ross McNaughton and James Cole (Paul Hastings) and David Gossen (Deutsche Bank), 'Cornerstone investments in IPOs: The new normal for European markets?', *PLC Magazine*, September 2015.
4. HKEx guidance letter HKEX-GL43-12, October 2012, updated in July 2013.

1.5

Types of cornerstone investors and the US option

There are many types of cornerstone investors and they come from a variety of countries around the world.

It should be noted, however, that US onshore institutions may only be included as cornerstone investors if the offer structure for the IPO in question includes a Rule 144A private placement to Qualified Institutional Buyers (QIBs), that is, in effect, large institutions in the US.

This also enables the management of the issuer to visit the US as part of the roadshow, which is conducted simultaneously with the institutional bookbuilding exercise. Failing this, US institutions may only participate through offshore vehicles, in what is known as a Regulation S (Reg. S) tranche. Generally, all or most of the IPOs above, say, US$250 million, include a Rule 144A private placement.

While some larger IPOs are sometimes not marketed to QIBs under Rule 144A (for example, in 2011, the US$890 million equivalent IPO on Bursa Malaysia of Malaysian offshore services provider to the oil and gas industry Bumi Armada was only marketed internationally pursuant to Reg. S), it is generally a good idea to include that option under the offer structure, since it considerably widens the pool of institutions that may be targeted as potential cornerstone investors (and/or other potential institutional buyers under the IPO).

Conversely, the drawbacks of doing so are the necessary involvement of US legal advisers, a somewhat more comprehensive disclosure regime (although this is less true nowadays than perhaps ten years ago) and, of course, potential liability of the issuer to US parties, who are generally known to be more litigious than investors from other jurisdictions.

1.5.1 Sovereign wealth funds

At the outset, cornerstone investors have included a number of well-known sovereign wealth funds, often from the Middle East. For example, Kuwait Investment Authority (KIA), an autonomous government body of Kuwait responsible for the management and administration of funds and assets entrusted to it by the Ministry of Finance of Kuwait, featured as a cornerstone investor in the Hong Kong IPOs of ICBC in 2006, ABC in 2010, as well as that of insurer AIA Group, again in 2010. It was also a cornerstone in the IPO of hospital owner and operator IHH Healthcare in Malaysia and Singapore, in 2012.

Qatar Investment Authority (QIA), through its strategic and direct investment arm Qatar Holding LLC, similarly invested in the IPOs of ICBC and ABC, as well as the IPO of oil palm plantation owner Felda Global Ventures in Malaysia in 2012.

Other sovereign wealth funds include Norway's Norges Bank Investment Bank Management, China Investment Corporation (CIC), the Abu Dhabi Investment Authority (ADIA), the Oman Investment Fund, Singapore's Temasek Holdings and Government of Singapore Investment Corporation (GIC), and Khazanah Nasional Berhad, the investment arm of the government of Malaysia. All of them have regularly featured as cornerstone investors, but usually only in the more sizeable IPOs.

It should be noted that the sovereign wealth funds from the Middle East in particular are thought to be interested only in large cornerstone participations, with individual tickets of at least US$100 million and, generally, a high multiple of that number. QIA invested the equivalent of US$2.8 billion in the IPO of ABC, while KIA subscribed for US$720 million in the IPO of ICBC and US$1 billion in that of AIA. Even in a (relatively) smaller IPO such as that of IHH Healthcare (whose offer size was approximately US$2 billion, pre-exercise of the overallotment option), KIA subscribed for more than US$130 million equivalent, making it one of only two cornerstone investors to subscribe for more than 5 per cent of the share capital of the company.

1.5.2 Supranational entities

More rarely, supranational entities can also be found as cornerstone investors. For example, the International Finance Corporation (IFC), a member of the World Bank Group, was a cornerstone investor in the IPO of IHH Healthcare.

1.5.3 Tycoons and ultra-high net worth individuals

Cornerstone investors initially also included a number of tycoons, or ultra-high net worth (UHNW) individuals, especially in Hong Kong IPOs. Examples include Mr Li Ka-shing, the richest person in Hong Kong, who has often invested through companies he controls, such as Cheung Kong (Holdings) or Hutchison Whampoa; Mr Cheng Yu-tung (deceased in 2016), who controlled Chow Tai Fook and New World Development; Mr Yung Chi-kin, the former chairman of CITIC Pacific; Mr Robert Kuok Hock-nien, the founder of the Kuok Group, which includes Kerry Properties and the Shangri-La hotel chain; Mr Peter Woo Kwong-ching, the chairman of Wheelock and The Wharf; and Mr Lee Shau-kee, a Hong Kong–based real estate tycoon and majority owner of Henderson Land, a conglomerate with interests in properties, hotels, restaurants, and Internet services.

Tycoons investing in IPOs as cornerstone investors are not limited to Hong Kong. Mr Chua Ma-yu from Malaysia has also featured, through his vehicle CMY Capital, as has Mr Gordon Tang from Singapore.

Such UHNW individuals generally invest through companies or special-purpose vehicles (SPVs), often incorporated offshore, in jurisdictions such as the British Virgin Islands (BVI) and the Cayman Islands. These have come under increasing scrutiny in Europe, following the leaks and disclosure of clients of Panamian law firm Mossack Fonseca, but, in Asia, the majority of cornerstone investors—and indeed even Chinese IPO issuers in Hong Kong—continue to be incorporated in such offshore jurisdictions.

1.5.4 Insurance companies

Also frequently subscribing as cornerstone investors in new issues are insurance companies. Examples include Hong Kong's AIA Group (which invested in the IPO of Far East Hospitality Trust in Singapore in 2012), mainland China insurer China Re (which was a cornerstone in the Hong Kong IPOs of China Development Bank Financial Leasing and China Merchants Securities in 2016), and Singapore's Great Eastern (a member of the Singaporean OCBC banking group), which bought into the IPO of energy company Malakoff in Malaysia, in 2015.

Insurance companies, and life insurance companies in particular, need to match long-term liabilities with assets of a similar maturity, so are generally known to have a long-term investment horizon, which makes them ideal targets to invest in a cornerstone investor capacity.

1.5.5 Pension funds

Again with a particularly long-term investment horizon—for obvious reasons—are pension funds. Examples include Kumpulan Wang Persaraan (Diperbadankan) (also known as KWAP), which manages the pension contributions of Malaysian civil servants and employees of statutory bodies and local authorities in Malaysia; and the Employees Provident Fund Board (EPF), also in Malaysia, which provides retirement benefits for members through the management of their savings.

1.5.6 Social security organizations, charities, and similar institutions

A number of social security organizations, charities, and similar institutions have also featured as cornerstones, particularly in Southeast Asia.

These have included Lembaga Tabung Haji (LTH) in Malaysia, whose functions are to administer the depositors' fund and all matters concerning the welfare of pilgrims (to Mecca); and Permodalan Nasional Berhad (PNB), also in Malaysia, which is an investment institution with a diverse portfolio of activities that include unit trust funds, property trust funds, property management, and asset management, and which was initially established to promote share ownership in the corporate sector among *Bumiputera* (that is, ethnic Malays).

1.5.7 Asset managers, 'long only' funds, and banks

Of course, traditional asset managers and, in particular, 'long only' funds (that is, a type of institutional investor known for its stable, long-term investment horizon, and for not using short-position hedging, unlike many hedge or alternative funds) are frequently seen too.

These have included, among others, CIMB Principal, Maybank Asset Management, and RHB Asset Management in Malaysia; BlackRock, Capital Group, Fidelity, and Wellington in the US; JF Asset Management (the Asia-Pacific equity investment arm of J.P. Morgan Asset Management), and Guoco Management and Value Partners in Hong Kong; and Aberdeen in Singapore.

Some of these funds also specialize in certain industry sectors. For example, APG Strategic Real Estate Pool in the Netherlands focuses more particularly on property and property-related investments.

Often times, such asset managers are owned by banks, such as Bank of China Group Investment Limited (BOCGI), the direct investment and fund management business of the Bank of China; and BOCOM Investment, an indirect wholly owned subsidiary of China's Bank of Communications.

Finally, although more rarely, the wealth management arms of banks have sometimes made cornerstone investments on behalf of private banking clients. DBS Bank invested the equivalent of US$36 million in the Singapore IPO of Keppel DC REIT in 2014, on behalf of such customers. However, investments by private banks are often considered relatively volatile and, in some cases, such institutions probably would not be chosen in a cornerstone capacity by the lead banks—at least not as primary targets.

1.5.8 Hedge funds

In addition to long only funds are hedge funds. The streamlined decision-making process of these alternative investment managers often makes them particularly well suited to investing in IPOs, where committing substantial amounts of money in what can be a relatively short space of time is often necessary. Names that have frequently appeared have included Havenport, Indus, Myriad, and, especially, Och-Ziff.

1.5.9 Corporate investors

Increasingly, however, cornerstone investors include corporates.

For example, Kencana, an investment holding company in Malaysia with a diversified investment portfolio ranging from oil and gas, engineering and construction to information technology services, education and training, as well as real estate, has featured a number of times in IPOs in Southeast Asia.

However, it is first and foremost in Hong Kong that corporates have been included as cornerstones in IPOs, especially in transactions by issuers from the Chinese mainland, who now also account for the vast majority of IPOs priced on HKEx (as well as across Asia, excluding Japan).

Sometimes, although not often, the industry sector of these corporates is similar, or at least relatively closely related, to that of the issuer. For example, as mentioned earlier, Archer-Daniels-Midland Company was a cornerstone in the Hong Kong IPO of Agricultural Bank of China in 2010. In turn, The Boeing Company invested as a cornerstone in the Hong Kong IPO of aircraft operating and leasing company BOC Aviation Limited in May 2016. Brazil's biggest producer of processed food, BRF (formerly known as Brazil Foods), also signed up as a cornerstone investor in the US$252 million Hong Kong IPO of COFCO Meat Holdings, which promotes large-scale hog farms and safe meat production in China, that same year.[1] Similarly, in its US$1.8 billion Hong Kong IPO in October 2016, China Resources Pharmaceutical Group lined up cornerstone investors who could actually benefit from its manufacturing of, and distribution network for drugs. They included Reckitt Benckiser, the maker of Durex condoms and Nurofen; Japan's Fujifilm, which morphed into a healthcare giant after first starting as a photography company; and Guangdong Hengjian Investment Holding, a supplier of medical devices, among other activities.[2]

In addition, such corporates appear to ever more be from the People's Republic of China, largely unrelated to the business activities of the issuer and, more often than not, state-owned enterprises (or SOEs). As of September 2016, mainland Chinese companies had provided 71 per cent of cornerstone

1. Jonathan Breen, 'COFCO Meat bags Brazilian cornerstone, JNBY opens IPO', *GlobalCapital*, 19 October 2016.
2. Joh Loh, 'Kaboom! CR Pharma listing fetches $1.8bn', *GlobalCapital*, 21 October 2016; Nisha Gopalan, 'Hong Kong IPOs' health shot', Bloomberg, 24 October 2016.

money that year, up from 55 per cent only two years before, according to an analysis conducted by Dealogic.[3]

This is especially true for the larger offerings. In 2015, according to Bloomberg, government buyers represented 62 per cent of the cornerstone shares in Hong Kong IPOs of US$1 billion equivalent or more.[4] In the first eight months of 2016, only a handful of international (that is, non-Chinese) institutional names came up as cornerstones in Hong Kong. They included Prudential Insurance of the US (in the IPO of Everbright Securities); Value Partners (in the flotation of Chinese broker DFZQ); and Oman Investment Fund and Fullerton (both in the offering by BOC Aviation)—out of a total of 61 cornerstones, a proportion of only 6.5 per cent by number.[5]

China Shipbuilding Industry Corporation (or CSIC), through a wholly owned subsidiary, made a US$184 million cornerstone subscription in the Hong Kong IPO of Everbright Securities in 2016. CSIC is a very large state-owned enterprise in China, authorized by the PRC central government to engage in investment and capital management, and was also a Fortune Global 500 company for six consecutive years. It owns a group of competitive enterprises specialized in the manufacturing and repair of marine equipment and research and development institutions in China. Arguably, its business is clearly different from that of Everbright Securities, one of China's largest securities brokerages as ranked by assets, and controlled by state-owned financial conglomerate China Everbright Group.

In that same IPO, China State Construction Engineering Corporation (or CSCE) (again, indirectly) invested the same amount as CSIC. CSCE is one of the largest construction and real estate conglomerates in China and is principally engaged in housing construction, infrastructure construction and investment, real estate development and investment, design, and prospecting, all businesses largely unrelated to the securities industry.

One issue with industrial corporations acting as cornerstone investors is that they are not ordinarily in the business of buying or selling securities, and their inclusion is usually done purely as a form of insurance to get the deal done. While they may enable a significant portion of a transaction to

3. Jennifer Hughes, 'Issues stack up with Hong Kong IPO cornerstones', *Financial Times*, 6 September 2016.
4. Fox Hu, 'Public goes missing from Hong Kong IPOs as state giants buy', Bloomberg, 13 November 2015.
5. Philippe Espinasse, 'Cornerstone summer party', *GlobalCapital*, 6 September 2016.

be covered by investor demand at an early stage, they will not top up their cornerstone allocations in the aftermarket, unlike institutional investors.

In fact, government-backed companies are not actually allowed to trade in the secondary market under Chinese law. For that reason, it is often the case that, when cornerstone tranches principally comprise of corporates, rather than professional investors (as is increasingly the case in Hong Kong), the share price performance of these IPOs after listing can be disappointing.

In 2014, Bloomberg reviewed the performance of 18 Hong Kong IPOs worth more than US$200 million each. Seven deals with international institutions as cornerstones gained on average 9.4 per cent from their offer prices, while 11 offerings with only Chinese cornerstones—by and large, all corporates—or none at all, dropped 9.9 per cent on average.[6]

Another concern associated with corporate cornerstone investors is to do with liquidity. According to the *Financial Times*, from mid-2014 to mid-2016, the proportion of institutional investors among cornerstone investors dropped from almost a third to only 11 per cent in Hong Kong IPOs. As a result, trading in those IPOs that each represented the equivalent of at least US$500 million accounted for only 4 per cent of the value of the free float per month, and those with a large proportion of cornerstone investors traded even less actively. By contrast, daily trading in New York hovered around the 13 per cent mark over the same period.[7]

In September 2016, *FinanceAsia* conducted a survey among market participants in the region, asking them whether cornerstone tranches had become too big in Hong Kong IPOs. More than 85 per cent of the respondents agreed, saying that it had become a market-wide problem,[8] largely on account of corporate investors.

Selected profiles of cornerstone investors, including a number of corporates and Chinese state-owned enterprises, are included in Appendix 8.

6. Fox Hu, 'Public goes missing from Hong Kong IPOs as state giants buy', Bloomberg, 13 November 2015.
7. Jennifer Hughes, 'Issues stack up with Hong Kong IPO cornerstones', *Financial Times*, 6 September 2016.
8. http://www.financeasia.com, accessed 28 September 2016.

1.6

Individual subscription amounts

Like the type of investors, the amounts for which individual cornerstone investors subscribe in IPOs (or, indeed, albeit more rarely, in follow-on offerings) also vary greatly.

At one end of the spectrum are single-digit amounts in millions of US dollars. For example, this would include the US$6.4 million subscribed by Prestigious Leader, an investment holding company; and the US$5 million subscribed by Sichuan Huifeng, another professional investor from the PRC, both in the US$41 million Hong Kong IPO of Sinco Pharmaceuticals in 2016.

At the other end of the scale are individual subscriptions of US$1 billion or more made by sovereign wealth funds from the Middle East, such as KIA and QIA, in the multibillion dollar IPOs and privatizations of Chinese state-owned banks in Hong Kong in the mid to late 2000s.

The individual amounts subscribed for depend of course in no small measure on the size of the company and IPO, as well as the nature of each investor. As outlined earlier, major funds from the Middle East are usually only interested in very large investments, in what are *de facto* multibillion dollar transactions.

Generally, however, the bookrunners will probably look at individual commitments in the region of US$50 million in the case of an IPO of US$1 billion or more, and perhaps half of that amount for more modest equity offerings. Only in the smaller IPOs would one normally find much lower individual subscription amounts.

Examples of amounts subscribed by individual cornerstone investors in IPOs in Hong Kong, Malaysia, and Singapore can be found in Appendices 1, 2, 3, and 4.

1.7

How many cornerstones are in an IPO?

Just like the individual subscription amounts, the number of cornerstone investors assembled to anchor an IPO varies significantly.

In smaller IPOs, the number will generally be in single digits and probably below five, so as to ensure enough liquidity in the aftermarket, since cornerstone investors are generally (although not always) shareholders with a relatively long-term investment horizon. In addition, cornerstone investors in Hong Kong must each abide by a six-month lock-up, which puts further strain on the aftermarket liquidity of IPOs.

For example, in the IPO of Sinco Pharmaceuticals (mentioned in the previous chapter), there were only two cornerstone investors since the IPO size was only just above US$40 million.

In larger deals, the number of cornerstone investors will often be greater. For example, in 2016, the US$1 billion Hong Kong IPO of DFZQ, a brokerage house from mainland China, accommodated 10 cornerstone investors, and there were no fewer than 22 cornerstone investors (the largest number of cornerstones ever assembled in an IPO at the time) in the US$2 billion (before exercise of the overallotment option) new listing of hospital operator IHH Healthcare in Malaysia and Singapore in 2012.

Usually, in the case of a sizeable offering, a large number of target investors (perhaps up to 50 or so) will be contacted at the outset of the process. Ultimately, however, the number of investors who actually decide to subscribe as cornerstones will normally only represent a fraction of that initial number, following discussions with the bookrunners and due diligence.

The process of gathering cornerstone investors will be discussed in detail in Part 3 below.

1.8

Tranche sizes and the question of liquidity

Cornerstone tranche sizes, that is the amount allocated to the cornerstone investor group in an IPO, is obviously a function of the individual subscription amounts received and the number of investors who ultimately choose to subscribe in the offering.

A key objective of the lead banks is always to de-risk the transaction, and therefore to have an (ideally) significant proportion of the IPO or follow-on offering already subscribed at the outset of the marketing process. Generally, that amount will be in the order of at least 30 per cent of the deal, but the size of the cornerstone tranche can on occasion be much larger.

For example, in 2016, the six cornerstone investors in the US$795 million IPO in Hong Kong of China Development Bank Financial Leasing subscribed for an astonishingly high 78.7 per cent of the deal (pre-overallotment option). Much of this was due to a single subscription (for the equivalent of US$335 million) by Three Gorges Capital. Also in 2016, six cornerstone investors, all corporates, took approximately 77 per cent of the much larger, US$7.4 billion equivalent IPO of China Postal Savings Bank in Hong Kong. They included a subsidiary of CSIC and Shanghai International Port Group for almost US$2.1 billion and just over US$2 billion, respectively; Victory Global Group, a unit of aviation conglomerate HNA Group for US$1 billion; and State Grid Corp. of China, the world's largest utility, for US$300 million. State-owned China Chengtong Holdings Group (US$150 million) and Great Wall Pan Asia Asset Management (US$100 million) also purchased stock in the offering as cornerstones.[1]

1. Fiona Lau and Elzio Barreto, 'China Postal Savings Bank $8.1 billion IPO mostly covered by cornerstone investors', Reuters, 12 September 2016; and Jun Luo and Fox Hu, 'China's Postal Savings Bank seeks up to $8.1 billion in IPO', Bloomberg, 13 September 2016.

In fact, and in Hong Kong in particular, the proportion of IPOs subscribed for by cornerstones has gradually increased, as compared to a few years ago. The main reason for this is probably the increase in market volatility that has plagued the Asian markets since the latest financial crisis. Launching a deal that is already significantly covered at the outset is therefore much more palatable to both the issuers and the underwriting investment banks.

In the first eight months of 2016, cornerstone investors in Hong Kong IPOs of US$500 million-equivalent or more subscribed for, on average, 61 per cent of these IPOs by value (pre-overallotment option).[2]

By contrast, no fewer than 17 cornerstone investors accounted for only 28.3 per cent of the US$13.9 billion Hong Kong IPO of ICBC in 2006. Similarly, in 2011, the cornerstones took just over 30 per cent of the US$10 billion IPO of Glencore in both London and Hong Kong.

As alluded to in Chapter 1.5, one of the consequences of effectively pre-placing such a large proportion of a deal with cornerstone investors, especially where the later are locked up for six months after listing as in Hong Kong, is a lower liquidity post-listing.

In August 2016, Reuters' *Breakingviews* cited Eikon data analysing 10 recent deals that had been heavily allocated to cornerstone investors, including the IPOs of China Huarong, China Re, and China Railway Signal. It showed that trading volumes for the last 10 days for those stocks averaged just 0.05 per cent of outstanding shares—only one-third of the liquidity of shares making up the Hang Seng index, and less than one-sixth of that of the constituents of the Dow Jones index in the US.[3]

The share price performance of newly listed companies can also be negatively affected because of the so-called 'overhang' of shares that exists as a result of the lock-up on cornerstones in Hong Kong IPOs (unlike in other jurisdictions, as we will see later), whereby the market anticipates that a significant amount of stock may be sold at, or soon after, the expiry of such lock-up, which in turn depresses the value of the securities.

Finally, another consequence of IPOs with large cornerstone tranches, and especially where those are predominantly comprised of Chinese state-owned enterprises and other corporates, is a valuation that is not as thoroughly

2. Philippe Espinasse, 'Cornerstone summer party', *GlobalCapital*, 6 September 2016.
3. Quentin Webb, 'Cornerstones send HK stocks to trading graveyard', Reuters *Breakingviews*, 31 August 2016.

scrutinized, unlike in transactions largely bought by international institutions, which traditionally conduct a thorough analysis of the investment case and financials of a company before committing funds to new issues. Accordingly, IPOs that are for the most part bought by corporate cornerstones can sometimes be overpriced, a consequence of a weaker—or narrow-ranging—price-discovery process.[4]

4. Quentin Webb, 'Hong Kong's cornerstone problem goes postal', Reuters *Breakingviews*, 25 August 2016; Jackie Horne, 'Mark Machin: Improving Asia equity capital markets', *FinanceAsia*, 8 August 2016.

1.9

What cornerstones bring to IPOs

There are two main benefits that cornerstone investors bring to IPOs.

First, because a significant proportion of the offerings in which they subscribe are effectively pre-sold at the outset, they considerably de-risk these transactions both for the issuer (and/or any shareholders) and the underwriters. The amount that must be raised from institutional and retail investors through the conventional marketing process is accordingly reduced, sometimes considerably so. This can come in handy, in particular when market conditions are more challenging, perhaps because of an increase in overall trading volatility.

Second, because cornerstone investors are usually well-known names, with a good reputation in the marketplace (such as major asset managers and tycoons), the fact that they agree to subscribe for an IPO or follow-on offering—which is publicized, for regulatory reasons, as well as for greater effect—encourages the wider pool of market participants, many of whom are not as sophisticated as them, and also do not have the resources to conduct extensive research and due diligence into the affairs of the listing candidate (even if the securities regulators now command significant disclosure on the part of IPO issuers in the expectation that such investors will do so).

Therefore, cornerstones provide leadership and the deals in which they participate often end up significantly oversubscribed. This, in turn, enables the bookrunners and the management or shareholders of the company to pick and choose the investors they like, when it comes to allocating stock after pricing, a luxury unknown in transactions in which demand only remains tepid.

Accordingly, cornerstone investors constitute a useful device to ensure the success of an equity capital markets offering. More, in a sense, by agreeing to subscribe, they actually also create successful deals. At least this was the case initially, when IPOs that had strong cornerstone support were virtually ensured of doing well in the aftermarket. In 2010, I even wrote on the website of the *Wall Street Journal* that 'their [the cornerstones] very involvement can contribute to creating sought-after offerings'.[1]

Increasingly, however, and in Hong Kong in particular, securing subscriptions from cornerstone investors has become virtually the only way that sizeable transactions can actually be completed, and especially thanks to the presence of price-insensitive[2] corporate and state-owned enterprise investor demand.

One consequence of this, for Chinese IPOs in Hong Kong, is that it has now become largely mandatory for investment banks to bring in cornerstone investors, not only to help maximize the valuation of the issuer, but also, importantly, to be assured of a senior role in the transaction.[3] Bringing in one or more cornerstones, more often than not, virtually guarantees a place as a global coordinator or bookrunner in the syndicate of underwriters.

This is less the case in Southeast Asia (in Malaysia and Singapore), primarily because of the absence of a compulsory six-month lock-up on cornerstones in these markets. This ensures that *bona fide* institutional investors there find it easier to commit to buying shares at an early stage, since they know they will not be restricted if they choose to dispose of some or all of their allocations, should the transaction fail to perform after listing. In today's market, where investors are required to mark-to-market losses incurred on securities investments, being able to sell quickly is often a must.

---

1. Philippe Espinasse, 'Cornerstone investors and ethics', *Wall Street Journal*, 22 December 2010.
2. Nisha Gopalan, 'Thank you, Mr. Postman', Bloomberg, 13 September 2016.
3. Jonathan Breen, 'Cornerstone craving starts to hurt IPO pitch process', *GlobalCapital*, 8 September 2016.

1.10
What is in it for the cornerstones?

The main reason investors participate in equity capital markets transactions as cornerstones is of course the guaranteed allocation that comes with their subscriptions. As previously mentioned, in a successful and heavily subscribed transaction, investors who have instead placed orders in the book can expect these to be heavily scaled back by the bookrunners.

Conversely, a cornerstone subscription is never reduced (at least, not in a material way). Simply put, cornerstone investors know how much stock they will receive at the start of the marketing process, and irrespective of its outcome. Obviously, this may be an issue if the offering sees weak investor response, as the cornerstones may end up with sizeable allocations in a transaction that likely will not perform well in the aftermarket—but that is a risk they must take.

Importantly, subscriptions made by cornerstone investors are not subject to adjustment in the event of a clawback, the mechanism through which more shares are allocated to retail investors at the expense of institutions, because of strong demand under the public offer tranche.

In Hong Kong in particular, there exists an automatic clawback mechanism, with a number of set 'triggers'. For IPOs on HKEx, the size of the retail tranche normally starts at 10 per cent of the IPO, and is then adjusted upwards depending on how many times this initial amount of 10 per cent has been subscribed by investors. If the amount of shares (or units) set aside for members of the public is more than 15 times subscribed, the size of the public offer tranche increases to 30 per cent. A subscription of more than 50 times brings it to 40 per cent, and then to a maximum of 50 per cent in the event of a subscription of 100 times or more.

Such a large subscription level is actually not difficult to achieve in the case of a small IPO, given the even lower amount of the transaction (that is, 10 per cent) initially set aside for retail buyers. This explains why a transaction like the US$35 million IPO of second-hand luxury handbag retailer Milan Station could be 2,179 times subscribed by members of the public in 2012. Incidentally, despite its small size, this IPO featured several cornerstone investors, including a celebrity sushi restaurateur and tycoons of local newspaper and jewellery businesses.

In the case of very large IPOs, however, such clawback triggers may be adjusted downwards, and the amount provisionally allocated to retail investors will probably be as low as 5 per cent to start with, so as to avoid too high an amount of shares automatically and ultimately being allocated to members of the public, whose trading pattern is usually much more volatile than that of institutions.

No such clawback triggers exist in Malaysia or Singapore, and these are unique to Hong Kong. Public offer tranches in these Southeast Asian markets usually only account for around 5 per cent and, at most, 10 per cent of the IPOs there.

In addition, in Malaysia only, a separate proportion of new listings must be set aside by law for the benefit of *Bumiputera* (that is, ethnic Malay) investors, but only in cases where 50 per cent or more of the net profit of a company is derived from activities actually conducted in Malaysia. When the threshold is lower than this level, this may still happen, but only on a voluntary, rather than compulsory, basis. Obviously, as with retail offers, the amount provisionally allocated to *Bumiputera* investors may be reallocated to other tranches if not fully taken up.

In any event, whenever a clawback is triggered, guaranteed allocations made to cornerstone investors (unlike those of institutions which place orders in the book of demand) are not affected—and remain unchanged, across all jurisdictions.

1.11
Obligations of cornerstone investors

The guaranteed allocations of cornerstone investors, however, do come with strings attached, especially in Hong Kong.

First of all, the names of cornerstone investors must always be disclosed in the prospectus for an IPO, together with a short narrative describing the nature of their business, perhaps including a handful of statistics, such as the amount of funds they have under management or, in the case of a listed company, its market capitalization at the most practicable date.

In Singapore (only), the domestic prospectus is called an 'offer information statement' (or OIS), but is essentially similar to the offer documents used in Hong Kong and Malaysia, with only minor differences.

In addition, the individual allocations made to each of the cornerstone investors are usually also disclosed, either in the narrative description, or in a table (or both). However, in Malaysia (and sometimes also in Singapore), the recent trend is to disclose only the amount allocated to all the cornerstone investors (that is, the aggregate amount of the entire cornerstone tranche). Examples (for Malaysia only) can be found in Appendix 3.

In (the rare) cases where individual cornerstones subscribe for a number of shares in excess of the disclosable amount of a shareholding (usually 5 per cent), then the amount of the subscription will be stated, and such investors will also be subject to continuing disclosure requirements, for example when their interest falls below or increases above disclosure thresholds. In the IPO of IHH Healthcare in Malaysia (with a dual listing in Singapore) in 2012, the individual amounts subscribed by the cornerstone investors were not disclosed, except for those by Malaysia's Employees Provident Fund (EPF) and Kuwait Investment Authority (KIA), each of which had bought more than 5 per cent of the company's share capital.

Among other obligations of cornerstone investors is a requirement for their subscriptions to be locked up for a period of time after the IPO. This now only exists in Hong Kong, where all cornerstone investors are required to hold on to their shares for a minimum period of six months, after listing and the start of trading.

There never was a requirement for cornerstone investors to be locked up in Singapore. This used to be market practice (although not a requirement under the Listing Rules) in Malaysia, but changed for the first time with the IPO of IHH Healthcare, where cornerstone subscriptions were only locked up above a certain threshold (in that transaction, all the subscriptions by cornerstone investors were exempt from a lock-up if they represented less than 50 million shares—worth about US$100 million—with only subscriptions above that amount locked up for six months). Accordingly, some investors found themselves with only part of their subscription locked up, and free to sell the remainder immediately, if they so wished. Most of the cornerstones in that deal were actually not locked up at all.

A similar arrangement existed in the subsequent US$1.5 billion IPO of pay-TV company Astro Malaysia, also in 2012. In that transaction, a lock-up was only imposed on cornerstones whose allocations exceeded 15 million shares, or about US$12 million, and for a period of three months only.

Finally, in 2014, in the US$225 million equivalent IPO of 7-Eleven Malaysia, no lock-up was imposed on cornerstone investors, from thereon effectively aligning market practice in Malaysia with that which had prevailed in Singapore.

However, for now at least, cornerstone investors are still required to be locked up in Hong Kong.

Other obligations of cornerstone investors include being independent from the issuer. No board representation on their part is allowed, and they are generally not entitled to any other direct or indirect benefits on top of their guaranteed allocation (for example, a waiver of brokerage commission—where applicable—buy-back arrangements, or an entitlement to a share of underwriting commissions).

While cornerstone investors can—and are actually encouraged to—place aftermarket orders (thereby supporting the share price upon start of trading by topping up their allocations), in Hong Kong (only) no 'double-dipping' is allowed.[1] This is the practice whereby a cornerstone investor can place an order in the institutional book of demand, separately from its guaranteed allocation as a cornerstone. No such restriction exists in Malaysia or Singapore, both markets generally seen as more flexible or accommodating than Hong Kong (although in practice it would be rare for a cornerstone investor to do so).

1. Tze-Gay Tan and Jeanne Ong, 'Cornerstone investors in IPOs—an Asian perspective', *Capital Markets Law Journal*, Vol. 8, No. 4, August 2013.

1.12

Anchor investors: Cornerstone investors by another name?

A number of prospective candidates for cornerstone subscriptions will usually be contacted by the bookrunners of an equity offering, sometimes months ahead of the actual launch of the transaction.

However, there may be instances where an investor is keen to subscribe for a large amount of stock in a deal, and at an early stage—just as cornerstone investors do—but does not want its name to be disclosed in the prospectus or, in the case of IPOs in Hong Kong in particular, to abide by a lock-up.

In such cases, this investor may still serve a purpose by subscribing to the offering as an 'anchor investor'.

Unlike for cornerstone investors, no regulations apply to anchor investors and their involvement is purely a matter of market practice. Just like cornerstone investors, anchor investors pay the offer price (they do not benefit from a discount to the IPO price) and also place early orders, so they greatly contribute to book momentum.

However, because they do not agree to the restrictions or obligations that are required of cornerstone investors, they cannot receive guaranteed allocations. Their orders may therefore be scaled back if the offering is significantly oversubscribed, or if securities are clawed-back from the institutional tranche in favour of the public offer tranche, as I have explained in Chapter 1.10.

Because the orders of anchor investors are often large in size, and also because of their early involvement (which helps to ensure, together with that of the cornerstone investors, that the book is covered at an early stage) there often exists an informal understanding with the bookrunners that they will be 'well looked after' when allocations are ultimately made to investors. There is, of course, no guarantee that this may happen as far as they are concerned.

Accordingly, anchor investors can effectively be considered as cornerstone investors by another name, in that their participation greatly helps issuers and the lead banks to de-risk transactions, and generate demand from a wider pool of investors at the outset of the marketing process. Usually, this objective is achieved in an IPO through gathering a combination of cornerstone as well as anchor investors.

In 2014, the Hong Kong IPO of Chinese pork producer WH Group—which was initially pulled, after no cornerstone investors could be secured—was successfully relaunched and completed (as a much smaller and cheaper offering), after a large number of anchor investors finally agreed to subscribe (on an undisclosed basis) for shares in the deal.

It should be noted that the term 'anchor investor' remains informal, and in particular never appears in a prospectus since their role is not, unlike that of cornerstones, a regulated practice. Like cornerstones, anchor investors can obviously place aftermarket orders, and will usually be encouraged to do so by the bookrunners. The best way to do this is to give these accounts an allocation which only represents part of the amount of securities they have placed an order for, hence the need for them to 'top it up', when trading begins.

Part 2

The legal framework

In Part 2, I will summarize the key rules relating to cornerstone tranches in each of the three markets of Hong Kong, Malaysia, and Singapore. For cornerstones, Hong Kong has the most comprehensive—and restrictive—regulatory regime, while the regimes in Malaysia and Singapore are generally considered more flexible.

2.1
Hong Kong

As compared to Malaysia and Singapore, the rules governing subscriptions by cornerstone investors in Hong Kong are relatively detailed and extensive.

In Hong Kong, the frontline regulator for IPOs is the Stock Exchange of Hong Kong, which sets out and administers the Listing Rules. A number of duties of the lead regulator for the securities industry in Hong Kong, the Securities and Futures Commission (SFC), have also effectively been delegated to the exchange.

However, the SFC still acts as a second regulator. Changes to the Listing Rules require its consent, and it is also able to comment on prospectuses and question issuers and the sponsor banks in connection with new listings. The SFC also retains investigation and enforcement powers in relation to listing matters.

At the time of writing, a proposal had been jointly tabled by the exchange and the SFC whereby the exchange's listing department would continue to decide on 'a large majority of initial listing applications and post-listing matters', while the ways in which the SFC's powers and functions are exercised and performed would be slightly enhanced. In particular, it was proposed that the SFC would now no longer look at every single IPO application as 'a second pair of eyes', but only focus on cases that have larger policy and market implications.

2.1.1 Offer structure and underwriting

In Hong Kong, subscriptions by cornerstone investors are part of the placement tranche, and there is therefore a *de facto* requirement for cornerstone offerings to be underwritten by the banks included in the syndicate of underwriters under the institutional portion (also known in Hong Kong as the international tranche) of an IPO. Such underwriting takes place after pricing and is therefore a 'soft' (or settlement) underwriting only, unlike the underwriting of the retail tranche, which is made at the outset. This is different from the approach in Malaysia or Singapore where cornerstone tranches are not required to be, but in practice still are, underwritten.

As already noted in Chapter 1.10, cornerstone subscriptions remain unaffected when a clawback in favour of public offer investors is triggered.

2.1.2 Basic requirements

In summary, the involvement of cornerstone investors is allowed (although obviously not compulsory) in Hong Kong IPOs, with the following conditions:

- The cornerstone investors must buy shares at the IPO offer price.
- They must abide by a lock-up for a minimum of six months after the listing date (which is also the settlement or closing date, as well as the date when trading starts). It should be noted that, rather than being imposed by the Listing Rules, this is a contractual arrangement with the issuer and the underwriters and that, as such, it can be waived (although in practice rarely is) by the lead banks.[1]
- As seen in Chapter 1.11, they do not receive any direct or indirect benefit from their involvement, other than the guaranteed allocation. In particular, no financial assistance must be granted to cornerstone investors and there must be no side letter or arrangement offering such benefits.
- They must be independent from the issuer and persons connected to the issuer (such as directors, associates, and shareholders of the issuer), although, as we will see in more detail in Section 2.1.5, 'business partners' of issuers and the like are acceptable as cornerstone investors.
- Details of the individual subscription, identity, and background of the cornerstone investors must all be included in the prospectus.

1. Nigel Davis and Melanie Mitchell, *Hong Kong Listed Companies: Law and Practice*, Wolters Kluwer, 2012.

2.1.3 Independence from the underwriters

In Hong Kong, cornerstone investors must not be 'connected clients' of the underwriters, which essentially means that proprietary trading accounts of the underwriting banks cannot act as cornerstone investors, although the private banking or wealth management arms, as well as asset management divisions of underwriting banks face no such restrictions—provided that the cornerstone subscriptions are made on behalf of parties independent of the underwriters (that is, *bona fide* end-investors), with the banks acting as agents or fiduciaries.

In specific circumstances when an asset manager is a connected client of a lead bank that manages funds on a non-discretionary basis (that is, who only takes orders from end-investors but makes no investment decisions of its own), the risk of it leveraging its relationship with connected brokers/ distributors to obtain actual or perceived preferential treatment is considered by the exchange to be low. This is because the asset manager is in such cases acting only 'as a pass through, simply aggregating orders placed by its clients, and not exercising any decision-making authority over the size of the order or its distribution among its client accounts'. Accordingly, the exchange will look 'through the asset manager' and treat the underlying investors as the persons receiving the allocation.[2]

Conversely, when the asset manager is a connected client of a lead bank that manages funds on a discretionary basis, confirmations to the exchange and other procedures may be required to ensure that no preferential treatment for such asset manager has taken place.[3]

2.1.4 Prohibition on 'double dipping'

As already mentioned in Chapter 1.11, cornerstone investors (and parties related to such cornerstone investors) must not place orders in the institutional book of demand on top of, or in addition to, their guaranteed allocations. The reason for this lies in a listing rule that prevents existing shareholders of an issuer from participating in an IPO if shares are offered to them on a preferential basis. Accordingly, cornerstone investors effectively cannot 'have

2. HKEx Guidance Letter HKEX-GL85-16, January 2016.
3. HKEx Guidance Letter HKEX-GL85-16, January 2016.

it both ways', and can only receive their guaranteed subscription as part of the allocation process.

As noted above, however, they are obviously free (and generally encouraged) to place aftermarket orders, so as to top up their cornerstone allocations, which provides further support for the share price after the start of trading. If and when they do so, shares purchased as part of such 'top-up orders' are obviously not locked up.

2.1.5 Disclosure

Prospectuses for Hong Kong IPOs subscribed for by cornerstone investors must include a section dedicated to the cornerstone tranche, and providing information on:

- the identity of each cornerstone investor;
- the amount subscribed by *each* cornerstone investor, as well as the percentage of shareholding it represents (both pre- and post-exercise of the overallotment option, if any); and
- the independence of each cornerstone investor. In this respect, it should be noted that cornerstone investors that are customers, suppliers, or even joint-venture partners of an issuer are generally acceptable, provided that such arrangements are disclosed in the prospectus. In addition, while each application is considered on a case-by-case basis, the Stock Exchange of Hong Kong will also normally give its consent to connected clients of an issuer to act as cornerstone investors if it is satisfied that the allocation to such connected clients represents genuine demand for securities in an applicant, and that they have not taken (or will not take) advantage of their position to receive an allocation for their own benefit at the expense of other placees (or the public), that is, that no actual or perceived preferential treatment has been given to them.[4] Examples of such cases are shown in Appendices 1 and 2.

It should also be noted that cornerstone subscription agreements are considered as material contracts entered into by the issuer and their terms must therefore be disclosed as such in the prospectus. This also means that

4. HKEx Guidance Letter HKEX-GL85-16, January 2016.

they must be made available for inspection by the public and delivered to the Companies Registry, as and when the prospectus becomes registered.

2.1.6 Conditions precedent

In Hong Kong, subscriptions by cornerstone investors are subject to, among other things, the following conditions precedent:

- the offer price having been agreed between the issuer and the underwriters;
- the underwriting agreement for the Hong Kong public offering (that is, the retail tranche of an IPO) and the sale and purchase agreement for the international offering (the institutional tranche of the deal) being entered into, and having become effective and unconditional;
- neither of the above agreements having been terminated;
- the Listing Committee of the Stock Exchange of Hong Kong having granted the listing of, and permission to deal in the shares (or other securities, such as units) of the issuer, and such approval or permission not having been revoked;
- no laws, statutes, or legislation having been enacted or promulgated which prohibit the consummation of transactions contemplated in the Hong Kong public offering, the international offering or the relevant cornerstone subscription agreements, and there being no orders or injunctions from a court of competent jurisdiction precluding or prohibiting consummation of such transactions; and
- each of the representations, warranties, undertakings, and confirmations of the cornerstone investors in the relevant cornerstone subscription agreements being accurate and true in all material respects, and there being no material breach of these on their part.

2.1.7 Protection in the event of clawback

In all jurisdictions, shares (or other securities, such as units) may be reallocated from the institutional offer to the public offer tranche by the bookrunners, and vice versa. However, in the case of Hong Kong IPOs, such clawback mechanism happens automatically, rather than at the behest of the lead banks, and depends of the level of oversubscription achieved by demand generated by members of the public, as we explained in Chapter 1.10.

Specifically, allocations made to cornerstone investors are not subject to clawback provisions, because they are pre-agreed and guaranteed in advance. Accordingly, only institutions placing orders in the book of demand will see the pool of shares to be allocated to them decrease in the case of strong demand by members of the public. Conversely, their allocations will be topped up if the public offer remains undersubscribed.

2.2
Malaysia

The frontline regulator for IPOs in Malaysia is *Suruhanjaya Sekuriti*, the Securities Commission Malaysia (SC). It reviews and vets prospectuses, and is also the authority for registering them.

In turn, Bursa Malaysia (the Kuala Lumpur stock exchange) is more of a listing platform and also supervises listed issuers. In that sense, arrangements in Malaysia are broadly similar to those seen in the US or the UK, where the Securities and Exchange Commission (SEC) or the UK Listing Authority (UKLA), respectively, act as regulators for IPOs, and where the New York Stock Exchange, Nasdaq or the London Stock Exchange maintain their respective exchange platforms and oversee companies that are listed on them.

Compared to Hong Kong, Malaysia offers a lot of flexibility when it comes to cornerstone investors. The SC's main focus is on disclosure and it regards matters such as pricing and lock-up arrangements purely as commercial decisions to be made by the issuer and the lead underwriters only.[1] In fact, investments by cornerstones are not really regulated as such in Malaysia.

The main item of legislation that applies to them is the Capital Markets and Services Act 2007, which provides that an agreement for the subscription or purchase of securities may be entered into prior to the SC approval being granted, provided that such agreement may not be binding until regulatory approval is actually received. As in Hong Kong, this is effectively dealt with through a condition precedent in the cornerstone subscription agreement.

1. Tze-Gay Tan and Jeanne Ong, 'Cornerstone investors in IPOs—an Asian perspective', *Capital Markets Law Journal*, Vol. 8, No. 4, August 2013.

2.2.1 Offer structure and underwriting

In Malaysia, cornerstone tranches usually form part of the placement tranche, although, as already noted, there is no specific regulation as such governing subscriptions by cornerstones in that jurisdiction.

For that same reason, there is no specific requirement for a cornerstone tranche to be underwritten, although in practice subscriptions by cornerstone investors are generally underwritten by the syndicate of banks for the institutional (or placement) tranche, and investment banks accordingly charge management, underwriting, and selling fees to the issuer and/or the selling shareholders on cornerstone tranches.

In addition, typically only institutional, accredited, or high net worth (UHNW) investors are approached in a cornerstone investor process in Malaysia.

Lastly, there are no restrictions on cornerstone investors acquiring additional IPO securities above and beyond their initial subscription by placing orders in the institutional book of demand, unlike in Hong Kong.

2.2.2 Basic requirements

As mentioned above, there are no requirements as far as the price paid by cornerstone investors is concerned, although in practice, this will always be the IPO or offer price (as is effectively the case in other markets).

The main difference with Hong Kong is that there now is no requirement for cornerstone investor lock-ups in Malaysia. As we have seen, market practice used to be for a lock-up of six months, which then became applicable to (part of) large subscription amounts only. This was then reduced to three months before being scrapped altogether.

In addition, another important difference is to do with disclosure (see Section 2.2.3).

Finally, as in other markets, cornerstones subscriptions in Malaysia are also outside the scope of any clawback (even though there are no compulsory clawback triggers in Malaysia, unlike in Hong Kong).

2.2.3 Disclosure

Information relating to cornerstones that must be disclosed to investors can be found in the prospectus guidelines issued by the SC. This includes:

- the number and type of securities to be sold (or issued, in the case of a primary offering) to cornerstone investors;
- the price of such securities;
- the identity of the cornerstone investors (usually with a short narrative describing each investor, as is also the case in Hong Kong);
- details of lock-up arrangements (if any); and
- details of the master cornerstone agreement entered into by the cornerstone investors (which, as a material contract, must be made available to the public for inspection in connection with the IPO, as is also the case in Hong Kong).

It should be noted that, in Malaysia, and also sometimes in Singapore, individual subscriptions by cornerstone investors are generally not stated, and only the aggregate amount subscribed by all of the cornerstones is disclosed. The main exception would be in the case of cornerstone investors subscribing for 5 per cent or more of a company's share capital, in which case they would be required to comply with the reporting requirements applicable to substantial shareholdings, on a continuing basis.

Malaysian prospectuses also include a statement or disclaimer to the effect that the identity of the cornerstone investors and the shares they have undertaken to subscribe for should not be taken as 'indicative of the merits of an IPO, and that prospective investors should read the prospectus in its entirety before deciding to subscribe by themselves'.

2.2.4 Conditions precedent

In Malaysia, cornerstone subscription agreements are conditional upon, among other things, the Malaysian underwriting agreement and the institutional placement agreement being entered into, having become unconditional and not having been terminated pursuant to their respective terms (which would include, as already mentioned in the introduction to Chapter 2.2, SC approval being granted).

In effect, this is similar to the arrangements that exist in Hong Kong (although these are usually not as extensively worded in Malaysia).

2.3 Singapore

In Singapore, all IPO prospectuses (or rather, offer information statements—OISs—as they are called there) must be registered with the Monetary Authority of Singapore (MAS) prior to the start of the public offer. However, as in Hong Kong, but unlike in Malaysia, the contents of the offer document are actually negotiated with the exchange (SGX), rather than with the securities regulator.

2.3.1 Offer structure and underwriting

It is quite unique that cornerstone tranches in Singapore are technically considered as outside the scope of an IPO, rather than part of the placement tranche.

This is a legal or technical consideration only, since, for all intents and purposes, and as in Hong Kong and Malaysia, subscriptions by cornerstone investors are generally underwritten by the syndicate underwriting the institutional (or placement) tranche. Such investment banks will accordingly charge management, underwriting, and selling fees to the issuer and/or selling shareholders on cornerstone tranches.

As in other markets, cornerstone investors in Singapore will generally be institutional or accredited investors, or high net worth (HNW) or ultra-high net worth (UHNW) individuals, although there is no legal restriction on who can actually be a cornerstone investor in a Singapore IPO.

2.3.2 Basic requirements

The basic requirements for cornerstone subscriptions in Singapore are generally similar to those seen in Malaysia.

Cornerstone investors in Singapore only benefit from a guaranteed allocation and there are no precedents to date where cornerstones would have subscribed for shares at a discount.

Unlike in Hong Kong and Malaysia, however, lock-ups, with a few rare exceptions, were never imposed on cornerstone investors in Singapore IPOs. This would only be in the case of a cornerstone connected to the issue manager (that is, the equivalent of a sponsor bank in Hong Kong, or principal adviser in Malaysia).

Lastly, as in other markets, cornerstones subscriptions in Singapore are also outside the scope of any clawback (even though there are no compulsory clawback triggers in Singapore, unlike in Hong Kong).

2.3.3 Disclosure

The Securities and Futures Act (Chapter 289) of Singapore requires that details of the nature of cornerstone subscriptions, as well as the number and characteristics of the securities to which they relate, must be disclosed.

In practice, disclosure will generally be similar to that seen in Malaysia. Traditionally, individual subscription amounts were disclosed, but these are now sometimes aggregated as one amount, as they are in Malaysia (except, again, in the case of cornerstone investors subscribing above a disclosable threshold).

In addition, because in Singapore cornerstone offerings are concurrent but separate from IPOs, disclosure relating to cornerstone subscriptions will often be found in the section of the prospectus in which ownership of the shares (or units) of the issuer is disclosed, rather than in a dedicated section, or in the plan of distribution (or underwriting) section. Except as mentioned above, however, disclosure will largely be similar to that in Hong Kong or Malaysia.

Finally, as in other markets, cornerstone agreements (or rather, the master subscription agreement) are usually included as material contracts for disclosure to the public in connection with an IPO.

2.3.4 Conditions precedent

As in Malaysia, the subscription of securities by cornerstone investors in Singapore IPOs is conditional upon the underwriting and placement agreements having been entered into, and not having been terminated, pursuant to their terms on, or prior to, the settlement date.

Part 3

How the process works in practice

Let us now turn to how the process of gathering cornerstone demand actually works. In Part 3, I will review the key steps and building blocks leading to the subscription of securities by a cornerstone until these are actually credited to its investment account, upon listing and the start of trading.

This starts with the banks pitching the opportunity to act as cornerstones to prospective investors, and this can only happen once the equity story has been clearly defined.

3.1

Defining the equity story

In order to kick off a cornerstone investor process, it is first and foremost necessary for the equity story (also known as the investment case) to have been largely finalized. This means that the prospectus (or offer document) needs to be in a reasonably well-advanced stage. In turn, it requires the lead bank(s) in charge of the marketing of the transaction to have conducted comprehensive due diligence into the affairs of the issuer, covering commercial, financial, and legal aspects. In particular, the following elements of disclosure will need to be in near-final shape before any prospective cornerstones can be approached:

- the timetable for the equity offering;
- the risk factors which may affect the business of the issuer;
- the use of proceeds (in cases where the issuer raises new money);
- the dividend policy;
- the capital structure and level of indebtedness of the issuer;
- the financials of the issuer for the period under review (which may, however, be updated at a later stage, also including a management discussion and analysis of financial condition and results of operations);
- an overview of the industry in which the issuer operates;
- the corporate structure of the group;
- a comprehensive description of the business of the company; and
- key management appointments (although the composition of the board of directors may perhaps not yet be finalized at that stage).

In most cases, it is likely that the above will require several months of work before the lead bank(s) is/are in a position to initiate contact with potential cornerstone investors. The main concern here is obviously to avoid any material changes at a later stage to what may first be presented to investors.

3.2
The initial approach

There are several important considerations related to the best timing to approach potential cornerstone investors.

First, as mentioned above, the degree of preparedness of the issuer. It is obviously undesirable to show investors a story that is only just half-baked, and in particular as far as the financials are concerned. It is also important for the bookrunner(s) to have visibility over any financials which may later be announced, to avoid them painting a picture that may be at odds with what may already have been disclosed.

Second, as with any marketing exercise, it is key to maintain momentum. Approaching potential investors at too early a stage may result in long lead times between that initial approach and the provision of additional information to them at a later stage.

Another risk in this regard is a possible change in the timetable of the offering. Aside from unfavourable market conditions, this usually occurs because of financial disclosure, when the lead bank(s), legal advisers, and auditors have identified that more work is needed on the accounts, perhaps because *pro forma* or interim financials need to be included in the offer documents. For example, the issuer may have conducted a material acquisition or disposal in the run-up to the offering, the financial effects of which may, in turn, need to be disclosed in the prospectus.

Alternatively, the period of 135 days between the publication of the last available financials (whether these are audited, or simply reviewed) and the publication of the offer document may have been exceeded under the offer timetable, requiring the computation of additional interim financials, so that the issuer and lead bank(s) may obtain clean comfort letters, including crucial 'negative assurance' language on the part of the auditors.

Negative assurance consists of a statement by the accountants that, as a result of performing specified procedures, nothing came to their attention that caused them to believe that specified matters do not meet a specified accounting standard (for example, that nothing came to their attention that caused them to believe that any material modifications should be made to the unaudited financial statements for them to be in conformity with generally accepted accounting principles).[1]

Next, there obviously needs to be good visibility regarding the timetable for the completion of the IPO by the time potential cornerstones are first approached.

Generally speaking, the initial approach to potential cornerstones will be made at least about two months before the pricing of an IPO. Because some of these investors may commit substantial amounts to the transaction, and at any price within the indicative range, they will need to carefully research the equity story and conduct due diligence of their own. This obviously takes time, especially when tens or even hundreds of millions of US dollars are at stake.

In addition, as we will see later, several legal agreements must be entered into between the issuer, the bookrunners, and each of the investors, so allowing enough time (but not too much!) to negotiate these documents is also necessary.

---

1. Lloyd S. Harmetz, Bradley Berman and Edward M. Welch, 'Frequently asked questions relating to comfort letters and comfort letter practice', Morrison & Foerster LLP, 2016.

3.3

Targeting potential cornerstones

The number of potential cornerstone investors to be contacted largely depends on the size of the IPO. Given the amounts subscribed by cornerstones (from, say, US$5 million to US$100 million or more apiece), contacting too many accounts may easily result in disappointment in the case of a small offering, not to mention possible negative implications in terms of aftermarket liquidity if too large a cornerstone tranche is ultimately allocated (and in Hong Kong in particular, given the requirement for a six-month lock-up there).

Conversely, contacting only a handful of accounts may leave issuers and their bookrunners short-changed when it comes to finally signing subscription agreements.

A good rule of thumb is, therefore, probably to contact around three times as many investors as may ultimately be allocated, which should allow for attrition, either because they are not attracted to the equity story, or because they are uncomfortable with the valuation of the business (or both), or the process itself (including what may be required of them in terms of disclosure and lock-up restriction).

The ratio between the number cornerstone subscriptions ultimately secured to the number of accounts initially contacted during the process is invariably known as the conversion or 'hit' rate. Obviously, the higher the hit rate the better, as far as the issuer and the bookrunners are concerned. A high hit rate shows that the targeting exercise was particularly accurate in the first place. Conversely, a low conversion rate points to the wrong accounts having been contacted by the bookrunners, or to an investment case or valuation that might perhaps be below par.

There may also be legal implications impacting the number of investors that are contacted. For example, in Singapore, potential cornerstones are often contacted pursuant to a private placement exemption under Section

282B of the Securities and Futures Act, which allows offers to be made to a maximum of 50 investors within a 12-month period, without triggering the need to publish a prospectus. It should be noted that such exemption focuses on offers made, rather than on acceptances received.

In any event, as a practical matter, around 50 is probably the maximum number of investors that can safely be contacted, even in the case of a multibillion dollar offering. Beyond that number, the legal work associated with the marketing of a cornerstone tranche becomes rather cumbersome, and the confidentiality of the exercise can probably no longer be ensured. If the targeting exercise done by the bookrunner(s) has been accurate, then there should be no need in most cases to contact a larger number of accounts anyway.

Within investment banks, those executives involved in the cornerstone process are invariably part of the 'front office', and are usually equity capital markets bankers from the firms' equity syndicate desks.

For large and prestigious IPOs, it is also relatively common nowadays for independent advisers to be involved, on top of the global coordinators and bookrunners. Such independent advisers are usually appointed first by the issuers, and help them and their shareholders organize beauty parades for the selection of the senior underwriters. They also assist in 'keeping the banks honest', since they generally do not have the conflicts of interest of the latter, in that their clients do not include investors, but merely the issuers (and/or sellers) of the securities. This phenomenon is more common in Europe (and the US), but is slowly gaining in popularity in Asia. When independent advisers are involved, they will more often than not closely monitor the targeting of, and marketing to, potential cornerstone investors by the lead banks.

3.4
Drawbacks of a 'free-for-all' approach

In Hong Kong, there has in recent years been a trend whereby a large number of investment banks are appointed in a bookrunner role on the more sizeable Chinese IPOs there. The more senior roles—global coordinator, and even sponsor banks—are then decided depending on which banks have sourced cornerstone accounts to effectively 'underwrite' part of the offering.

In theory, this sounds like a good deal for issuers and their shareholders: the banks that are actually pulling their weight are ultimately rewarded with more senior positions in the syndicate, which inevitably leads to a larger share of the commission pool for them. In addition, because such commission pool is expressed as a percentage of the proceeds—and remains unchanged irrespective of the number of firms appointed to lead the offering—issuers appear to get more 'bang for their buck', with more banks helping to market the deal for what is effectively the same cost, casting a wider net to secure more demand from institutional investors.

Unfortunately, such reasoning completely ignores the dynamics associated with the marketing of securities to investors in a capital markets transaction. The net result of such a 'free-for-all' approach, where dozens of firms roam the marketplace, marketing a potential investment often to the same accounts is usually nothing short of a recipe for disaster.[1]

First, when 20 or 25 banks are appointed in a senior role, the execution work for the corporate finance phase of the transaction will often suffer. The group of bookrunners will invariably be split between 'active bookrunners', who effectively run the show, and 'passive bookrunners', who do very little and are only in for the ride and the league table credit that their bookrunner

1. Philippe Espinasse, 'Alibaba—the genie is out of the bottle', *GlobalCapital*, 18 March 2004; and anonymous, 'Sizing up Asia's growing syndicates', *GlobalCapital*, 19 June 2013.

title conveys. Because the commission pool ends up being shared among perhaps two dozen houses, rather than just five or six, these transactions often end up being staffed by more junior and less experienced investment bankers, leading to shortcomings in the quality of the advice provided, and much 'reinventing of the wheel' on their part. The better qualified managing directors and heads of teams will simply focus the bulk of their time on more lucrative transactions, leaving most of the execution work to associates and junior vice-presidents. In addition, the involvement of a large number of working parties will obviously generate much inefficiency, for obvious reasons.

Second, the lack of coordination in the marketing efforts of such a large number of houses inevitably leads to different messages being communicated to investors. Because many of the key investors will each receive a dozen or more calls, their portfolio managers will easily become annoyed with the process. Such an arrangement raises obvious questions as to which firm or firms are actually in charge, and may even lead some accounts to simply pass on the opportunity altogether, because they become increasingly uncomfortable with the whole process.

This was painfully illustrated by the infamous US$6 billion Hong Kong IPO of Chinese pork producer WH Group in April 2014, when the issuer and its shareholders lined up no fewer than 28 bookrunners (some media articles even suggested 29) to secure cornerstone demand, ultimately generating none, and leading to the offering being postponed, only to be successfully relaunched as a much smaller and cheaper, US$2 billion deal in July of that same year—and with two lead banks only.[2] While no cornerstones ultimately subscribed to the deal, even the second time around, anchor investor demand finally enabled the lead banks to complete the offering.

Finally, it must be noted that, in Hong Kong only, appointing at a later stage additional investment banks as IPO sponsors (rather than merely as global coordinators or bookrunners) may result in a delay to the overall transaction timetable. Under the new IPO sponsor regime, which came into effect in 2013, there must now be a minimum period of two months between the formal appointment of the latest sponsor to be contracted by the issuer (through the signing of an engagement letter) and submission by the issuer of the listing application to the exchange. The reason for this is to ensure that

2. Prudence Ho, 'WH Group raises $2.05 billion in Hong Kong IPO', Reuters, 29 July 2014.

the banks working on the listing application and advising the company on the listing rules have enough time to conduct due diligence into the affairs of the issuer before the draft prospectus is submitted for review by the IPO department of HKEx.[3]

3. Philippe Espinasse and Syren Johnstone, *Study Manual for the IPO Sponsor Examinations in Hong Kong*, Hong Kong Securities and Investment Institute, 2013.

3.5

Cornerstone marketing and multi-bookrunner syndicates

Accordingly, instead of a free-for-all arrangement, marketing to potential cornerstone investors with a multi-bookrunner syndicate is best conducted through a collaborative approach.

This starts with each of the bookrunner banks devising a shortlist of accounts believed to be interested in the offering, based on the IPO size, their prior investment patterns, and/or affinity with a certain industry sector. Then, each bookrunner will be responsible for contacting a set number of investors.

The best way to decide which bookrunner has responsibility for which institutions is for the banks to each pick names in turn, until the agreed number of target accounts has been attained. Of course, to ensure fairness, each bookrunner will be responsible for contacting exactly the same number of investors as the other houses. A different arrangement may be made in cases where some bookrunners are more senior than others, for example with larger individual underwriting amounts.

Alternatively, names may be assigned by the issuer (or an independent adviser) to each of the bookrunners although it is probably best in most circumstances to let the banks decide first among themselves, if at all possible.

What is key under such an arrangement, however, is that each target investor is contacted by one investment bank, and one bank only. This avoids repetitive calls by various syndicate members to the same account, as well as different messages about the investment case and offering being conveyed to the market. Crucially, it also empowers the banks to deliver (or not, as the case may be) demand from potential individual cornerstone investors. For example, this technique was used to great effect in the multibillion dollar IPO of IHH Healthcare in Malaysia and Singapore, which ultimately delivered 22 cornerstone subscriptions through six different bookrunner banks.

For its initial approach to potential cornerstones, each bookrunner must use exactly the same script as the other firms and this should also be vetted by the legal advisers to the issuer and/or underwriters. The main concern here is to avoid asymmetry of information, that is, certain investors being made privy to more information, or to information that may be different from that included (or ultimately to be included) in the prospectus. The contents of the script are discussed in the following section and a sample is shown in Appendix 5.

3.6 The bookrunner script

As mentioned in Chapter 3.5, the script should be exactly the same for all the bookrunners involved in the transaction, to ensure consistency in the messages relayed to investors.

First, the script should refer to the call being made on behalf of the issuer (and/or any selling shareholder(s)), and perhaps also to news that may have appeared in the media about the IPO.

Ideally, it should clarify that the discussion is entirely based on publicly available information and that, at this stage, the investor will not be 'crossed', that is, brought 'over the Chinese Wall' for compliance purposes, and therefore made privy to information not already in the public domain.

The script should then mention that the investor has been shortlisted by the issuer and the bookrunners to become a potential cornerstone investor in the IPO, and that only a select group of investors is being approached at this stage, so as to create a 'club-like' feeling of exclusivity.

It should also clarify that, to ensure efficiency and one point of contact, only one firm (obviously the bank making the investor call) has been appointed as the syndicate bank to coordinate with the investor on exploring a cornerstone subscription in the proposed IPO, and that, importantly, no other houses will be talking to the investor about this opportunity.

The script then typically includes summary background information about the company, its market positioning, track record and strategy, but without going into too much detail. In particular, no information that may still be confidential at this stage should be communicated and probably not more than a handful of key metrics should be provided.

The script should also most likely mention the valuation methodology agreed among the lead banks for the valuation of the business, and provide a ballpark amount (or—even better—a range) for the equity value of the issuer.

Next would come an indication of the timetable for the IPO, including a target date for the launch of the IPO and the date by which cornerstone subscriptions will need to be locked down, that is, by when the subscription agreements must be finalized and signed.

The script should also mention that potential cornerstone investors would, in due course, be given access to management of the company (if applicable—see Section 3.8.4) to conduct due diligence, perhaps undergo one or more site visits, and also be provided with a draft of the offering circular prior to publication.

An indication of the minimum cornerstone investment size (if applicable) and of the lock-up, if any, should also be given.

Finally, the script will typically end by conveying that, should the investor be interested in exploring this opportunity further, it will first be required to sign a non-disclosure agreement, since the bookrunners will not be in a position to provide any additional information without such a document being signed. Effectively, if the portfolio managers want to know more, they must at that point become insiders.

3.7 The non-disclosure agreement (NDA)

The next step in the cornerstone investor process is, therefore, the negotiation of a non-disclosure agreement (NDA), also sometimes called confidentiality agreement. It cannot be overemphasized how time-consuming this can be when perhaps up to 40 or 50 agreements must be negotiated simultaneously between the issuer, the bookrunners (even if one of them takes the lead in each case) and each of the potential cornerstone investors, and sufficient time must absolutely be allowed for this to take place.

To retain control of the process, it is always better for the issuer and the bookrunners to use a template drafted by their own legal advisers, rather than one devised by the investor or its own lawyers.

While, inevitably, this document will be negotiated between all parties and some amount of horse-trading will necessarily take place, an NDA remains a fairly standard contract and investors (or their legal departments, rather than the portfolio managers) will generally know which changes deviating from the initial template are likely to be accepted.

3.7.1 The issue of governing law

A practical way of negotiating the NDA is usually to appoint a dedicated individual from the firm (or firms) of lawyers advising the issuer to lead the negotiations. In this respect, the governing law of the NDAs will be an important consideration.

The investors targeted through the cornerstone process may include a mix of domestic and international names. For example, for a Singapore IPO, they may include Singaporean investors as well as accounts from the rest of Asia, the Middle East, or Europe (including the UK), as well as the US.

International investors will most likely be more comfortable with the NDA being drafted under English or New York law, while Singaporean investors may, in turn, prefer to use Singaporean law, for obvious reasons. Accordingly, depending on the profile of the target list of investors, more than one law firm or individual lawyer may need to be involved.

As noted earlier, the NDA is generally entered into between the issuer, each of the bookrunners, and each investor, so a minimum of three signatories (and probably more in the case of sizeable transactions) is required.

The NDA states that the investor is considering whether to make an investment in the securities of the issuer and that, for this purpose, the company has agreed to furnish it with certain information that is non-public, confidential, and/or proprietary in nature relating to, or in connection with, the proposed offering. This includes, but is not limited to, the investments, business, and structure of the company. Defined terms (in particular what exactly constitutes confidential information) typically follow.

Subject to the terms of the NDA, the investor then confirms that it shall hold all such information (including all analyses, compilations, notes, studies, memoranda, and other documents prepared by the investor or its representatives to the extent that the same contain, reflect, or are derived from the information) provided by the issuer in strict confidence.

Further, the investor acknowledges that some or all of such information is or may become price-sensitive information and that its use may be regulated or prohibited by applicable legislation relating to insider dealing. In addition, the information so provided generally remains the property of the company.

Lastly, while the information disclosed is deemed confidential, the NDA usually includes a disclaimer to the effect that the company does not accept responsibility for the accuracy, reliability, completeness, or reasonableness of such information.

3.7.2 Investor undertakings

Typically, the investor undertakes, without the company's prior written approval:

- to take reasonable procedures and measures in order to maintain the confidentiality and prevent unauthorized use and disclosure of the confidential information;

- not to make copies of such information, except as permitted;
- to procure that any of its representatives abide by the same obligations, and to be responsible for their actions;
- except as required by law, a court order or regulatory requirements, and as otherwise permitted, not to make any disclosure or announcement concerning (i) the possibility of the IPO taking place; (ii) any related investigations, discussions, or negotiations taking place; (iii) the fact that the investor has requested or received information from the company; and (iv) any terms, conditions, or other facts with respect to the proposed IPO or the investor's proposed investment in the company (including the status of such investment).

In addition, the investor typically undertakes to notify the company of any unauthorized disclosure of the information or any other breach of the provisions of the NDA, and to use its best efforts to assist the company in connection with any proceedings the company may institute to deal with such breach of confidence.

The investor also generally agrees to return or destroy any information provided within a set period of time (typically seven days or less) upon termination of the discussions relating to a proposed cornerstone investment in the company or, in any case, upon notification by the company. It should be noted that returning or destroying confidential information does not actually release the investor from its obligations under the NDA.

3.7.3 Permitted disclosure

Essentially, disclosure of the information given to the investor may only be made to the following people:

- its directors, officers, employees, agents, advisers, and affiliates, for the purposes of considering and evaluating the investor's proposed investment in the company;
- any independent auditors engaged to review the investor's proposed investment; and
- any other independent advisers to the investor, again with respect to the proposed investment in the company.

In addition, where the NDA imposes any obligations on such investor's representatives, the investor must procure that such persons must comply with these obligations and it also agrees to be responsible for any breach of the NDA by the representatives.

3.7.4 Disclosure required by law

In cases where the investor is required by applicable laws, a court order or regulatory requirements to disclose the information given to it, it must generally notify the person to which disclosure is required to be made that the information is the confidential information of the company. It must also give the company an opportunity and provide assistance to it to resist the disclosure or protect the confidentiality of such information.

It is also often expected that where disclosure must be made, it must only be limited to what counsel advises the investor to disclose.

3.7.5 Exclusions

It is common for an NDA to exclude the following from the definition of what constitutes confidential information:

- information which, at the date of disclosure, is already in the public domain or which subsequently enters the public domain;
- information which is already lawfully known to the investor prior to its disclosure by the company, and which is, or becomes, free of any obligation of confidentiality;
- information which, after execution of the NDA, is lawfully acquired by the investor from a third party who did not, whether directly or indirectly, acquire the information from the company under any obligation of confidentiality;
- subject to the provisions discussed in Section 3.7.4, information which is required to be disclosed by law, by order of a court of competent jurisdiction, or regulatory authority; and
- information which is independently developed by the investor without use of the confidential information.

3.7.6 Consequences of breach

In the event that the investor is found to be in breach of its obligations under the NDA, the agreement includes a provision to the effect that the company shall have the right to sue the investor and/or its representatives to seek monetary and/or other damages. This may include the company seeking to obtain injunctive or other equitable relief against the investor.

This may even extend to alleged and threatened breaches of the provisions of the NDA, rather than actual breaches of the agreement.

3.7.7 Duration of the confidentiality agreement

The NDA becomes effective from the date of its execution and remains in force until the earlier of:

- the date on which the confidential information becomes public (other than as a result of any act or omission or default by the investor or its representatives); or
- a period of one year (or, at most, two years) from the date of the agreement.

It is rare for an NDA entered into in relation to a cornerstone investor process to extend beyond a year, and it would hardly ever extend beyond two years in any event. By then, it is likely that the IPO would have happened (with disclosure of such information in the prospectus and other public offer documents), or that much of the information would have become obsolete anyway.

3.7.8 Other provisions included in the agreement

If the IPO includes a Rule 144A tranche (that is, if it is marketed to large onshore institutions in the US), the investor will be asked to certify that it is:

- a Qualified Institutional Buyer (QIB) as defined in Rule 144A under the US Securities Act of 1933 (and also a 'qualified purchaser' [as defined in Section 2(a) (51) (A) of the US Investment Company Act of 1940]); or, alternatively,
- not a US person and located outside the United States (within the meaning of Regulation S [or Reg. S] under the Securities Act).

In addition, the obligations under the agreement may not be assigned or transferred to another party without the prior agreement in writing of the other signatories.

3.7.9 Additional considerations in the case of spin-offs

There are additional issues in terms of disclosure and confidentiality in the case of spin-offs, that is, when a listed company seeks a separate, stand-alone listing for one of its businesses or division. This can also happen when a listed company sponsors the listing of a REIT or business trust, which is a relatively common occurrence in Malaysia and Singapore in particular (but less so in Hong Kong).

The main concern in such a case is that selective news about the IPO may in turn have implications on the share price of the parent (or sponsor company). Accordingly, it would be fairly usual in such cases to include, in the NDA, a provision preventing potential cornerstone investors from trading the securities of the parent, until news of the proposed IPO are made public.

Obviously, this may become an issue when the securities of the parent are particularly liquid and actively traded, or when the investor is already a shareholder, or owns other securities of the parent (such as convertible or other bonds).

An alternative to a trading ban can therefore be the publication of a redacted prospectus, so that the parent company or sponsor can make an announcement about the proposed IPO. This approach has so far been used in Hong Kong only.[1] In any event, in Hong Kong, spin-off listings must be announced at the time of submission of the application proof (that is, the draft prospectus) for review by the stock exchange (or the equivalent for an overseas listing). This would typically be at least a couple of months before the pricing of the IPO, so around the time prospective cornerstones are normally approached anyway.

In Hong Kong, spin-offs are usually not accepted by the exchange within three years of listing of the parent. In addition, there as in other markets, the parent must retain a sufficient level of operations and assets to support its

1. Tze-Gay Tan and Jeanne Ong, 'Cornerstone investors in IPOs—an Asian perspective', *Capital Markets Law Journal*, Vol. 8, No. 4, August 2013.

separate listing status (and in particular meet the minimum profit requirement and other quantitative tests).

Spin-off listings can also create issues in terms of independence of directorships and management, as well as the administrative capabilities of the two companies. There must also be clear commercial benefits for both the parent and the entity that is being spun-off, with no adverse effects on the shareholders of the parent in particular. Ongoing and future connected- and related-party transactions can also create issues that must be remedied prior to listing (unless suitable waivers can be obtained from the exchange).

3.8
What happens after the NDA has been signed

After the NDA has been signed by the issuer, the bookrunner(s), and potential cornerstones, come marketing activities and due diligence by the investors. In a nutshell, the investment banks will try to convince the investors to part with their money and to subscribe for the securities to be issued by the company (and/or sold by its shareholders), while the investors will carefully study the equity story and investment opportunity to decide whether or not to come in as cornerstones in the IPO.

In a way, this is not really different from what happens in connection with a normal bookbuilding exercise, except that it will usually be conducted over a much longer period of time, owing to the significant amounts to be invested by each of the participants.

There is no hard and fast rule on how this phase of the process may be conducted and it varies from deal to deal. Normally, potential cornerstone investors will first and foremost be provided with a draft of the offering circular (or prospectus) by way of additional information on the issuer.

It is also a good idea to use a project or code name when referring to the transaction in all communication with potential cornerstone investors, so as to increase the level of confidentiality—and avoid leaks.

3.8.1 The draft offering circular

As mentioned earlier, the draft prospectus will most likely be pretty much in near final form by then. However, it is important to remember that it is still a draft and, as such, not a document that can be legally relied on to make a decision whether or not to invest in the securities issued and/or sold in an IPO.

3.8.1.1 No reliance on the draft offering circular

Accordingly, there will be an acknowledgement in the cornerstone subscription agreement (should one later be signed with that particular investor) that the information contained in any draft preliminary offering circular or the draft prospectus lodged with any stock exchange or regulator (depending on the jurisdiction in which the IPO is being conducted), or any other draft documentation provided to the investor on a confidential basis or otherwise publicly available, remains subject to change, and should not be relied upon by the investor in determining whether to invest in the securities.

When such a document(s) is/are provided to the investor, it/they may also be accompanied by a disclaimer or letter making such non-reliance clear, to ensure additional legal protection for the issuer and the bookrunner(s). As with all other IPO investors, the investor will be deemed to have received information contained in the published, final offering circular, and to have relied on it in determining whether or not to invest.

Further, the cornerstone subscription agreement will also state that, notwithstanding the fact that any information concerning the company may have been furnished to the investor, the company and the bookrunners (as well as their respective advisers and affiliates) make no representation and give no warranty or undertaking as to the accuracy or completeness of any such information not contained in the offering circular. As such, none of them will have any liability to the investor or its representatives resulting from the use of such information.

3.8.1.2 Review of the draft offer document

Even though it is not a document that can legally be relied on by potential cornerstones, and may still be subject to completion and amendment, the draft prospectus nevertheless provides them with a wealth of information about the issuer.

Since it is also a document that is at an advanced stage of drafting, it is likely to include most of the information required by an investor when deciding to subscribe for tens or hundreds of millions of US dollars in the securities of the company.

Among other topics, the draft offer document will probably include all or most of the following, in addition to the timetable for the proposed IPO:

- a summary and highlights of the prospectus and selected financial information and operating data;
- a glossary and list of defined terms;
- risk factors pertaining to the company's operating environment, business and investment in the securities;
- information on the company's future plans and use of proceeds (in the case of a primary offering, if applicable);
- information on the company's dividend policy;
- details of the issuer's capitalization and indebtedness;
- a management discussion and analysis of financial condition and results of operation (that is, an analytical review of key line items in the accounts);
- an overview of the industry in which the company operates, by way of an independent market research (IMR) report;
- the corporate structure of the group;
- a detailed overview of the business;
- information on the management and directors of the company (if already appointed);
- information on the company's capital and its principal shareholders;
- a review of related/connected-party transactions (commonly known as 'RPTs') and potential conflicts of interest;
- general and statutory information;
- consolidated financial statements for the period under review (perhaps subject to updating at a later stage, for example if interim accounts are yet to be published);
- details of material assets, material contracts, and intellectual property; and
- the parties to the transaction.

3.8.2 Due diligence questions

Once they have reviewed the offer document, potential cornerstone investors will, more often than not, have a number of questions as part of their due diligence into the business of the company and group.

Again, an important consideration in this respect is not to disclose more information to them than what will ultimately be disclosed to other investors in the IPO, to avoid asymmetry of information and potential insider trading issues down the line.

Because, invariably, a large number of investors will have been contacted—and especially in the case of large offerings—answering such questions can be particularly time consuming on the part of the management of the issuer and investment banks leading the IPO. Accordingly, a practical way of addressing them is to group all questions together and to circulate to all potential investors a written *addendum* to the draft prospectus they have seen, answering all the questions at the same time. This has the additional advantage of putting all investors on the same footing, in that all investors are provided with exactly the same data, and can also see what questions other accounts have asked.

Depending on the volume of questions received, and on the time needed to compile answers, one or more rounds may be needed to address all the questions received by the bookrunners.

As an alternative, or in addition to the above, one or more conference calls may also be arranged, whereby management will answer the questions over the telephone for the benefit of all investors. While this also works well, setting out information in writing makes it perhaps easier to keep track of what information has actually been disclosed as part of the exercise, so that the draft prospectus can be updated at a later stage. It may also be the case that management may not have the information at hand while on the conference call, in which case they will need to revert to the investors in writing in any event. In all cases, one must avoid disclosing forward-looking information such as profit forecasts, which may not ultimately be included in the offer documents.

3.8.3 Site visits

Depending on the business of the company, it may also be appropriate to arrange one or more site visits. For example, if the issuer boasts impressive or particularly innovative production facilities, it may pay to get investors to actually see some of these. Examples would include, among others, large-scale open-pit mines, or retail businesses with a novel concept.

Again, to avoid spending too much time catering to investors as part of the cornerstone process, it is probably a good idea to arrange a day or two where investors can all visit the company together. This is also a good opportunity for them to ask questions along the way, and to clarify some issues, which they may not yet have fully grasped. Ideally, the members of management hosting such site visit(s) should be broadly the same as those who will later embark on the roadshow, to be undertaken simultaneously with the bookbuilding exercise, that is, the chairman, CEO, CFO, or finance director, and perhaps one or two other senior members, such as the heads of part of the business or division, perhaps assisted by one or two more junior members of the finance department. This also serves as a good early rehearsal for the IPO roadshow itself.

3.8.4 Roadshows and reverse roadshows

In cases where visiting corporate sites may not be appropriate (perhaps for security reasons or, alternatively, because the company's headquarters and other sites primarily only consist of offices where there is not all that much to see), it may be useful for management to instead simply meet with investors in a neutral setting (such as a hotel conference centre). Such a meeting—or meetings—can then take the form of a management presentation (as will later be done with the research analysts of the members of the underwriting syndicate, and also with potential investors during the bookbuilding process), together with a questions and answers session at the end.

There are several ways such a roadshow can be arranged.

One is for management to visit individual investors one by one (that is, a series of one-on-one meetings) over the space of a week or so, which will imply the corporate team traveling around the world (as will be done in the later stages of the IPO). Another can be for management to hold group presentations in the various financial centres where investors are located (for example, in Hong Kong, the Middle East, London, and New York). It should be noted that, in the case of Singapore IPOs, potential cornerstone investors typically do not benefit from separate management meetings.[1]

For those investors in hard-to-reach locations, where perhaps only one or a handful of potential cornerstone accounts may be located (say, in Australia), it is also possible for management to answer questions over the telephone or by videoconference.

1. Tze-Gay Tan and Jeanne Ong, 'Cornerstone investors in IPOs—an Asian perspective', *Capital Markets Law Journal*, Vol. 8, No. 4, August 2013.

Alternatively, management may decide to arrange a 'reverse roadshow', where investors visit the corporate headquarters (as they would on a site visit) instead, which has the advantage of being quicker, and also for management to address investors in a more familiar environment and setting. Obtaining answers to some questions may perhaps require certain calculations or digging out more information, which may be more easily done from the company's offices than when the chairman and CEO are on the road on the other side of the world. As ever, keeping track of the information actually provided is essential for the reasons already stated earlier.

As will later be the case with the research analysts from the syndicate of underwriters, it is a good idea to remind prospective cornerstone investors to agree and undertake not to seek from the company, its directors or advisers, whether directly or indirectly, any material information including forward-looking information (whether qualitative or quantitative) concerning the company that is not reasonably expected to be included in the prospectus to be issued by the company; or publicly available.[2]

2. HKCFEF Limited, Hong Kong Sponsor Due Diligence Guidelines, September 2013.

3.9

Firming up the bids

Once the potential cornerstone investors have reviewed the information provided by the issuer and the bookrunners and obtained answers to the questions they have asked—through meetings with management, conference calls, or further correspondence, they will be asked to confirm their interest (or not, as the case may be) in subscribing to the offering in a cornerstone capacity.

While cornerstone investors commit to buying securities at any price within and up to the top end of indicative price range, their feedback on valuation is very important in that it, in no small measure, contributes to the later setting of that range, especially when the cornerstone tranche is a sizeable one. The 'price talk' between the lead banks and the cornerstones (and the price sensitivity they may have) therefore becomes essential when it comes to actually pricing a deal.

To maintain momentum, it is important to ensure that the cornerstones communicate at an early stage such commitments in principle. A book with their expressions of interest can then be compiled by the bookrunners.

Invariably, some investors will end up declining to participate, perhaps because they are ultimately not comfortable with the business model of the company, or they find the valuation too demanding (bearing in mind that cornerstones are asked to commit to buying at any price within the IPO price range, including the top end), or they are unwilling to see their name disclosed in the prospectus, or to abide by a six-month lock-up, in the case of a Hong Kong IPO. In the latter two cases, some of these investors may perhaps still choose to participate in the IPO at an early stage as anchor investors (see Chapter 1.12).

Once the bookrunners have a fix on the actual demand that can be gathered from cornerstones, three things need to happen.

First, in the event that the cornerstone 'shadow book' is sizeable, it may be necessary to scale back some or all of these investors' commitments. The advantage is that cornerstones will often buy more securities in the aftermarket to top up their allocations, thereby providing support for the share price upon the start of trading.

Second, demand by the cornerstone investors will usually be expressed as a mix that will include US dollar amounts, local currency amounts (for example, Hong Kong or Singapore dollars, or the Malaysian ringgit, or even the reference currency for the investor in question, for example, the renminbi in the case of an investor from mainland China). Ultimately, it is worth bearing in mind that all allocations under the IPO, including allocations to cornerstone investors, will actually need to be made in shares (or in units, in the case of a REIT or business trust), and that individual allocations will also need to be expressed as a multiple of the board lot, to avoid odd-lot allocations being made.

Such adjustments do not need to be made at this early stage, but it should be made clear that minor changes will probably be necessary upon allocation of the book after pricing, to address these important considerations.

Third, each cornerstone investor will be asked to sign a subscription agreement evidencing its individual commitment.

3.10
The subscription agreement

As with the NDA, it is best for the issuer and the bookrunners to have drafted the template for the subscription agreement. Such master agreement—which, as previously mentioned, is usually put on display at a later stage for the benefit of members of the public—can then be negotiated with individual cornerstones before it is finalized and ready for execution. The parties to the agreement are also the same as for the NDA, that is, the issuer, the bookrunners, and each individual investor.

Again, inevitably, there will be several rounds, going back and forth with each cornerstone investor to finalize this document, and some amount of horse-trading will take place. However, as is the case for the NDA, the parties to the agreement are generally familiar with the process and know what, and how much, can be negotiated. Such negotiations are also often conducted over a relatively short space of time (perhaps two to three weeks at most), so there are limitations to what can be changed from the initial template.

The subscription agreement evidences the fact that, subject to certain conditions, the investor is now prepared to make an equity investment in the company through the subscription of securities issued by the company (and/or sold by existing shareholders).

An example of cornerstone subscription agreement can be found in Appendix 7.

3.10.1 When must the agreements be signed?

Essentially, the cornerstone subscription agreements must in all cases be signed before the start of bookbuilding (that is, the offering to institutional investors) and publication of the preliminary offering circular—also known as a red or 'red herring'—used for marketing under the institutional tranche. The reason for this is that the bookrunners want to be in a position to announce before the offer (that is, the gathering of demand from institutions) starts in earnest that a substantial portion of the deal has already been taken up by cornerstone investors (and which ones).

In the event that anchor investors have expressed early demand for the securities on offer, then, more often than not, the lead banks will also be able to communicate to the wider marketplace that the entire IPO is already covered by the end of the first day of bookbuilding. This will enable them to build on this momentum to ensure that the IPO ends up multiple times subscribed, which in turn will also likely (although not systematically) mean a better valuation for the issuer and selling shareholders.

This, of course, ultimately depends on the price limits (or lack thereof) and quality of the orders received through the cornerstone process and in the book of demand. Ideally, the book of demand should include a significant core of orders by large professional investors, with a reasonably long-term investment horizon, also known as 'long only' funds.

In practice, in Southeast Asia (that is, in Malaysia and Singapore), the cornerstone subscription agreements will need to be signed before 'public exposure', that is when the draft prospectus is displayed online for the benefit of members of the public, to effectively mirror information in the pre-deal research reports that are sent to institutional investors (only). Members of the public are also able to comment on the draft offer documents (which they, however, rarely do).

This generally happens around midway through pre-deal investor education (PDIE), otherwise known as pre-marketing, the process through which the research analysts of the underwriting banks meet with institutional investors and gather their feedback to enable the lead banks and the issuer to agree on a bookbuilding price range, at which point the IPO will be formally marketed to investors. Because PDIE typically lasts for two weeks, the cornerstone agreements must be signed roughly a week before bookbuilding starts.

In Malaysia, public exposure is made for 15 days on the website of Suruhanjaya Sekuriti, the Securities Commission Malaysia, the regulator for the securities industry. In Singapore, the prospectus is displayed for a roughly similar period of time on Offers and Prospectuses Electronic Repository and Access (better known as OPERA), an Internet-based, electronic information system established by the Monetary Authority of Singapore, the country's *de facto* central bank and securities regulator.

The preliminary prospectus remains a draft and, as such, is subject to completion and amendment. It therefore also carries a disclaimer.

A typical disclaimer in Singapore would read as follows:

> The information in this Preliminary Prospectus is not complete and is subject to further amendments and completion in the final Prospectus to be registered by the Monetary Authority of Singapore. Under no circumstances shall this Preliminary Prospectus constitute an offer to sell or any solicitation of an offer to buy, nor shall there be any sale of securities in any jurisdiction on the basis of this Preliminary Prospectus. Certain information (including dates and times) and statements in this Preliminary Prospectus refer to events which have not occurred or been completed and may or may not have occurred or been completed by the time the final Prospectus is registered by the Monetary Authority of Singapore, which may or may not occur. We may not sell the Offering Shares until the Prospectus is delivered in its final form. A person to whom a copy of this Preliminary Prospectus is issued must not circulate this copy to any other person. No reliance may be placed for any purpose whatsoever on the information contained in this Preliminary Prospectus or on its completeness. By accepting this Preliminary Prospectus, you agree to be bound by the restrictions set out herein.

In Malaysia, the following disclaimer, which is even shorter, is prominently displayed on the website of the Securities Commission:

> The prospectuses displayed here have not been registered with the SC and are only for comments to be made by the public. THEY SHOULD NOT BE USED FOR MAKING ANY INVESTMENT DECISION. Securities cannot be offered and application for securities cannot be accepted until the prospectus has been registered by the SC. The SC shall not be liable for any non-disclosure on the part of the corporation and takes no responsibility for the contents of the prospectuses, makes no representation as to their accuracy or completeness and expressly disclaims any liability whatsoever for any loss howsoever arising from or in reliance upon the whole or any part of the contents of the prospectuses. [emphasis in source]

Hong Kong also has public exposure for prospectuses—with a few twists. First, the draft prospectus sent to the exchange for review (also known as an Application Proof) is simultaneously published (in both English and Chinese) on HKEx News, a website operated by the Stock Exchange of Hong Kong, and dedicated to listed company information, shareholding disclosures, and issuer-related information. This happens roughly two months before the pricing of the IPO and, at that stage, although substantially complete, the prospectus is still very much in draft form, and subject to any comments the exchange's listing division may have.

This is broadly similar to the publication of draft prospectuses on the US Securities and Exchange Commission's (the SEC's) Electronic Data Gathering, Analysis, and Retrieval (EDGAR) system.

Subsequently, following the listing hearing by the exchange's Listing Committee, another draft of the prospectus is also published online, on that same website. At this juncture, it is of course a much more advanced version and known as a post-hearing information pack (or PHIP). Unlike in Malaysia or Singapore, however, this draft is substantially redacted and does not include equity capital markets information such as the underwriting or plan of distribution section, as well as, crucially, information on cornerstone investors.

As in Malaysia and Singapore, draft prospectuses posted online in Hong Kong (both the application proof and the PHIP) all carry a warning statement to investors. A typical warning for a PHIP (which is similar to that used for an application proof, although longer and much more wordy than the disclaimers used in Malaysia or Singapore) would read as follows:

> The publication of this Post Hearing Information Pack ('PHIP') is required by The Stock Exchange of Hong Kong Limited (the 'Exchange')/the Securities and Futures Commission (the 'Commission') solely for the purpose of providing information to the public in Hong Kong.
>
> This PHIP is in draft form. The information contained in it is incomplete and is subject to change, which can be material. By viewing this document, you acknowledge, accept and agree with the Company, its sponsor(s), advisers or members of the underwriting syndicate that:
>
> (a) this document is only for the purpose of providing information about the Company to the public in Hong Kong and not for any other purposes. No investment decision should be based on the information contained in this document;
>
> (b) the publication of this document or supplemental, revised or replacement pages on the Exchange's website does not give rise to any obligation of the Company, its sponsor(s), advisers or members of the underwriting syndicate

to proceed with an offering in Hong Kong or any other jurisdiction. There is no assurance that the Company will proceed with the offering;

(c) the contents of this document or supplemental, revised or replacement pages may or may not be replicated in full or in part in the actual final listing document;

(d) the PHIP is not the final listing document and may be updated or revised by the Company from time to time in accordance with the Rules Governing the Listing of Securities on The Stock Exchange of Hong Kong Limited;

(e) this document does not constitute a prospectus, offering circular, notice, circular, brochure, or advertisement offering to sell any securities to the public in any jurisdiction, nor is it an invitation to the public to make offers to subscribe for or purchase any securities, nor is it calculated to invite offers by the public to subscribe for or purchase any securities;

(f) this document must not be regarded as an inducement to subscribe for or purchase any securities, and no such inducement is intended;

(g) neither the Company nor any of its affiliates, advisers or underwriters is offering, or is soliciting offers to buy, any securities in any jurisdiction through the publication of this document;

(h) no application for the securities mentioned in this document should be made by any person nor would such application be accepted;

(i) the Company has not and will not register the securities referred to in this document under the United States Securities Act of 1933, as amended, or any state securities laws of the United States;

(j) as there may be legal restrictions on the distribution of this document or dissemination of any information contained in this document, you agree to inform yourself about and observe any such restrictions applicable to you; and

(k) the application to which this document relates has not been approved for listing and the Exchange and the Commission may accept, return or reject the application for the subject public offering and/or listing.

If an offer or an invitation is made to the public in Hong Kong in due course, prospective investors are reminded to make their investment decisions solely based on the Company's prospectus registered with the Registrar of Companies in Hong Kong, copies of which will be distributed to the public during the offer period.

Accordingly, because the PHIP for a Hong Kong IPO is redacted, members of the public will only find information on the cornerstone investors in the public offer prospectus that is published at the start of the retail offering (that is, towards the end of the bookbuilding process) or, more likely, through the media, which will often relay such information, since it appears in the preliminary offering circular published for the benefit of institutional investors (only) at the start of bookbuilding.

3.10.2 Nature of the investment

Under the subscription agreement, the investor agrees that it subscribes for the securities at the IPO (or offer) price. Similarly, the company agrees that it will allot and issue such securities to the investor, and the company and the joint bookrunners further agree that they will cause the securities to be allocated to the investor.

The number of shares to be allocated to the investor is equal to the amount in currency subscribed for by the investor (excluding brokerage commissions) divided by the IPO price, rounded down (or up) to the nearest whole board lot. In any event, the number of shares to be subscribed by the investor remains subject to final determination by the company and the bookrunners (but is, in practice, always roughly equivalent to what is stated in the subscription agreement).

Separately, the investor also agrees to pay a brokerage commission to the bookrunners (typically 1 per cent of the amount of the IPO allocation received by the investor).

Lastly, in the case of IPOs in Malaysia or Singapore only, the investor and its affiliates are normally entitled to also apply for, or place an order through the bookbuilding process for the securities, in addition to those securities to be subscribed by, and allocated to the investor pursuant to the subscription agreement. As we have seen earlier, such 'double-dipping' is not allowed in Hong Kong.

3.10.3 Conditions precedent

Under the agreement, the subscription of securities by the investor remains subject to a number of conditions. In particular:

- the underwriting agreement for the public offering and the placement agreement for the institutional placement being entered into and having become unconditional (in accordance with their respective original terms, or as subsequently varied by agreement of the parties), by no later than the time and date specified in these agreements;
- completion of the admission of the securities to listing on the relevant stock exchange; and
- none of the above underwriting or placement agreement having been terminated in accordance with their respective terms.

It should be noted that execution of the underwriting agreement (for the retail offer) and placement agreement (for the institutional offer) are normally conditional upon each other. Accordingly, should the issuer and the bookrunners fail to agree on a price for the IPO, then no placement agreement will be signed, the underwriting agreement (signed as a 'hard underwriting' commitment prior to the start of the public offer) will become void, and the subscription agreements signed by the cornerstone investors will simply lapse.

3.10.4 Closing and delivery

Under the subscription agreement, the investor agrees to subscribe for the securities through the bookrunners upon (and, in Singapore only, contemporaneously with) the closing (that is, the settlement) of the placement, at such time and in such manner as shall be determined by the bookrunners.

Normally, for an IPO, such closing or settlement date will be on the same day as the listing and start of trading for the securities. Payment for the securities subscribed for, as well as payment of brokerage commissions to the bookrunners, therefore, takes place on that same date and (pretty much) at the same time.

The brokerage commission is normally payable to the joint bookrunners together and apportioned among them pursuant to whatever formula has been agreed between them and the issuer. As previously mentioned, for an IPO, the amount of such brokerage commission is typically equal to 1 per cent of the amount of shares allocated to each investor.

When the group of bookrunners is relatively small (say, single digits), more often than not, the brokerage pool will be split equally among them.

However, when many bookrunners are appointed by the issuer, brokerage may remain competitive and only the bookrunner which originated a cornerstone order may be entitled to it. The latter obviously does not encourage a spirit of cooperation among the lead banks and should therefore be avoided if at all possible.

Delivery of the securities to the investor is made through the central depositary system operated by, or working with, the relevant stock exchange, following receipt of payment.

The agreement also provides for circumstances where the investor fails to meet its obligations (that is, to pay for the shares it has agreed to subscribe for) or the securities fail to be admitted to listing. In such cases, the investor shall be deemed to have forfeited and waived all rights, benefits, and claims in relation to the securities.

In particular, if the investor has already paid for the securities, the relevant bookrunner (or bookrunners) holding the payment for the securities and related brokerage and/or the company (in the event that such monies are then held by the company or by a third party to its order) undertake(s) to return such amount to the investor, without any interest, within a set period of time (usually, a week or so).

Conversely, if the securities have been validly allotted and issued to the investor, and in the case of a capital raising only, then a capital reduction of the share capital of the company will be required for payment to be made from the monies held by the company. Accordingly, the company undertakes to procure such capital reduction to be effected as soon as reasonably practicable, and then to pay the investor back after a set period of time.

3.10.5 Restrictions on the investor

Restrictions on the investor essentially provide for cases where a lock-up is imposed on the securities subscribed. As we have already seen, nowadays this is only the case for IPOs listed in Hong Kong.

When the subscription agreement includes an investor lock-up, this does not simply focus on the outright sale of securities but also applies to options and warrants related to the securities. In particular, it provides for circumstances where the investor may:

- pledge the securities;

- transfer the securities to another party;
- contract to sell the securities;
- sell any option or contract to purchase the securities;
- purchase any option or contract to sell the securities;
- grant any option, right or warrant to purchase, lend, or otherwise transfer or dispose of any securities or warrants, or any securities convertible into or exercisable or exchangeable for the securities or warrants; or
- enter into any swap or other agreement or any transaction that transfers, in whole or in part, the economic consequence of ownership of the securities or warrants.

In addition, the investor usually also agrees, during the period of the lock-up, not to take any steps to issue new shares or other securities that are convertible or exchangeable into those subject to the lock-up, or to authorize the disposal of any such securities of the company without the prior written consent of the lead banks (which is rarely granted, although I am aware of at least one precedent in the case of a Hong Kong IPO in 2007).

Finally, the subscription agreement may also include a clause to the effect that, should the investor wish to dispose of the securities within a period extending beyond that of the lock-up (perhaps up to a year or so), it will give the company and the lead banks reasonable notice of such intended disposal (say, a week or thereabouts) and use all reasonable endeavours to ensure that such disposal is not only in compliance with all applicable laws and regulations, but also that it will not create a disorderly or false market.

3.10.6 Acknowledgements and warranties

3.10.6.1 Acknowledgements by the investor

First, the investor is asked to acknowledge that the company and the bookrunners will be under no liability whatsoever to the investor should the IPO not proceed for any reason. This is logical as performance of the subscription agreement is entirely subject to the transaction reaching completion, that is, the securities being listed and starting to trade on the stock exchange. If the deal fails to reach that ultimate stage for any reason, then the agreement will simply lapse.

Second, the investor is also asked to acknowledge that the subscription agreement, certain background information on the investor, and the relationship and arrangements between the parties to the subscription agreement will be required to be described in the prospectus and other marketing materials for the IPO.

In addition, as already noted, the subscription agreement constitutes a material contract required to be filed with regulatory authorities and/or made available for public inspection in connection with the offering.

Third, the investor is also asked to confirm that the issuer and the lead banks have no obligation to consider the interests of the investor in determining the IPO price. Indeed, they may have interests that conflict with those of the investor in doing so (that is, to sell at as high an IPO price as possible, subject to investor demand, whereas an investor will obviously generally try to pay as little as possible for the securities).

Further, the investor is required to accept the securities subject to the terms and conditions of the articles of association of the company.

Most importantly, the investor is required to acknowledge that, in reaching its investment decision, it has not relied on any preliminary information furnished to it by the company and the bookrunners. As mentioned in Section 3.8.1.1, no reliance can be placed by the investor on information contained in the preliminary offering circular (which is subject to change) or other documents provided to it on a confidential basis. Accordingly, the company and the bookrunners make no representation and give no warranty or undertaking as to the accuracy or completeness of any information not contained in such offering circular. The consequence of this is that they will have no liability to the investor resulting from the use of such information.

Lastly, the investor is asked to acknowledge that similar subscription agreements may be entered into with other cornerstones, either at the same time, or at a later stage (although before the closing of the transaction).

3.10.6.2 Warranties and undertakings by the investor

The cornerstone subscription agreement also includes 'standard' warranties and undertakings, in relation to capital markets transactions. In particular, the investor is asked to confirm that:

- it has been duly incorporated and is validly existing under the laws of its place of incorporation;
- it has full power, authority, and capacity to perform its obligations under the subscription agreement;

- there are no laws in any jurisdictions to which the investor is subject that may affect the execution and delivery of the subscription agreement (and, in turn, the acquisition of the securities by the investor);
- it will provide to the company and the bookrunners information that may be required by the relevant stock exchange or regulator, as well as other governmental, public, monetary, or other authorities;
- it will indemnify on demand the company and the bookrunners against losses, costs, expenses, claims, actions, liabilities, proceedings, or damages resulting from a breach of the subscription agreement by the investor;
- it is acquiring the securities for investment purposes only (and not for redistribution to other parties); and
- it has knowledge and experience in financial and business matters (and its ordinary business is to buy or sell or invest in shares or debentures, and that it is experienced in securities transactions) and is therefore capable of evaluating the merits and risks of the prospective investment.

The investor also confirms that it has received all the information it considers necessary or appropriate for deciding whether to acquire the securities. Obviously, in the case of a corporate cornerstone investor, such representation and warranty may perhaps be slightly tweaked, since its ordinary business may not necessarily be to buy, sell or invest in shares or debentures.

Furthermore, it is usual for the subscription agreement to include certain warranties and undertakings on the part of the investor with respect to US securities laws, as follows:

- that the investor is aware that the offer and sale of the securities has not been and will not be registered under the US Securities Act (that is, that there is no listing in the US and no offering to members of the public in the US), or the laws of any state or other jurisdiction in the US;
- that it is not located within the US or, if so, that it is a Qualified Institutional Buyer (or QIB, that is, a large institutional investor) and purchasing the securities pursuant to a private placement under Rule 144A and that the securities may not be offered, resold, pledged, or otherwise transferred except to offshore US investors or to QIBs;
- that it is not an affiliate of the company;
- that it is not purchasing the securities with a view to any resale or distribution pursuant to a public offering in the US; and

- that it has not purchased the securities as a result of any general solicitation or general advertising (as defined in Regulation D under the US Securities Act), including advertisements, articles, notices, or other communications published in any newspaper, magazine, on a website, or in or on any similar media or broadcast (that is, the investor has purchased the securities pursuant to a private placement only).

In addition, the investor warrants and undertakes the following:

- The investor will comply with any and all applicable selling restrictions in the offering circular. These set out the jurisdictions in which private placements may be made to institutional investors, without the need to conduct local public offers to sell or issue shares to members of the public. Ideally, the offer document should include selling restrictions in respect of all the jurisdictions in which the cornerstone investors and other institutions that are allocated shares are both located and incorporated.
- If it is purchasing the securities through a wholly owned subsidiary, such subsidiary will remain so until at least the expiry of any lock-up period.
- None of the materials which may have been provided to the investor constitutes an offer to acquire, purchase or subscribe for any securities in jurisdictions where such offer, solicitation or sale is not permitted and, in particular, that the subscription agreement does not, in any way, constitute an offer of securities for sale in the US or any other jurisdiction.
- It has conducted its own investigation into the affairs of the company and obtained its own independent advice.
- It is not a party related to the company.
- It is an institutional investor (or the equivalent—the definition of which varies from jurisdiction to jurisdiction).
- It will comply with any requirements imposed or which may be imposed by the relevant stock exchange or regulator in connection with the IPO.

Lastly, the investor confirms that the narrative describing it (which is usually included as a schedule to the subscription agreement) is accurate and consents to its inclusion in the preliminary offering circular and prospectus. It also agrees to provide additional information as may be required by the exchange or regulatory authorities. Information provided by a cornerstone investor normally includes, in addition to its legal name:

- its place of incorporation;

- its company number and certificate of incorporation number;
- its principal activities and ultimate controlling shareholder;
- details of other interests in the industry in which the issuer operates; as well as
- a short description of, or narrative on, the investor for insertion in the offer documents.

Examples of such narratives can be found in Appendix 8.

3.10.6.3 Representations and warranties by the company

The representations and warranties made by the company in a cornerstone subscription agreement are usually kept to a minimum. This document is first and foremost about the cornerstone investor purchasing the securities and the company—and its directors in particular—already take full responsibility for the contents of the offering circular, which is the only document which the cornerstone can legally rely on for information pertaining to the issuer.

Accordingly, the company usually only represents and warrants that:

- it has been duly incorporated and is validly existing under the laws of its country of incorporation;
- the issue and sale of the securities will, upon admission to listing, be fully paid and free from all options, liens, charges, mortgages, pledges, claims, equities, encumbrances, and other third party rights, and that these shall rank *pari passu* with other securities to be listed on the exchange;
- it has full power, authority, and capacity to enter into, and perform its obligations under the subscription agreement and the agreement constitutes valid and binding obligations of the company (and is therefore enforceable against the company); and
- there are no laws in any jurisdictions to which the company is subject that may affect the execution and delivery of the subscription agreement.

3.10.6.4 Representations by the bookrunners

As noted, the cornerstone subscription agreement is fundamentally a contract between the issuer and the investor. Accordingly, the bookrunners will generally only represent that they can delegate their rights, duties, powers, and discretions under the agreement to any of their affiliates, to cater for the fact that different subsidiaries or other group companies may be involved when selling securities across various jurisdictions.

3.10.6.5 Announcements and confidentiality

Even though the NDA has already been signed at that stage, the subscription agreement usually also contains a short clause, which states that the transactions contemplated in that document remain confidential and must not be disclosed by one party without the prior written consent of the other.

However, such information can be disclosed to legal and financial advisers and employees of each signatory, provided that they abide by the same confidentiality obligations. It may also be disclosed if required by any law, regulatory authority, or stock exchange rules (which addresses the issue of publication of details of the cornerstone tranche in the offer documents, at which point the arrangements actually become public).

3.10.6.6 Governing law

Considerations pertaining to governing law for the subscription agreement are similar to those applicable to the non-disclosure agreement. Usually, the subscription agreement will be under English or New York law in the case of international investors, and under Hong Kong, Malaysian, or Singaporean law in the case of domestic buyers.

3.11 Finalizing the allocations and settlement

3.11.1 Pricing the deal

Once the agreements have been signed, the subscriptions made by the cornerstone investors can be reflected in the preliminary offering circular and prospectus. As noted earlier, in Malaysia and Singapore (only), this will first appear in the exposure drafts available on the websites of the Securities Commission Malaysia and Monetary Authority of Singapore respectively.

The preliminary offering circular is a document published for the benefit of institutional investors and sent to them (only) as bookbuilding starts (which is also when the management roadshow begins). When this happens, it is usual for financial journalists to pick up on the information that a cornerstone tranche has been assembled, especially in the case of a large, visible, and notable IPO.

Details of the cornerstone subscriptions, accordingly, often appear in, or on the likes of the *Financial Times*, *Wall Street Journal*, Bloomberg, Reuters, *FinanceAsia*, *The Edge*, or *GlobalCapital*; and perhaps on a syndicated basis, in the *South China Morning Post* in Hong Kong, *Straits Times* in Singapore, and *Business Post* or *The Star* in Malaysia. Chinese-language and *Bahasa Malaysia* publications also commonly relay the information, as appropriate.

After publication in the preliminary offering circular, details of the cornerstone tranche will also appear in the public offer prospectus (or, in Singapore, the OIS), which is published for the benefit of retail investors. In Hong Kong, this is actually the only offer document in which such information will be made available to members of the public, since the online 'exposure drafts' are always redacted, and do not include information on the equity capital markets aspects of an IPO.

Once the institutional and retail offers have closed, the issuer—and any selling shareholder(s)—as well as the bookrunners must price the IPO, having regard to the demand received from all investors. If the deal has been heavily oversubscribed at any level within the price range, and if the book of demand includes enough quality institutional investors in particular, then it is likely that the offering will be priced at, or near, the top end of the range.

Conversely, in cases where the IPO is only marginally oversubscribed, or when the quality of the investor base is found to be lacking, or when there has been significant price sensitivity, then the deal will likely be priced at, or towards, the bottom end of the range. In some cases, the IPO may even be priced below the indicative price range (although this is rare in Asia, and is more of a practice in the US), or the deal may also be postponed in cases where investor demand is particularly weak. In Asia, pricing above the range would require the members of the public who have already subscribed (and paid) for their shares at the top end of the price range to consent to this (see Section 3.11.5). Again, this is more of a practice in the US.

More often than not, however, the book will be priced somewhere in between the bottom and the top end of the range.

After pricing has been agreed, the sale and purchase agreement, pursuant to which the syndicate of underwriters underwrites the shares comprised in the institutional (or international) tranche, is signed. The underwriting agreement for the public offer tranche will already have been signed (with conditions, including the subsequent signing of the sales and purchase agreement) prior to the launch of the public offer, since retail offerings, unlike institutional placements, must be 'hard' underwritten. In other words, the underwriters must have committed to buying the shares before they can offer them to members of the public. This is different from the 'soft' (also known as settlement) underwriting for orders placed by institutional investors.

A number of other documents are signed and delivered at that point, and bring down due diligence is also conducted, details of all of which can be found in my book *IPO: A Global Guide* (now in its second edition), published by Hong Kong University Press, but these are beyond the scope of this book on cornerstone investors.

3.11.2 Cornerstone investors and underwriting obligations

Increasingly, the senior underwriting investment banks argue that, in the event of one or more cornerstone investors defaulting, their own 'soft' underwriting obligations under the institutional tranche should fall away. The argument they generally use is that such accounts are so essential to the completion of the deal that one or more of their subscriptions not reaching the closing stage can constitute a material event, which then needs to be disclosed to other investors (including members of the public), who must accordingly decide whether to remain in or out of the deal themselves.

To my mind, such an argument is quite far-fetched: equity issuers (and their advisers) should instead ask themselves why such cornerstone subscriptions might not ultimately make it to the closing. In such a case, three scenarios are probably applicable:

- The first scenario concerns an issue with the investor itself, for example significant (and unexpected) redemptions on the part of the end-investors of, or the disclosure of fraud at, say, a major hedge fund. In such a case (a 'Bernard Madoff' type of event), it is probably preferable for all the parties concerned that the account should drop out—provided that there is still enough demand for the deal to be fully subscribed, or even oversubscribed. Such an event can rather easily be explained to the wider market, and should not affect the outcome of a deal.
- The second case might involve an unforeseen 'macro' event, for example, a major terrorist attack in one of the world's main financial centres, such as the multiple assaults on New York and other US locations on 11 September 2001. However, this would also likely trigger the *force majeure* clause in the underwriting and sale and purchase agreements, providing the underwriters with an 'out', as has long been capital markets practice.
- The last scenario may arise in relation to the issuer itself, say, a major disaster at one of the company's key production facilities, which may in turn open a wider set of issues and concerns. If and when that happens, it may perhaps not be advisable to proceed with the IPO in the first place.

A possible solution is for the issuer and the underwriters to agree on a threshold, expressed as a number of shares, the settlement of which might be in default, beyond which the underwriters' obligations would actually be repealed. This can allow for one, or perhaps even several cornerstones to default—a most unlikely scenario—before the underwriters can legally back away from their commitments.

However, this only really works in the case of fairly large IPOs. In a small transaction, the presence or absence of a single digit number of cornerstones can often readily make or break the outcome of a deal.

3.11.3 Allocating the IPO

3.11.3.1 Institutional investors

Only when pricing has been agreed can the book of demand be allocated. For institutions, this is a process that is conducted largely manually, and more of an art than a science. Each investor (other than the cornerstones, whose allocations are guaranteed and already pre-agreed) is first assigned a quality ranking or grading, agreed among the syndicate desks of the bookrunner banks. This can be a rather lengthy process.

'Allocation runs' are then made using algorithms whereby, for example, the best ranked investors receive, say, 75 per cent of the shares (or securities) they have applied for; the second-best ranked investors, 50 per cent; and so on. Usually, institutional investors are ranked into four or five categories.

Once the allocation runs result in a number of shares that is close to the number of shares offered in the institutional portion of the IPO (including shares subject to any overallotment option—usually around 15 per cent of the shares comprised in the IPO—but excluding the shares subscribed by the cornerstone investors), manual adjustments are then made on a line-by-line basis, to ensure that investors receive round numbers of shares and, importantly, multiples of the board lot (that is, the minimum number of shares in which the latter can be traded on the exchange).

All allocations are made on the basis of shares (or units, for REITs and business trusts), so any orders placed in US dollars or other currency must at that point be converted into shares at the offer price.

At this stage, minor adjustments may also be made to the cornerstone allocations, but the amounts they have subscribed for will, by and large, be those they ultimately receive upon settlement of the offering. At this juncture, changes made to the cornerstone allocations are not material and relate to issues such as exchange rates or the board lot, taking into account the final IPO price. It should be remembered that when the cornerstone investors signed the subscription agreements, the offer price was not yet known, hence these minor adjustments (which are readily provided for under the agreements, as previously explained in Section 3.10.2).

3.11.3.2 Retail investors

Unlike institutional allocations, allocations to retail investors are calculated mechanically, since it would be unpractical to distinguish between the 'quality' of various members of the public as shareholders.

Retail allocations are therefore made by the registrar appointed by the company, using a balloting process, based on the number of shares applied for by each investor. Bands of numbers of shares are determined, and allocation runs calculated accordingly, having regard to other considerations such as a willingness on the part of the company to allocate shares to any applicant (or not, in which case some applications will be unsuccessful and some investors will receive no shares at all), or a cap on the absolute number of shares a single retail investor may actually receive.

Here too, board lots must be taken into account, to ensure that retail investors receive only multiples of the number of shares in which the latter can actually be traded on the exchange.

3.11.4 Placing letters

'Placing' letters are then sent to all 'institutional' investors (including the cornerstone investors) by the bookrunner(s). Essentially, such letters serve to confirm the exact amount of shares each institution will receive, and also ask the institutions to revert by way of acknowledgment, including their securities accounts details.

Placing letters also commonly include US representations and warranties, similar to those shown in Section 3.10.6.2, which each investor is asked to (re)confirm.

3.11.5 Settlement

A few days later, settlement takes place on the same day as listing and the start of trading. Institutional investors (including the cornerstone investors) receive the securities they have subscribed for, in exchange for payment to the company and/or any selling shareholders, through one or more of the bookrunner banks. Normally, one bank will act as the settlement agent on behalf of the others to ensure an orderly process. In developed markets such as Hong Kong, Malaysia, and Singapore, settlement is made on a DVP (delivery versus payment) basis, so the crossing of securities and money is pretty much simultaneous.

The process for retail investors is different, and essentially the same across all of the above three markets. To apply in an IPO, members of the public are always asked to pay for the securities in advance, at the top end of the indicative price range. In Hong Kong in particular, many retail investors enter into on-margin, borrowing arrangements with Hong Kong retail banks or brokers to finance such investments. If the IPO is priced below the top end of the range, they then receive (together with their allocation of securities) a refund for the difference between the price they have paid for and the actual IPO price, as well as between the number of shares they have applied for, and the number of shares they ultimately receive as an allocation, bearing in mind that a number of retail investors will—as will indeed some institutions—inflate their orders in a bid to receive more shares, especially in a well-subscribed transaction.

3.11.6 Overallotment options and cornerstones

In many IPOs, and especially the larger ones, it is common for the offer structure to include what is known as an overallotment option, or Greenshoe (a name derived from that of the first company, the Green Shoe Company, which used that device in the US).

A Greenshoe is nothing more than an extra amount of securities, on top of the 'firm' shares that are otherwise comprised in the IPO, and it is allocated to institutional investors (only) at the same time as the other shares. Such extra shares are usually borrowed, either from a large, legacy shareholder, or from the company itself, for example in the case where there are Treasury shares (that is, shares issued by the company and held by the company for its own account). Alternatively, a Greenshoe may also be allocated using new securities issued by the company, although this can be an issue in the case of REITs or business trusts, since it increases the number of units in issue, and therefore affects the dividend per unit (DPU).

The purpose of a Greenshoe is to allow the price of the securities to be stabilized in the aftermarket, after start of trading, should it ever fall below the offer price during a period of up to 30 days after listing. To do this, one of the bookrunners—known as a stabilizing agent or manager—will, on behalf of the syndicate, simply buy shares in the market, effectively covering the short created at the time of allocation (and returning such shares to the lending party).

There is an option linked to this additional amount of shares, whereby the latter (when not bought back) can actually be sold or issued under the IPO, but only if the share price trades at or above the IPO price. Without going into too much detail, a Greenshoe can therefore be exercised in full, partially, or not at all, depending on how the share price performs after listing. In addition, unlike in the US, in Asia no 'naked short' can be used by the stabilizing manager above and over the Greenshoe to stabilize a new issue. The Greenshoe also cannot be 'refreshed' (that is, where the stabilizing agent reallocates Greenshoe shares to investors after buying them back in the market).

Greenshoes typically represent around 15 per cent of the amount of shares comprised in an IPO.

Because allocations made to cornerstone investors are pre-agreed in advance, the Greenshoe is normally allocated to the other institutional investors only. Accordingly, should the Greenshoe be exercised (in full or in part), the percentage of the shares in issue (or indeed in the IPO) represented by a cornerstone allocation will actually decrease as a result. In effect, cornerstone investors are protected from the reallocation of shares under a clawback from the institutional tranche to the public offer tranche, but their aggregate allocation—unlike that of other institutional investors—will not increase as a result of exercising the overallotment option.

Part 4

Issues associated with cornerstone investors

The cornerstone process in Asia has initially worked well, ensuring the success of many transactions over a period of more than 15 years. In particular, many multibillion dollar IPOs in the region (including new listings around the US$20 billion mark by several Chinese and other regional financial institutions) would perhaps not have been possible, absent significant subscriptions by cornerstone investors.

However, the practice now increasingly raises issues, most of which are in relation to IPOs in Hong Kong.

As we saw earlier, the main reason for including cornerstone investors in capital markets transactions is to raise the confidence of the wider pool of investors, and to encourage them to participate in new issues. Effectively, by participating in IPOs, cornerstones provide leadership and momentum, that is, a form of 'stamp of approval' or vote of confidence.

Increasingly, however, cornerstone investors have become the only way some IPOs can be completed at all, by sourcing price-insensitive and 'friendly' demand, which would not otherwise be found through normal marketing channels.

While cornerstone investors always made possible the launch of more challenging offerings, especially against volatile market conditions, their presence has now become effectively *de rigueur* in any sizeable offering in the region, and this may not necessarily be for the better. Many market participants have therefore complained that cornerstone tranches have become too large, as brought to light by the *FinanceAsia* survey, previously mentioned in Chapter 1.5.

In addition, the practice raises other issues, a number of which have been picked upon by financial commentators over the years.

4.1
Ethics

There is no doubt that cornerstone investors are, in a way, 'favoured' by the bookrunners. They are approached at an early stage in IPOs and given the opportunity to subscribe in large amounts in these offerings, well before other investors.

And while they must abide by some additional requirements (although, in fact, very few of them in the case of IPOs in Malaysia and Singapore, as we have seen earlier), they actually pay the same price as any other investors. They are therefore part of a shortlist that benefits from a 'first look' opportunity, broadly equivalent to a right of first refusal, leading some observers to talk of an inside game and unfair behaviour.[1]

Governance activist David Webb argued at the time of United Co. Rusal's US$2.2 billion IPO in Hong Kong in January 2010 that 'the presence of cornerstone investors is of no value to investment decisions', while Low Chee Keong, an associate professor in corporate law at the Chinese University of Hong Kong, also questioned the fairness of the practice, saying that 'it was at best difficult to justify their existence' and that 'at worst, one could contend that cornerstones serve primarily to prefer a select group of investors by the underwriters', and may [even] constitute 'a sophisticated form of bribery'.[2]

This concern has actually become more prevalent, given the increasing weight of cornerstone investors in new issues, and in Hong Kong more than anywhere else. In October 2016, *The Economist* noted that, in Hong Kong, cornerstones 'accounted for 13 per cent of total IPO values in the first decade

1. Philippe Espinasse, 'Cornerstone investors and ethics', *Wall Street Journal*, 22 December 2010.
2. Low Chee Keong, 'Cornerstone investors and initial public offerings on the Stock Exchange of Hong Kong', *Fordham Journal of Corporate and Financial Law*, Vol. XIV, No. 3, 2009.

of the century'. Since then, cornerstone investment as a percentage of Hong Kong's deal volume has steadily increased (with a small dip between 2012 and 2014), to an astonishing 60 per cent.[3]

In 2014, the Financial Services Development Council (FSDC) in Hong Kong noted in a publication, that 'in recent years, cornerstone investment has become an increasingly important part of the Hong Kong IPO process and that cornerstone investments of a combined size exceeding 70 per cent of a global offering are not unheard of'.[4] We have already seen in Section 1.5.9 that such levels have even recently been exceeded on a few occasions, obviously a worrying development as far as the liquidity of new issues is concerned (and also given the requirement for a six-month lock-up in Hong Kong).

The practice is clearly not illegal, but can it really be said to be ethical?

---

3. Anonymous, 'Chinese IPOs in Hong Kong: Cornering the market', *The Economist*, 1 October 2016.
4. 'Positioning Hong Kong as an international IPO centre of choice', Hong Kong Financial Services Development Council (FSDC), June 2014.

4.2

Cornerstone investors: A way around market forces?

In a guidance note issued in February 2013,[1] the IPO Transactions Department of the Stock Exchange of Hong Kong noted that, in 2012, among the 50 newly listed companies on the Main Board of the exchange, the cornerstone placings ranged between 6 per cent and 66 per cent of the total offering size of IPO shares. In 2011, the range was between 9 per cent and 76 per cent. It also added that more cornerstone placings were seen when market conditions were difficult.

In 2011, the (relaunched) Hong Kong IPO of China Outfitters, a Chinese designer and manufacturer of casual menswear and accessories (under the brand names JEEP, Santa Barbara Polo, and Racquet Club, among others), included three cornerstone investments that made up almost 75.7 per cent of the offer size, equivalent to almost 15.3 per cent of the company's issued capital. Because the issuer initially failed to gather demand for its shares in a previous attempt at listing, it can reasonably be argued that, without the presence of these three cornerstones, the IPO could never have been completed.

A similar observation can be made in the case of the Hong Kong IPO of pork producer WH Group in July 2014, whose IPO was successfully relaunched after an aborted first attempt in April of that same year. While no 'formal' cornerstones were actually secured at the second attempt, early orders reportedly received from approximately 30 anchor investors (see Chapter 1.12) made it possible to finally complete the much trimmed US$2 billion equivalent new listing.[2]

---

1. HKEx Guidance Letter HKEX GL51-13, February 2013.
2. Philippe Espinasse, 'Cornering elusive cornerstones', *The Peak Hong Kong*, September 2014.

In its report (see Chapter 4.1), the FSDC also noted that 'one undesirable side effect of IPO cornerstone investment is that it takes the pricing process further away from the normal market forces, and may have a distortive effect on the company's market value' and that 'in sluggish market conditions, the success of an IPO often hinges on the ability of the deal managers and the listing applicant to attract cornerstone investors'.

It added that 'the aftermarket performance of companies with a significant cornerstone component in their IPOs proves to be sub-optimal', having calculated that those transactions with cornerstone tranches that represented more than 50 per cent of the offer had significantly underperformed the wider market,[3] a finding similar to those in later studies by financial journalists and media publications (see Section 1.5.9).

The Economist went even further, saying that companies are actually 'using cornerstones to evade market forces'.[4]

In other words, cornerstone investors have, in many cases, become little more than a device to get deals done, irrespective of demand for the securities by the wider pool of investors. And, more often than not, reality soon catches up with these issuers—and their shareholders.

3. 'Positioning Hong Kong as an international IPO centre of choice', Hong Kong Financial Services Development Council (FSDC), June 2014.
4. Anonymous, 'Chinese IPOs in Hong Kong: Cornering the market', *The Economist*, 1 October 2016.

4.3
Disclosure

As we have seen earlier, one requirement across all markets is that the names of the cornerstones and other key details related to them must be disclosed in the offer document.

There are of course a few variations: individual cornerstone allocations are generally not disclosed in Malaysia, nor are they, at least from time to time, in Singapore. However, in all cases, the name of each cornerstone investor must be accompanied by a short narrative describing the individual account, for the benefit of potential participants in the IPO.

The issue here is that such narratives often do not say very much, on occasion merely describing cornerstones as holdings incorporated in offshore jurisdictions, which invest across a range of industries. This is probably appropriate when the individual behind the company is a well-known tycoon (and identified as such), but does not really help in cases where the ultimate shareholder is a virtually unknown entity, or even not mentioned altogether. Examples of such narratives are set out in Appendix 8.

In October 2016, in a long column published on his website,[1] Hong Kong–based governance activist David Webb complained that such an individual 'of which he had never heard before' was only 'given seven lines of glowing biography in the cornerstone description'. Further, he identified that the individual in question only owned a maximum of 1 per cent of the actual investing company—a joint venture—and that its other shareholder was in turn owned by two Chinese individuals, also unknown entities, and that even the Chinese version of the prospectus did not contain their Chinese character

1. http://www.webb-site.com, David M. Webb, 'Hiding behind the cornerstones', accessed 6 October 2016.

names. Webb concluded by saying that 'simply naming shareholders, without their background, was meaningless disclosure'.

Not only is the background information provided on cornerstone investors sometimes lacking in substance, it can on occasion also be frankly misleading. In that same column, Webb described how cornerstone investors who took 31 per cent of the IPO of a bank in Hong Kong had secretly laid off their risk by issuing derivatives to a property developer from the same city (in mainland China). None of these arrangements were described in the IPO prospectus, and the identity of the margin lender who could potentially end up owning the shares was not disclosed either.

This obviously raises issues about whether these transactions were entered into to evade the restrictions imposed by the six-month lock-up, and whether the issuer and the lead banks (including the IPO's sponsors) had also consented to (or even worse, contributed to financing) the arrangement.

Webb also found out that such cornerstone investors had participated in that same capacity in other IPOs in Hong Kong, and questioned whether they had entered into similar secret arrangements to bypass the lock-ups in other offerings.

4.4

The lock-up requirement

Perhaps one of the main issues with cornerstone investors is the requirement that their subscriptions be locked up after an IPO. As we have seen, this is now only the case in Hong Kong, where a six-month lock-up post listing remains mandatory.

Such a requirement has several consequences.

First, the lock-up creates an 'overhang' of shares in the market, which not only reduces trading liquidity, as noted by Hong Kong's FSDC,[1] but also depresses the share price of the company near the expiry of the lock-up, because the market generally expects significant sales of shares to be forthcoming—either because the cornerstones want to lock in capital gains, or finally dispose of a loss-making holding to which they were forced to cling on to.

Second, the FSDC also noted 'a wider conceptual issue' between 'the existence of a large and illiquid "overhang" and the concept of a minimum public float, which is a key principle of the Hong Kong market'.

Indeed, there have been many issues in Hong Kong about companies that have not taken adequate action to address a low public float, thereby, in the words of the Hong Kong exchange, 'denying reasonable access to the market and preventing its proper functioning, depriving shareholders of trading their shares and/or realizing their investments in the market'.[2]

Imposing a lock-up on cornerstone investors would therefore seem at odds with such a principle, as well as with market practice in the other Asian

---

1. 'Positioning Hong Kong as an international IPO centre of choice', Hong Kong Financial Services Development Council (FSDC), June 2014.
2. Philippe Espinasse, 'Doing away with Hong Kong's free-float rule', *GlobalCapital*, 3 August 2016.

markets where cornerstone investors can be found, chiefly in Malaysia and Singapore. In 2008, the Stock Exchange of Hong Kong toyed with the idea of introducing a concept of a minimum 'market float' (excluding investors or shareholders subject to a lock-up), within the public float for listed companies, so as to ensure sufficient aftermarket liquidity, but this was ultimately not adopted.[3]

Third, the lock-up on cornerstone investors increasingly leads to 'the wrong type' of cornerstones being assembled, that is, corporates—and especially state-owned enterprises—and 'friends and family' types of investors, who are not particularly concerned about a restriction on their ability to immediately trade the shares post-listing or even about the actual valuation of the company.[4] And, as we have already seen, Chinese SOEs in particular are not actually allowed to trade in the secondary market under Chinese law, further adding to the concerns over liquidity.

Arguably, the quality of cornerstone investors gathered in IPOs in Malaysia and Singapore is often much higher than in Hong Kong, with cornerstone tranches in these first jurisdictions regularly exhibiting sovereign wealth funds, pension funds, well-known asset managers, tycoons, and some of the larger hedge funds, all of which have generally been noticeably absent as cornerstone investors in Hong Kong IPOs, sometimes for years.

---

3. Nigel Davis and Melanie Mitchell, *Hong Kong Listed Companies: Law and Practice*, Wolters Kluwer, 2012.
4. Philippe Espinasse, 'Game of thrones in the SAR', *GlobalCapital*, 1 November 2016.

4.5
Recent developments

In February 2017, China's State Administration of Foreign Exchange (SAFE) announced that investors from the PRC would now be able to invest directly into Hong Kong IPOs as cornerstone investors. Previously, such accounts were only able to do so through offshore-incorporated companies, or under China's Qualified Domestic Institutional Investor (QDII) scheme, which only permitted onshore Chinese investors to invest outside of the country up to a certain limit, and within a foreign exchange quota.

However, SAFE also explained that this new development would come with strings attached. Investors would be required to bring back onshore proceeds from a partial or full disposal of the cornerstone holdings (obviously after the expiry of the compulsory six-month lock-up). It also stated that investors would be required to exit their positions 'at a certain time', although the holding period was not specified at the time of writing.[1]

Given the significant flight of capital from China in recent months and years, this initiative was generally seen at the time of its announcement as a good way for the country to manage its capital outflows, and increase its foreign exchange reserves. The new arrangement was also considered to potentially have a positive impact on Hong Kong IPOs, as it would increase the number of investors from mainland China able to subscribe in a cornerstone capacity into new issues. Some observers, however, pointed out that the dominance of state-owned firms and other large corporates was unlikely to be eroded, and also that it would take time to educate the wider pool of firms now able to subscribe at an early stage into Hong Kong IPOs.

---

1. Jonathan Breen, 'China lays out new path for cornerstones to HK IPOs', *GlobalCapital*, 9 February 2017.

Similarly, it may also take time for seasoned investors in the Hong Kong market to familiarize themselves with what could be a large pool of relatively unknown names, perhaps to some extent negating one of the advantages of including cornerstones in IPOs in the first place.[2]

2. Jonathan Breen, 'No quick fix for HK's cornerstone problem', *GlobalCapital*, 14 February 2017.

Conclusion

There is now no escaping the presence of cornerstone investors in new equity offerings in some of Asia's key markets. Once an optional device in the bookrunners' toolkit to help them complete challenging transactions or, alternatively, a technique used by issuers to reward institutional shareholders with which they had established strategic relationships, cornerstones have now become an essential component of the offer structure to bring sizeable IPOs to market in the region.

There are several reasons behind this development.

The volatile trading environment, a legacy of the global subprime financial crisis, is probably partly to blame. The lead banks now increasingly need to rely on a core group of large allottees to de-risk equity offerings. Launching major transactions without such backing has become largely unthinkable. From a 'nice-to-have', cornerstones have become a 'must-have' feature of pretty much any deal, and especially in Hong Kong.

In effect, cornerstone tranches in Hong Kong have become a bit of a 'magic trick', and maybe even the *only* trick to getting large IPOs done in the city. The well-respected *Economist* observed, after the H-share IPO of Postal Savings Bank of China in September 2016, that 'instead of bringing in savvy investors who might persuade others to hop aboard, [China's] state-owned firms are cramming in other friendly state-backed investors to ensure their IPOs are successful'.[1] Its columnist even added that cornerstones were 'a classic case of China Inc. in action' as the state was 'shifting money from pocket to pocket . . . with limited [IPO] participation from outside investors'.

1. Anonymous, 'Chinese IPOs in Hong Kong: Cornering the market', *The Economist*, 1 October 2016.

The quality of the new issues now coming to market is perhaps also a reason for the increasingly widespread use of the practice. This is again especially true in Hong Kong, where the overwhelming majority of equity issuance in recent times has been by Chinese banks, brokers, and insurance companies. At the time of writing, the weight of the financial sector in the Hang Seng Index was almost 45 per cent. The growing issue of non-performing loans in the PRC, as well as the recurring freeze imposed by the regulatory authorities on domestic IPOs, has led many such issuers to instead seek capital in the neighbouring territory, just across the border from the Chinese mainland.

Irrespective of the industry sector, Hong Kong is also increasingly a listing venue for Chinese, rather than international, issuers. The former now account for more than 60 per cent and almost 70 per cent of the exchange's market capitalization and equity turnover, respectively. In the first quarter of 2016, 92 per cent of the IPO funds raised in Hong Kong were by Chinese companies.[2]

In addition, Chinese banks and brokers, rather than members of the bulge-bracket, international houses, or local brokers, now represent the lion's share of bookrunner roles (at least by number) in Hong Kong IPOs.

The irony is that much of the equity they contribute to raising now comes from investors from their own domestic market, rather than international investors, and that many of the former are now basically using Hong Kong, once a major marketplace for international fund managers to buy into primary issues, as a convenient conduit for such investments.

At the time of writing, there was a significant valuation gap between Chinese stocks listed in Hong Kong and their counterparts in Shanghai or Shenzhen, lending further impetus to this development.

There are signs that the Chinese authorities may be starting to recognize that the issue now needs to be addressed: in October 2016, China's SAFE, the country's foreign exchange regulator, started asking Chinese investors to submit requests for approval if they wanted to buy substantial amounts of Hong Kong currency for IPO investments in the city.[3] Such approval,

2. Philippe Espinasse, 'From the Kingdom to the Middle Kingdom', *GlobalCapital*, 10 May 2016.
3. Fox Hu and Steven Yang, 'China cornerstone buyers get clearer path to Hong Kong IPOs', Bloomberg, 1 November 2016.

however, is not needed in the case of Chinese investors who already have adequate foreign currency funds located offshore, including in Hong Kong.

With cornerstone investments largely made through subsidiaries incorporated in the British Virgin Islands, it is doubtful whether this move will actively help stem the flood of IPO investments from the mainland into Hong Kong's new issues. Furthermore, the root of the problem probably lies more in the existence of the compulsory lock-up in Hong Kong than in cross-border fund flows regulations. Some commentators at the time went as far as to suggest that the city's IPO market might even get a boost from these new rules, since they may smoothen the path for Chinese cornerstone investors to subscribe into Hong Kong new listings (which may now perhaps be the case under the new procedures decreed by SAFE allowing them to bypass the QDII scheme, and which came into effect in February 2017—see Chapter 4.5 above).

Cornerstone investors have served the Asian equity capital markets well, but now is perhaps the time for a rethink, and in Hong Kong more than anywhere else. The practice, however, continues to work well in Southeast Asia, not least because the rules there—and in particular the absence of a compulsory lock-up—make it much more palatable to institutional players.

As to whether cornerstones will increasingly feature (and perhaps even become regulated) in new offerings in Europe, or indeed in the US, only time will tell.

In February 2017, Snap Inc., the owner of messaging app Snapchat disclosed that it expected investors buying up to 25 per cent of its US$3.4 billion IPO to agree to be locked up for a year. This may perhaps be the start of a 'new normal' for new listings beyond Asia's shores.[4]

4. Lauren Hirsch and Olivia Oran, 'Snap expects some IPO investors to hold stock for a year', Reuters, 28 February 2017.

Appendix 1

Recent examples of cornerstone tranches in Hong Kong

Issuer	IPO size pre-Greenshoe (US$m equivalent)	Cornerstone investors (*indicates investors related to the issuer or to one of its shareholders)	Amount subscribed (US$m equivalent)
Postal Savings Bank of China	7,430	CSIC Investment:	2,090
(September 2016)		Shanghai International Port:	2,044
		Victory Global Group:	1,000
		State Grid Overseas:	300
		China Chentong Holdings:	150
		Great Wall Pan Asia:	100
		Total:	**5,684.0**
		Number of cornerstones:	6
		Percentage of IPO size:	76.5%
Everbright Securities	1,105	China Shipbuilding Capital:	184.0
(August 2016)		CSCEC Capital (Hong Kong):	184.0
		Hengjian International:	184.0
		China Life:	80.0
		BOCOM Investment:	50.0
		Dazhong HK:*	30.0
		PICA:*	30.0
		Mercuries Life:	20.0
		Total:	**762.0**
		Number of cornerstones:	8
		Percentage of IPO size:	69.0%

(continued on p. 125)

Issuer	IPO size pre-Greenshoe (US$m equivalent)	Cornerstone investors (*indicates investors related to the issuer or to one of its shareholders)	Amount subscribed (US$m equivalent)
DFZQ	1,000	Hung Jia Finance:	100.0
(June 2016)		BOCOM Investment:	99.0
		Great Boom Group:	50.0
		Pinpoint Asset Management:	50.0
		CES Global Holdings:	30.0
		Shanghai Electric:	30.0
		SIIC Treasury:	30.0
		Value Partners:	30.0
		Yunnan Energy:	30.0
		CM Securities:	25.0
		Total:	**474.0**
		Number of cornerstones:	10
		Percentage of IPO size:	47.4%
China Logistics Property Holdings	432	Joy Orient:	120.0
(June 2016)		Anbang Investment:	60.0
		LRC. Belt and Road:	20.0
		China Fintech:	20.0
		Total:	**220.0**
		Number of cornerstones:	4
		Percentage of IPO size:	50.9%

(continued on p. 126)

Issuer	IPO size pre-Greenshoe (US$m equivalent)	Cornerstone investors (*indicates investors related to the issuer or to one of its shareholders)	Amount subscribed (US$m equivalent)
Greentown Service Group	198	Greentown China:*	35
(June 2016)		Zhejiang Silicon Paradise:	31
		China Orient:	25
		Total:	**91**
		Number of cornerstones:	3
		Percentage of IPO size:	46.0%
China Development Bank Financial Leasing	795	Three Gorges Capital:	335.0
(June 2016)		China Re Group:	95.0
		Hengjian International:	65.0
		Fortune Eris:	50.0
		BOCGI:	41.0
		CCCC International:	39.5
		Total:	**625.5**
		Number of cornerstones:	6
		Percentage of IPO size:	78.7%

(continued on p. 127)

Issuer	IPO size pre-Greenshoe (US$m equivalent)	Cornerstone investors (*indicates investors related to the issuer or to one of its shareholders)	Amount subscribed (US$m equivalent)
BOC Aviation	1,121	China Investment Corporation:	99.5
(May 2016)		Silk Road Fund:	99.5
		China Development Bank:	59.7
		China Life Franklin AM:	49.7
		Oman Investment Fund:	49.7
		Hony Capital:	49.7
		Elion Resources:	49.8
		Fullerton:	37.8
		Fosun International:	34.8
		The Boeing Company:	29.8
		China South Industries:	29.8
		Total:	**589.8**
		Number of cornerstones:	11
		Percentage of IPO size:	52.6%
Yadea Group Holdings	165	Keenway International:	20.0
(May 2016)		Kunsheng Investment:	10.0
		Total:	**30.0**
		Number of cornerstones:	2
		Percentage of IPO size:	18.2%
Nameson Holdings	77	Fast Retailing:*	9.0
(March 2016)		Shima Seiki:	5.0
		Talent Charm:	5.0
		Total:	**19.0**
		Number of cornerstones:	3
		Percentage of IPO size:	24.7%

(continued on p. 128)

Issuer	IPO size pre-Greenshoe (US$m equivalent)	Cornerstone investors (*indicates investors related to the issuer or to one of its shareholders)	Amount subscribed (US$m equivalent)
China Zheshang Bank Co., Ltd.	1,675	Zhejiang Provincial Seaport:	508.0
(March 2016)		Yancoal International:	203.0
		Shaoxing Lingyan:	127.0
		Shenwan Hongyuan:	100.0
		Alipay:	30.0
		Total:	**968.0**
		Number of cornerstones:	5
		Percentage of IPO size:	57.8%
Bank of Tianjin Co., Ltd.	943	Fortune Eris:	270.0
(March 2016)		Sinotak:	100.0
		Tewoo Investment:	50.0
		Tianfang Jincheng:*	50.0
		Ruifuxiang Investment:	30.0
		Teda HK:*	30.0
		Hui Ding:	30.0
		Total:	**560.0**
		Number of cornerstones:	7
		Percentage of IPO size:	59.4%
Sinco Pharmaceuticals Holdings Limited	41	Prestigious Leader:	6.4
(February 2016)		Sichuan Huifeng:*	5.0
		Total:	**11.4**
		Number of cornerstones:	2
		Percentage of IPO size:	27.8%

Appendix 2

Older examples of cornerstone tranches in Hong Kong

Issuer	IPO size pre-Greenshoe ('H' shares only) (US$m equivalent)	Cornerstone investors (*indicates investors that were existing or potential business partners at the time)	Amount subscribed (US$m equivalent)
AIA Group Limited *(October 2010)*	14,780	Kuwait Investment Authority (KIA):	1,000.0
		Guoco Management:	250.0
		Kumpulan Wang Persaraan (Diperbadankan) (KWAP):	200.0
		Mr Peter Woo Kwong-chin (Wheelock/Wharf):	200.0
		GuoLine Capital:	100.0
		Hong Leong Financial Group:	50.0
		NWS Financial Management (New World):	49.7
		Chow Tai Fook (Mr Cheng Yu-tung):	49.7
		Hong Leong Assurance:	20.0
		Total:	**1,919.4**
		Number of cornerstones:	9
		Percentage of IPO size:	13.0%
Agricultural Bank of China *(June 2010)*	10,425	Qatar Investment Authority (QIA):*	2,800.0
		Kuwait Investment Authority (KIA):	800.0
		Standard Chartered Bank:*	500.0
		Rabobank Groep:*	250.0
		Seven Group:*	250.0
		Temasek Holdings:	200.0
		China Resources:	200.0
		China Travel Service:	150.0
		Archer-Daniels-Midland:*	100.0
		Cheung Kong (Holdings) (Mr Li Ka-shing):	100.0
		United Overseas Bank:	100.0
		Total:	**5,450.0**
		Number of cornerstones:	11
		Percentage of IPO size:	52.3%

(continued on p. 131)

Issuer	IPO size pre-Greenshoe ('H' shares only) (US$m equivalent)	Cornerstone investors (*indicates investors that were existing or potential business partners at the time)	Amount subscribed (US$m equivalent)
Industrial and Commercial Bank of China *(October 2006)*	13,900	Kuwait Investment Authority (KIA):	720.0
		China Life Insurance (Group):	565.0
		Gov. of Singapore Invest. Corp. (GIC):	360.0
		China Life Insurance (Hong Kong):	255.0
		Mr Cheng Yu-tung (Chow Tai Fook/New World):	205.0
		Mr Lee Shau-kee (Henderson Land):	205.0
		Qatar investment Authority (QIA):	205.0
		Sun Hung Kai Properties (Kwok family):	205.0
		United Overseas Bank:	205.0
		Mr Peter Woo Kwong-chin (Wheelock/Wharf):	205.0
		Mr Kuok Hock-nien (Kuok Group/Shangri-La):	205.0
		Mr Chen Din-hwa (Nan Fung):	185.0
		Cheung Kong (Holdings) (Mr Li Ka-shing):	100.0
		Hutchison Whampoa (Mr Li Ka-shing):	100.0
		CITIC Pacific:	100.0
		Mr Yung Chi-kin (CITIC Pacific):	100.0
		Mrs Chen Wai-wai (Nan Fung):	20.0
		Total:	**3,940.0**
		Number of cornerstones:	17
		Percentage of IPO size:	28.3%

Appendix 3

Recent examples of cornerstone tranches in Malaysia

Issuer	IPO size pre-Greenshoe (US$m equivalent)	Cornerstone investors (*indicates investors that were existing or potential business partners at the time)	Amount subscribed (US$m equivalent)
Malakoff Corporation Berhad *(April 2015)*	766	CIMB-Principal:	Not disclosed
		Corston-Smith Asset Management:	Not disclosed
		Eastspring Investments (Malaysia):	Not disclosed
		Great Eastern Life:	Not disclosed
		Hong Leong Asset Management:	Not disclosed
		Kencana Capital:	Not disclosed
		Lembaga Tabung Haji (LTH):	Not disclosed
		Maybank Asset Management:	Not disclosed
		Maybank Islamic Asser Management:	Not disclosed
		Pertubuhan Keselamatan Social:	Not disclosed
		RHB Asset Management:	Not disclosed
		UOB Asset Management:	Not disclosed
		Total:	**268**
		Number of cornerstones:	12
		Percentage of IPO size:	35.0%

(continued on p. 134)

Issuer	IPO size pre-Greenshoe (US$m equivalent)	Cornerstone investors (*indicates investors that were existing or potential business partners at the time)	Amount subscribed (US$m equivalent)
IHH Healthcare Berhad	1,996	AIA:	Not disclosed
(July 2012)		Blackrock:	Not disclosed
(Also simultaneously listed in Singapore)		Capital Group:	Not disclosed
		Capital International:	Not disclosed
		CIMB-Principal:	Not disclosed
		CMY Capital (Mr Chua Ma-yu):	Not disclosed
		Eastspring Investments (Malaysia):	Not disclosed
		Employees Provident Fund (EPF):	178
		Fullerton:	Not disclosed
		Gov. of Singapore Invest. Corp. (GIC):	Not disclosed
		Hotel Properties Limited (HPL) (Mr Ong Beng Seng):	Not disclosed
		Hwang Investment:	Not disclosed
		International Finance Corporation (IFC):*	Not disclosed
		JF Asset Management:	Not disclosed
		Keck Seng:	Not disclosed
		Kencana Capital:	Not disclosed
		Kuwait Investment Authority (KIA):	134
		Lembaga Tabung Haji (LTH):	Not disclosed
		Newton:	Not disclosed
		Och Ziff:	Not disclosed
		Permodalan Nasional Berhad (PNB):	Not disclosed
		Usaha Tegas:	Not disclosed
		Total:	**1,085**
		Number of cornerstones:	22
		Percentage of IPO size:	54.4%

(continued on p. 135)

Issuer	IPO size pre-Greenshoe (US$m equivalent)	Cornerstone investors (*indicates investors that were existing or potential business partners at the time)	Amount subscribed (US$m equivalent)
Felda Global Ventures Holdings Berhad *(May 2012)*	3,120	Asia Fountain Investment:	Not disclosed
		FIL Investment Management (Fidelity):	Not disclosed
		GuoLine Capital:	Not disclosed
		Qatar Holding:	Not disclosed
		Value Partners:	Not disclosed
		Employees Provident Fund (EPF):	Not disclosed
		Permodalan Nasional Berhad (PNB):	Not disclosed
		Lembaga Tabung Haji (LTH):	Not disclosed
		Kumpulan Wang Persaraan (Diperbadankan) (KWAP):	Not disclosed
		AIA:	Not disclosed
		CMY Capital (Mr Chua Ma-yu):	Not disclosed
		Hong Leong Foundation:	Not disclosed
		Total:	**920**
		Number of cornerstones:	12
		Percentage of IPO size:	29.5%

Appendix 4

Recent examples of cornerstone tranches in Singapore

Issuer	**IPO size pre-Greenshoe (US$m equivalent)**	**Cornerstone investors (*indicates investors that were existing or potential business partners at the time)**	**Amount subscribed (US$m equivalent)**
Keppel DC REIT	410	AEW Asia:	22.4
(December 2014)		DBS Bank:	20.0
		DBS Bank private banking clients:	36.0
		Eastspring Investments (Singapore):	20.8
		Fortress Capital:	28.8
		Mr Gordon Tang:	12.0
		Mr Lim Chap Huat:	16.0
		Myriad:	12.0
		Wellington:	48.0
		Total:	**216.0**
		Number of cornerstones:	9
		Percentage of IPO size:	52.7%
OUE Commercial Real Estate Investment Trust	277	Summit SPV:	80
(January 2014)		Mr Gordon Tang:	20
		Mrs Chen Huaidan:	20
		Mr Yang Dehe:	16
		RHB Asset Management:	8
		Total:	**144.0**
		Number of cornerstones:	5
		Percentage of IPO size:	52.0%

(continued on p. 138)

Issuer	IPO size pre-Greenshoe (US$m equivalent)	Cornerstone investors (*indicates investors that were existing or potential business partners at the time)	Amount subscribed (US$m equivalent)
Far East Hospitality Trust *(August 2012)*	525	Aberdeen:	28.0
		AIA:	44.0
		APG Strategic Real Estate Pool:	40.0
		Havenport:	12.0
		Hwang Investment:	36.0
		Indus:	16.0
		JF Asset Management:	36.0
		Lion Global Investors:	20.0
		Myriad:	12.0
		NTUC:	36.0
		Total:	**280.0**
		Number of cornerstones:	10
		Percentage of IPO size:	53.3%

Appendix 5

Sample script for an initial approach to potential cornerstone investors by bookrunner banks

Good morning/afternoon, we are calling on behalf of [shareholder] and [issuer]. As you may have seen in the media, [issuer] is contemplating an IPO of up to US$ [offering target size] later this year, with a listing on [stock exchange].

For the avoidance of doubt, this discussion is entirely based on public information and this is not a wall-cross situation.

We are contacting you because you have been shortlisted by [issuer] and the [joint] bookrunner[s] as a potential cornerstone candidate for the IPO of [issuer]. We are only approaching a limited/selected group of potential cornerstone investors at this stage.

To ensure efficiency, and one point of contact, [name of responsible joint bookrunner] has been appointed as the syndicate bank to coordinate with you on exploring a cornerstone investment in the proposed IPO. We will be the only investment bank that will be talking to you in relation to this opportunity.

As you may be aware, [short description of the company, its market positioning, track record and strategy].

We believe the IPO of [issuer] will be a successful offering and are accordingly expecting strong interest in cornerstone participation.

The [joint] global coordinator[s] and [joint] bookrunner[s] has/ [have, together,] considered various valuation methodologies and agreed on the following as the most appropriate for [issuer]: [Brief summary of the valuation methodology for the issuer].

We expect the equity value of [issuer] to be in the region of US$ [amount]. The IPO timing is [target launch date] and any cornerstone commitments would have to be locked down by [target date for signing of cornerstone subscription agreements], so we have approximately [X] [months] to explore this opportunity with you.

Potential cornerstone investors would, in due course, be given access to management to conduct due diligence meetings [Note: outside Singapore], site visits, and will also be provided with draft offering circulars prior to publication. The minimum cornerstone investment is US$ [amount]. [Indication of a lock-up requirement, if any].

If you are interested and can meet the requirements of minimum size, [lock-up], and timeline, we would be delighted to move this process forward with you. The first stage would be to work with your legal team on signing a non-disclosure agreement, so that we can furnish you with more information on [issuer].

Do let us know your initial thoughts on this opportunity and if you would like to move forward with an NDA. We are limited as to further information disclosure at this juncture without your signing an NDA.

Appendix 6

Example of a non-disclosure agreement for potential cornerstone investors

Important disclaimer: This is an example of a non-disclosure agreement for an initial approach to potential cornerstone investors for an initial public offering with two joint bookrunners, and whose offer structure includes a private placement pursuant to Rule 144A in the United States of America. This template is provided for illustration purposes only and should not be used for any proposed or actual non-disclosure agreement without input from a registered firm of legal advisers advising under English, Malaysian, or Singapore law, as appropriate.

This agreement (the 'Agreement') is made on [date] between:

[issuer] (the 'Company'), a company incorporated in [country] with its registered office at [address];

[first bookrunner], having its registered office at [address];

[second bookrunner], having its registered office at [address]; and

[investor], having its registered office at [address] (the 'Investor').

Whereas:

(i) The Company is proposing an initial public offering (the 'Offering') of its ordinary shares (the 'Shares'). It is intended that the Shares be listed on [stock exchange];

(ii) the Investor is considering whether to make an investment in the Shares; and

(iii) for this purpose, the Company has agreed to furnish to the Investor certain information that is non-public, confidential and/or proprietary in nature relating to, or in connection with, the proposed Offering, including but not limited to the investments, business and/or structure of the Company. Subject to the terms of this Agreement and in consideration thereof, the Investor agrees to be bound by the terms set out herein.

It is agreed as follows:

1. Interpretation

In this Agreement, except to the extent that the context otherwise requires:

'Affiliate' means any entity that directly or indirectly, through one or more intermediaries, controls, or is controlled by, or is under the common control of the Investor.

'Applicable Laws' means all applicable laws of [country].

'Information' means any and all information (including oral communication, information on computer disk or visual presentation) furnished by the Company, any one or more of its related corporations, its officers (including directors and alternate directors), shareholders (including, for the avoidance of doubt, any selling shareholders), employees, agents and/or advisers, including without limitation, the Joint Global Coordinators, to the Investor, relating to the proposed Offering, including but not limited to the investments, business and/or structure of the Company.

Notwithstanding the foregoing, the term 'Information' does not include information that:

(i) becomes generally available to the public other than as a result of a disclosure by the Investor or anyone to whom the Investor transmits the Information in breach of this Agreement;

(ii) was available to the Investor, known to the Investor or in the Investor's possession on a non-confidential basis prior to disclosure by the Company and/or any one or more of its related corporations; or

(iii) becomes available to the Investor on a non-confidential basis from a source, other than the Company and/or any one or more of its related corporations, and that source is not bound by any obligation of confidentiality with the Company or any of its related corporations.

'Joint Global Coordinators' means [names of global coordinators].

'Parties' means the Company and the Investor, and 'Party' refer to any one of them.

'Related corporation' in relation to any party means the holding company of another corporation, the subsidiary of another corporation or the subsidiary of the holding company of another corporation.

2. Confidentiality

2.1 Subject to the terms of this Agreement, the Investor shall hold all Information (including all analyses, compilations, notes, studies, memoranda, and other documents prepared by the Investor or its Representatives—as defined in Clause 4 below—to the extent that the same contain, reflect, or are derived from the Information) in strict confidence and, except as permitted under this Agreement, shall not, without the prior written consent of the Company:

(a) disclose, or cause or permit the disclosure, whether intentionally or negligently, of the Information to any person, in any manner whatsoever, in whole or in part; or

(b) use the Information for any purpose whatsoever, other than for the purpose of evaluating its proposed investment in the Company.

The Investor acknowledges that some or all of the Information is or may become price-sensitive information and that the use of such information may be regulated or prohibited by applicable legislation relating to insider dealing and the Investor hereby undertakes not to use any Information for any unlawful purpose.

All Information (whether or not developed or modified by the Investor or its Representatives) is and shall remain the property of the Company. The disclosure does not constitute a grant of any express or implied right to the Investor to or under any patents, copyrights, trademarks, or trade secret information except as otherwise provided herein or under a separate written agreement. The Company reserves without prejudice the ability to protect its rights under such patents, copyrights, trademarks, or trade secrets.

3. Investor's undertakings, representations and warranties

3.1 The Investor hereby undertakes:

(a) to take reasonable procedures, protection, and measures and continue to keep such procedures, protection, and measures in place, in order to maintain the confidentiality and prevent unauthorized use and unauthorized disclosure of the Information;

(b) not to make any copies of the Information or reproduce it in any form or part with possession of the Information except for (i) the purpose of supplying the same to those permitted to access the Information in accordance with this Agreement; or (ii) internal document retention purposes pursuant to any applicable law or regulation;

(c) to procure and ensure that any Representative to whom the Information is to be made available pursuant to Clause 4 observes the obligations contained in this Agreement regarding the Information, and the Investor hereby agrees to be responsible for any breach of the obligations contained in this Agreement by such permitted persons;

(d) that except as required by Applicable Laws, court order, or regulatory requirements and with respect to those parties specified in Clause 4, it will not, and will procure that its Representatives do not, make any disclosure or announcement concerning, or otherwise publicize (i) the possibility of the Offering taking place; (ii) any other investigations, discussions, or negotiations taking place; (iii) any arrangement with the Company or any of its related corporations connected in any way with the proposed Offering; (iv) the fact that the Investor has requested or received Information from the Company and/or its related corporations; or (v) any terms, conditions, or other facts with respect to the proposed Offering or the Investor's proposed investment in the Company, including the status thereof, without the Company's prior written approval;

(e) to notify the Company immediately by telephone and in writing, in accordance with Clause 16 of this Agreement, upon becoming aware of, or having reasonable grounds for suspecting any potential or actual unauthorized disclosure of the Information or any other breach of the provisions of this Agreement, and will use its best efforts to assist the Company in connection with any proceedings which the Company may institute against such person for breach of confidence or otherwise;

(f) at its expense, within [seven (7) days] of termination of discussions concerning the Investor's proposed investment in the Company and, in any event, on receipt of a written demand from the Company, to return or destroy all written Information provided to the Investor or its advisors, employees, and Affiliates (including expunging all information from any computer or electronic storage facility or any other device containing Information) and to confirm to the Company that this obligation has been complied with, save that the Investor is not required to return or destroy such Information to the extent that it is required by law or regulation or its internal filing policy to keep them or the Information is located on an off-site server as a result of the automatic backup of data in the usual operations of the Investor (for example, for archive, disaster recovery or other purposes) and is not readily available to the Investor, provided that the Investor shall safeguard the confidentiality of the retained Information in accordance with the terms of this Agreement;

(g) that neither the return of any Information or destruction or expunging of any of the same from its records will release it from its obligations under this Agreement;

(h) to keep confidential or destroy, at the Company's discretion, all analyses, compilations, notes, studies, memoranda, or other documents prepared by the Investor or its advisors to the extent that the same contain, reflect, or are derived from the Information; and

(i) to do anything reasonably required by the Company to restrain a breach or threatened breach of this Agreement or any infringement or threatened infringement of the rights of the Company arising out of this Agreement by any person, whether by court proceedings or otherwise, provided that where the abovementioned person is a person other than the Investor or any of its Affiliates, such restraining action shall be at the expense of the Company.

4. Permitted disclosure

Subject to Applicable Laws and the terms of this Agreement, the Investor agrees to transmit the Information only to the following:

(a) its directors (including alternate directors), officers, employees, agents, advisers and Affiliates who need to know the same for the purposes of considering, evaluating, advising on or furthering the Investor's proposed investment in the Company;

(b) any independent auditors engaged to review the Investor's proposed investment in the Company; and

(c) any other independent advisers to the Investor with respect to its proposed investment in the Company;

(collectively, the 'Representatives') provided that prior to receipt of any Information, such Representatives shall agree to keep such Information confidential on the same terms as set out in this Agreement.

For the avoidance of doubt, where this Agreement imposes any obligations on the Investor's Representatives, such obligation shall be deemed to include an obligation on the Investor to procure that such persons comply with such obligations and the Investor hereby agrees to be responsible for any breach of this agreement by the Representatives.

5. Disclosure required by law

If the Investor is required by the Applicable Laws, court order or regulatory requirements to disclose the Information to a third person (including, but not limited to, any court of competent jurisdiction, government, securities exchange, supervisory or regulatory body) the Investor must:

(a) where practicable before doing so: (i) immediately notify the Company by telephone and in writing in accordance with Clause 16 of this Agreement; and (ii) give the Company a reasonable opportunity and provide reasonable assistance to take any steps that the Company consider necessary to resist the disclosure or protect the confidentiality of the Information; and

(b) notify the third person that the Information is the confidential information of the Company.

In the event that the Company is unable to resist the disclosure or protect the confidentiality of the Information, the Investor will furnish only that portion of the Information which the Investor is advised by counsel is required by the Applicable Laws, court order or regulatory requirements (such advice being disclosed to the Company).

6. Consequences of breach

The Investor acknowledges that the Information is highly confidential and that monetary damages would not be an adequate remedy for any breach of the Investor's obligations under this Agreement.

Consequently, if the Investor, or its directors, officers, employees, agents, advisers or Affiliates, breach or threaten to breach any of the Investor's obligations under this Agreement, the Investor agrees that the Company shall, subject to Applicable Laws, have the right, in addition to any other rights or remedies available at law or in equity, to obtain, to the fullest extent available under Applicable Laws, injunctive or other equitable relief against the Investor and any of its directors, officers, employees, agents, advisers, or Affiliates for such alleged, threatened, or actual breach and to have the provisions of this Agreement specifically enforced.

The Company shall not have to prove special damages in order for this Agreement to be enforced or to be entitled to remedies hereunder unless Applicable Laws (or a governmental authority having competent jurisdiction thereunder) dictate otherwise. Nothing contained herein shall be construed as prohibiting the Company from taking any further actions against the Investor.

7. No representation

The Investor acknowledges and agrees that none of the Information has been subject to verification, and none of the Company or any one or more of its related corporations nor any of their respective directors, officers, employees, shareholders, agents, representatives, or advisers, including the Joint Global Coordinators, accepts responsibility for or makes any representation or gives any warranty or undertaking, whether express or implied, with respect to the accuracy, reliability, completeness, and reasonableness of the Information or any oral communication in connection with the Information (or that the Information remains unchanged after the date thereof) and none of the Company or any one or more of its related corporations nor any of their respective directors, officers, employees, shareholders, agents, representatives, or advisers, including the Joint Global Coordinators, shall be liable to the Investor or any of its agents, employees, or Affiliates or anyone else for any damages, whether direct, indirect, special incidental or consequential, arising from or relating to the Information, or any errors or omissions therein.

The Investor acknowledges and agrees with the Company that the Information does not constitute or form part of any offer or invitation to sell or issue, or any solicitation of any offer to purchase or subscribe for, any of the Shares, nor shall it or any part of it form the basis of, or be relied on in connection with, any contract or investment decision; and any purchase of the Shares will be made solely on the basis of the information contained in the offering memorandum or prospectus of the Company.

8. US Securities Act

The Investor and its agents represent and certify that it is/they are (a) (A) qualified institutional buyer(s) as defined in Rule 144A under the US Securities Act of 1933 (the 'Securities Act') and is/are (a) 'qualified purchaser(s)' (as defined in Section 2(a) (51) (A) of the US Investment Company Act of 1940 (the 'Investment Company Act')) or (B) not (a) US person(s) and is/are located outside the United States (within the meaning of Regulation S under the Securities Act).

9. Rights of third parties

[Insert an appropriate third party exclusion provision under the relevant governing law].

10. Release

To the extent permitted by law, the Investor releases the Company and each of its officers (including directors and alternate directors), shareholders, employees, agents, and advisers, including without limitation, the Joint Global Coordinators, and each of their officers (including directors and alternate directors) (each, a 'Relevant Person') from all liability for any loss of any kind (including, without limitation, damages, costs, interest, loss of profits, or special damage) (whether foreseeable or not) suffered by the Investor, its officers, employees, advisers, and/or Affiliates acting on any Information, unless such loss is due to the fraud, gross negligence, or wilful deceit of the Relevant Person.

11. Amendment

This Agreement may not be modified or amended, and no provision hereof may be waived, except by a written instrument executed by all of the Parties.

12. Assignment

Neither Party may, without the prior written consent of the other, assign, hold on trust, or otherwise transfer the benefit of all or any of the other Party's obligations under this Agreement, or any benefit arising under or out of this Agreement save that the Company shall be entitled to transfer its rights and obligations arising under or out of this Agreement to any of its related corporations.

13. Severability

If any of the provisions of this Agreement is found to be invalid for any reason whatsoever, such invalidity shall not affect the validity and operation of the other remaining provisions of this Agreement.

14. Waiver

The failure by the Company to exercise or delay in exercising a right or remedy provided by this Agreement or by law does not constitute a waiver of such right or remedy or a waiver of other rights or remedies, nor will any single or partial exercise of it preclude any further exercise.

15. Law and jurisdiction

This Agreement and all matters arising from, or connected with it are governed by, and shall be construed in accordance with [English/Malaysian/Singaporean] law. The Parties hereby irrevocably and unconditionally submit to the non-exclusive jurisdiction of the courts of [England/Malaysia/Singapore].

16. Notice

Any notice or other communication under this document must be in writing and addressed to:

If to [issuer], to it at:

[address]

Fax No.: [ ]

Attention: [ ]

If to [first joint bookrunner], to it at:

[address]

Fax No.: [ ]

Attention: [ ]

If to [second joint bookrunner], to it at:

[address]

Fax No.: [ ]

Attention: [ ]

17. Counterparts

This Agreement may be entered into in any number of counterparts, each of which when executed and delivered (whether in original or facsimile) shall be an original, but all the counterparts together shall constitute one and the same instrument.

18. Duration

This Agreement shall be effective from the date hereof and shall remain in force until the earlier of (i) the date on which the Information becomes public (other than as a result of any act or omission or default by the Investor or the Representatives) or (ii) [one (1)] year from the date of this Agreement. No modifications or alterations may be made to this Agreement without the express written consent of each of the parties hereto.

In witness whereof this Agreement has been entered into on the date stated at the beginning.

[Issuer]

By: ______________________________

Name: ____________________________

Title: _____________________________

[JOINT BOOKRUNNER]

By: ______________________________

Name: ____________________________

Title: _____________________________

[JOINT BOOKRUNNER]

By: ______________________________

Name: ____________________________

Title: _____________________________

Appendix 7

Example of an international cornerstone subscription agreement

Important disclaimer: This is an example of a cornerstone subscription agreement drafted under English law for an initial public offering with two joint bookrunners, and whose offer structure includes a private placement pursuant to Rule 144A in the United States of America. This template is provided for illustration purposes only and should not be used for any proposed or actual subscription agreement without English law input from a registered firm of legal advisers.

This agreement (the 'Agreement') is made on [date] between:

[issuer], a company incorporated in [country], whose registered address is [address] (the 'Company');

[cornerstone investor], a company incorporated in [country], whose registered address is [address] (the 'Investor');

[first joint bookrunner], a company incorporated in [country], whose registered office is [address] ('FB', also known as the 'Coordinator'); and

[second joint bookrunner], a company incorporated in [country], whose registered office is [address] ('SB') (with FB and SB together known as the 'Joint Bookrunners').

Whereas:

The Company is proposing to undertake an initial public offering (the 'Initial Public Offering') of up to [number of shares] ordinary shares of [nominal value] each in the Company ('Shares') comprising: (A) a public issue ('Public Issue') of up to [number of shares] [new] Shares comprising an offering of new Shares, subject to clawback and reallocation, to, by way of ballot, the public in [country] (the 'Public Offering'); and (B) an offering of [new] Shares, subject to claw-back and reallocation, to foreign institutional and selected investors outside the United States in reliance on Regulation S and QIBs in the United States in reliance on Rule 144A or pursuant to any other applicable exemption from registration under the Securities Act (as defined herein) (the 'Placement').

The Joint Bookrunners are acting as the joint bookrunners for the Placement (as defined herein).

[Separate from, but concurrent with the Initial Public Offering [Note: in the case of a Singapore listing only]], the Investor is prepared to make an equity investment in the Company through the subscription of the Investor Shares (as defined herein) from the Company (the 'Cornerstone Placement') subject to, and on the basis and terms set out in this Agreement.

It is agreed as follows:

1. Definitions and interpretation

[Insert definitions, as relevant for the agreement]

1.1. In this Agreement:

1.1.1. references to 'Clauses' and 'Schedules', are to clauses of, and schedules to, this Agreement;

1.1.2. headings are for convenience only and shall not affect the construction of the Agreement;

1.1.3. the Schedules form an integral part of the Agreement and any reference to this Agreement shall include the Schedules; and

1.1.4. any provision of this Agreement which is expressed to bind (i) more than one Joint Global Coordinator or Joint Bookrunner; or (ii) the Company and the Joint Global Coordinators or the Joint Bookrunners, shall, save where inconsistent with the context, bind each of them severally and not jointly and severally.

2. Investment

2.1. Subject to the conditions referred to in Clause 3 being fulfilled (or waived by the Investor) and other terms and conditions of this Agreement:

2.1.1. the Investor will subscribe for, and the Company will allot and issue, and the Company and the Joint Bookrunners will cause to be allocated to the Investor, the Investor Shares at the Placement price; and

2.1.2. the Investor will pay the Joint Bookrunners brokerage in respect of the Investor Shares.

2.2. For the avoidance of doubt, the number of Investor Shares shall be calculated in accordance with Schedule 1 and shall be subject to final determination by the Company and the Joint Bookrunners.

2.3. Subject to Clause 5, the Investor and its affiliates are entitled to apply for or place an order through the bookbuilding process for the Shares in the Placement (in addition to the Investor Shares to be subscribed by and allocated to the Investor pursuant to this Agreement) [Note: in Malaysia and Singapore only].

3. Agreement conditional upon completion of initial public offering

The Investor's obligation to subscribe for, and the Company's obligation to issue, and the Company's and the Joint Bookrunners' obligations to cause to be allocated, the Investor Shares in Clause 2.1 are conditional upon: (i) the underwriting agreement for the Public Offering and the placement agreement for the Placement being entered into and having become unconditional (in accordance with their respective original terms or as subsequently varied by agreement of the parties thereto) by no later than the time and date as specified in these underwriting or placement agreements; (ii) completion of the admission to [stock exchange]; and (iii) none of the aforesaid underwriting or placement agreement having been terminated in accordance with the terms therewith.

Nothing in this Agreement, including this Clause 3, shall (a) create, be deemed to create, or imply any duty or obligation, on or on the part of, any of the Company or any Joint Bookrunner to enter into any underwriting or placement agreements in a specific form or at all, or (b) create or be deemed to create or imply any right of the Investor or any duty or obligation of the Company to the Investor in or under any underwriting or placement agreements, including with respect to termination thereof.

4. Closing

4.1. Subject to Clause 3, the Investor will subscribe for the Investor Shares through the Joint Bookrunners [contemporaneously with the closing of the Placement], at such time and in such manner as shall be determined by the Joint Bookrunners.

4.2. The Investor shall make payment for the Investor Shares and the related brokerage on such date (the 'Payment Date') as the Coordinator shall notify the Investor, which notice shall include, inter alia, the payment account details, the final price per Share at which the Investor will be acquiring the Investor Shares and the total amount payable by the Investor hereunder (which total amount shall be the amount payable by the Investor unless there is manifest error). Payment for the Investor Shares and the related brokerage shall be made on the Payment Date so notified in [currency] by same day value credit in clear funds and without any deduction or set-off.

4.3. The delivery of the Investor Shares shall be made on such date (the 'Delivery Date') as the Coordinator shall notify the Investor. Delivery of the Investor Shares to the Investor shall, subject to receipt of payments in Clause 4.2, be made through the central depository system operated by [stock exchange], on the Delivery Date so notified, and on the same basis on which the Issue Shares are delivered to the other investors which acquire the Shares under the Placement through the Joint Bookrunners.

4.4. Delivery of, and payment for, the Investor Shares may also be made in any other manner which the Company, the Joint Bookrunners, and the Investor may agree in writing.

4.5. If the Investor fails to meet the obligations under Clause 4.2 (whether in whole or in part), the Investor shall be deemed to have forfeited and waived all rights, benefits, and claims in relation to the Investor Shares.

4.6. If admission to [stock exchange] has not occurred by [time] a.m. ([country] time) on [date] (or such later date as is agreed between the Company and the Joint Global Coordinators) or, if the conditions set out in the underwriting agreement for the Public Offering and the placement agreement for the Placement are not satisfied or waived by the date and time specified therein, or if any of the aforesaid underwriting or placement agreements shall be terminated on or before such time or date (each a 'Termination Event'), the obligation of the Investor to subscribe for and the Company's obligations to issue and the Company's and the Joint Bookrunners' obligations to cause to be allocated, the Investor Shares shall cease and if, at the time of the Termination Event, payment for the Investor Shares and the related Brokerage has been made and:

4.6.1. the Investor Shares have not been allotted and issued to the Investor, the relevant Joint Bookrunner(s) holding the payment for the Investor Shares and related brokerage (if applicable) and/or the Company (in the event that such monies are then held by the Company or by a third party to its order), as the case may be, undertakes to return or procure the return to the Investor, without any interest, no later than [seven] business days after the date of the Termination Event a sum equal to all monies then held by the relevant Joint Bookrunner(s) and/or the Company in connection with the subscription of the Investor Shares; or

4.6.2. the Investor Shares have been validly allotted and issued to the Investor and a capital reduction of the share capital of the Company is required for payment to be made from the monies held by the Company, the Company undertakes to procure such capital reduction to be effected as soon as reasonably practicable thereafter and then pay to the Investor within [seven] business days of such capital reduction taking effect a sum equal to all monies paid by the Investor to the Company towards the subscription of the Investor Shares under this Agreement;

and this Agreement will terminate and be of no effect, provided that termination of this Agreement pursuant to this Clause 4.6 shall be without prejudice to the accrued rights or liabilities of any party to the other parties in respect of the terms herein at or before such termination.

5. Restrictions on the Investor

The Investor agrees that, without the prior written consent of the Company and the Joint Global Coordinators, it will not, whether directly or indirectly, at any time during the period of six months following the date of admission to [stock exchange] (the 'Lock-up Period') (i) offer, pledge, sell, transfer, contract to sell, sell any option or contract to purchase, purchase any option or contract to sell, grant any option, right or warrant to purchase, lend, or otherwise transfer or dispose of any relevant shares or warrants or any securities convertible into or exercisable or exchangeable for relevant shares or warrants; or (ii) enter into any swap or any other agreement or any transaction that transfers, in whole or in part, the economic consequence of ownership of relevant shares or warrants, whether any such transaction described in sub-paragraph (i) or (ii) above is to be settled by delivery of relevant shares or warrants of the Company or such other securities, in cash or otherwise.

In addition, the Investor also agrees, during the same period, not to take any steps to issue new relevant shares or other securities that are convertible or exchangeable into relevant shares, nor to authorize the disposal of any relevant shares owned by the Company without the prior written consent of the Joint Global Coordinators. [Note: these clauses on lock-up are for IPOs listed in Hong Kong only.]

The Investor understands that the Company and the Joint Bookrunners are relying upon this agreement in proceeding toward consummation of the Offering. The Investor further understands that this agreement is irrevocable and shall be binding upon the undersigned's heirs, legal representatives, successors, and assigns.

In the event of a disposal of any relevant shares by the Investor at any time within 12 months after the expiry of the Lock-up Period [Note: if applicable], the Investor will give the Company and the Joint Global Coordinators not less than [seven] days' notice of such intended disposal and will use all reasonable endeavours to ensure that any such disposal is in compliance with all applicable laws and regulations and will not create a disorderly or false market.

6. Acknowledgements and warranties

6.1. The Investor acknowledges and confirms to each of the Company and the Joint Bookrunners that:

6.1.1. the Company, the Joint Bookrunners, and their respective affiliates and parties involved herein, make no representation and give no warranty or undertaking that the Placement and/or the Public Offering will proceed or be completed (within any particular time period or at all) and will be under no liability whatsoever to the Investor in the event the Placement and/or the Public Offering does not proceed or is not completed for any reason;

6.1.2. this Agreement, certain background information of the Investor and the relationship and arrangements between the parties contemplated by this Agreement will be required to be described in the public documents and other marketing materials for the Initial Public Offering and, specifically, this Agreement will be a material contract required to be filed with regulatory authorities and/or made available for public inspection in connection with the Initial Public Offering;

6.1.3. the Placement price is to be determined by agreement between the Company and the Joint Global Coordinators (for themselves and on behalf of the initial purchasers under the Placement) following, and on the basis of, an international roadshow and bookbuilding and such other factors as the Company and Joint Global Coordinators may take into consideration and the Investor shall not have any right to raise any objection thereto. The Company and Joint Global Coordinators may not, and have no obligation to, consider the interests of the Investor in determining the Placement price (other than the price limitation set out in Clause 2.1.1) and the Company and Joint Global Coordinators may have interests that conflict with those of the Investor in determining the Placement price and these interests will not be disclosed to the Investor;

6.1.4. the Investor Shares will be acquired by the Investor through the Joint Bookrunners in their capacity as underwriters in the Placement to institutional investors;

6.1.5. it will accept the Investor Shares on and subject to the terms and conditions of the articles of association of the Company;

6.1.6. the information contained in this Agreement, the draft preliminary offering circular, the draft prospectus lodged with [stock exchange/regulator] or any other draft documentation provided to the Investor on a confidential basis or otherwise publicly available is subject to change and will not be relied upon by the Investor in determining whether to invest in the Investor Shares and the Investor is deemed to have the information contained in the offering circular and relied on it in determining whether to invest in the Investor Shares;

6.1.7. notwithstanding that any information concerning the Company may have been furnished to the Investor by or on behalf of the Company on or before the date hereof, each of the Company and the Joint Bookrunners and their respective advisers and affiliates makes no representation and gives no warranty or undertaking as to the accuracy or completeness of any such information not contained in the offering circular and none of the Company, the Joint Bookrunners and their respective advisers, or their affiliates has or will have any liability to the Investor or its affiliates or advisers resulting from the use of such information; and

6.1.8. at or around the time of entering into this Agreement or at any time hereafter but before the closing of the Placement, the Company and the Joint Bookrunners have entered into, or may enter into, agreements similar to this Agreement with one or more other investors as part of the Placement.

6.2. The Investor represents, warrants, and undertakes to each of the Company and the Joint Bookrunners that:

6.2.1. it has been duly incorporated and is validly existing under the laws of its place of incorporation;

6.2.2. it has full power, authority, and capacity, and has taken all actions required to enter into and perform its obligations under this Agreement, and this Agreement constitutes valid and binding obligations of the Investor and is enforceable against the Investor, in accordance with its terms;

6.2.3. the execution and delivery of this Agreement, the acquisition of the Investor Shares, and the performance by the Investor of its obligations under this Agreement shall not contravene or result in a contravention of the laws of any jurisdiction to which the Investor is subject in respect of the transactions contemplated under this Agreement or which may otherwise be applicable to the Investor in connection with its acquisition of the Investor Shares;

6.2.4. it shall provide to the Company, the Coordinator and their respective affiliates promptly upon request, such information as may be required by [stock exchange/regulator] and other governmental, public, monetary, or regulatory authorities or bodies, or securities exchange;

6.2.5. it [and the Investor's parent/ultimate holding company] will on demand indemnify and hold harmless each of the Company, the Joint Bookrunners of the Offering and their respective officers, directors, employees, staff, affiliates, agents, representatives, and advisers ('Indemnified Parties') against any and all losses, costs, expenses, claims, actions, liabilities, proceedings, or damages (whether consequential or otherwise) resulting from a breach of this Agreement, or any act or omission hereunder, by or caused by the Investor or its officers, directors, employees, staff, affiliates, agents, representatives, associates, or advisors which may be made or established against any Indemnified Party in connection with, directly or indirectly, the subscription of the Investor Shares, the Investor Shares or this Agreement in any manner whatsoever and against any and all costs, charges, losses or expenses which any Indemnified Party may suffer or incur in connection with or investigating, preparing, disputing or defending any such claim, action or proceedings on the grounds of or otherwise arising out of or in connection therewith;

6.2.6. it is acquiring the Investor Shares for investment purposes without a view to making a distribution of any of the Investor Shares acquired by it hereunder;

6.2.7. in making the decision to acquire the Investor Shares, the Investor has not received any advice or recommendation, and has not relied on any investigations that the Company or the Selling Shareholders or any of their respective affiliates or any of its representatives or advisers (including, without limitation, the Joint Bookrunners) may have made in connection with the Initial Public Offering, and the Investor has such knowledge and experience in financial and business matters that it is capable of evaluating the merits and risks of the prospective investment in the Investor Shares and is capable of bearing the economic risks of such investment, including a complete loss of its investment in the Investor Shares, and it has received all the information it considers necessary or appropriate for deciding whether to acquire the Investor Shares;

6.2.8. [its ordinary business is to buy or sell or invest in shares or debentures and] it is experienced in transactions of investing in the securities of companies in a similar stage of development;

6.2.9. it is aware that the offer and sale of the issue Shares, including the Investor Shares, has not been and will not be registered under the US Securities Act, or the laws of any state or other jurisdiction in the United States;

6.2.10. it is not within the United States, not any affiliate of the Company or a person acting on behalf of such an affiliate and it and any account for whom it is purchasing the Investor Shares is purchasing such Investor Shares, or the beneficial interest therein, in an offshore transaction made in reliance on Regulation S under the Securities Act;

6.2.11. it is not purchasing the Investor Shares with a view to any resale or distribution thereof within the meaning of the US Securities Act; and furthermore, if the Investor is acquiring the Investor Shares as a fiduciary or agent for one or more investor accounts, it has investment discretion with respect to each such account and it has full power and authority to make the representations, warranties, acknowledgements, and agreements herein on behalf of each such account;

6.2.12. the Investor Shares may not be offered, resold, pledged, or otherwise transferred except (i) to a person whom the Investor and any person acting on its behalf reasonably believe is a QIB purchasing for its own account or for the account of a QIB in a transaction meeting the requirements of Rule 144A, (ii) in an offshore transaction complying with Rule 903 or Rule 904 of Regulation S, (iii) pursuant to the exemption from registration under the US Securities Act provided by Rule 144 thereunder (if available), or (iv) pursuant to registration or another applicable exemption from registration under the US Securities Act, and that, in each case, such offer, resale, pledge or transfer must be made in accordance with any applicable securities laws of any state of the United States and the Investor agrees to give any subsequent purchaser of such Investor Shares notice of any restrictions on the transfer thereof;

6.2.13. its purchase of the Investor Shares is not and will not be the result of 'directed selling efforts' (as defined in Regulation S) made in respect to the Investor Shares;

6.2.14. it has not purchased the Investor Shares as a result of any general solicitation or general advertising (as defined in Regulation D under the US Securities Act), including advertisements, articles, notices, or other communications published in any newspaper, magazine, on a website or in or on any similar media or broadcast over radio or television, or any seminar or meeting whose attendees have been invited by means of general solicitation or general advertising;

6.2.15. it understands that neither the Company nor any of the Joint Bookrunners makes any representation as to the availability of Rule 144A or as to the availability of any exemption under the Securities Act for the reoffer, resale, pledge, or transfer of the Securities;

6.2.16. it will comply with any and all applicable selling restrictions in the Offering Circular;

6.2.17. to the extent any of the Investor Shares are held by a wholly owned subsidiary of the Investor, the Investor shall procure that subsidiary to remain a wholly owned subsidiary of the Investor for so long as such subsidiary continues to hold any of the Investor Shares before the expiry of the Lock-up Period [if applicable];

6.2.18. it has received (and may in future receive) information that may constitute material, non-public information in connection with its investment in (and holding of) the Investor Shares, and it will not, and will use its reasonable efforts to ensure that its affiliates, directors, officers, employees, advisers, and representatives do not, provide such information to third parties or acquire, purchase, sell or otherwise trade, directly or indirectly, in the shares of the Company or their respective affiliates or associates in a manner that could result in any violation of the securities laws of the United States, [country] or any other applicable jurisdiction relevant to such dealing; for the avoidance of doubt, none of the materials which may have been provided to the Investor constitutes an invitation or offer to acquire, purchase or subscribe for any Shares or securities in any jurisdictions where such offer, solicitation or sale is not permitted and this Agreement does not, in any way, constitute an offer of securities for sale in the United States or any other jurisdiction;

6.2.19. it has conducted its own investigation with respect to the Company and the Investor Shares and obtained its own independent advice (legal and otherwise) to the extent it considers necessary or appropriate or otherwise has satisfied itself concerning, without limitation, the tax, legal, currency, and other economic considerations related to the investment in the Investor Shares;

6.2.20. it is not a 'related party' (as defined in the [stock exchange] listing requirements) of the Company and its acquisition of the Investor Shares shall not constitute a 'related party transaction' (as defined in the [stock exchange] listing requirements) or result in the Investor becoming a related party (as defined in the [stock exchange] listing requirements) of the Company and will, immediately after completion of this Agreement, be independent of and not acting upon or accustomed to take instructions from, or, directly or indirectly funded or backed by, or acting in concert with any related party of the Company in relation to the control of the Company or any acquisition, disposal, voting, or any other disposition of securities in the Company;

6.2.21. it is a person falling within [applicable definitions for institutional investors in Hong Kong, Malaysia, or Singapore];

6.2.22. it will comply with any requirements imposed or which may be imposed by [stock exchange] in connection with the Initial Public Offering and the Investor has complied and will comply with all applicable laws and regulations in all jurisdictions relevant to the acquisition of the Investor Shares; and

6.2.23. the Investor shall provide, upon request, to the Company and the Joint Bookrunners and their respective affiliates as soon as reasonably practicable and to the extent legally permissible, any such information as may be required by [stock exchange/regulator] and other governmental, public, monetary, or regulatory authorities or bodies, or securities exchanges.

6.3. The Investor warrants to each of the Company and the Joint Bookrunners that the description set out in Schedule 2 in relation to it and the group of companies of which it is a member is true and accurate and is not misleading. Without prejudice to the provisions of Clause 6.1.2, the Investor irrevocably consents to the mention and inclusion in the public documents of its name and all or part of the description set out in Schedule 2 may be included in the public documents and other marketing materials in respect of the Initial Public Offering. The Investor undertakes to notify the Company and the Joint Bookrunners immediately if any such information ceases to be accurate or complete or becomes misleading. The Investor further undertakes promptly to provide such further information and/or supporting documentation (to the extent such documentation is readily available) relating to it, its ownership and/or otherwise relating to the matters referred to in Schedule 2 which may reasonably be required by the Company and the Joint Bookrunners to ensure compliance with applicable companies or securities registration, applicable laws, regulations, and listing rules and/or the requests of competent regulatory authorities, including, without limitation, [stock exchange/regulator].

6.4. The Investor understands that the acknowledgements and confirmations in Clause 6.1 and the representations, warranties, and undertakings in Clause 6.2 are required in connection with [country] laws and regulations and the securities laws of the United States, among others. The Investor acknowledges that the Company, the Joint Bookrunners and others will rely upon the truth and accuracy of the Investor's representations and acknowledgements set forth therein, and it agrees to notify the Company and the Joint Bookrunners immediately in writing if any of the representations or acknowledgements therein ceases to be accurate and complete or becomes misleading.

6.5. The Company represents and warrants that:

6.5.1. it has been duly incorporated and is validly existing under the laws of [country];

6.5.2. the issue and sale of the Investor Shares will, upon admission to [stock exchange], be fully paid and free from all options, liens, charges, mortgages, pledges, claims, equities, encumbrances, and other third party rights and shall rank pari passu with the Shares then in issue and to be listed on [stock exchange];

6.5.3. it has full power, authority, and capacity, and has taken all actions required to enter into and perform its obligations under this Agreement, and this Agreement constitutes valid and binding obligations of the Company and is enforceable against the Company in accordance with its terms; and

6.5.4. the execution and delivery of this Agreement and the performance by the Company of its obligations under and subject to this Agreement shall not contravene or result in a contravention of the laws of any jurisdiction to which the Company is subject in respect of the transactions contemplated under this Agreement.

7. Announcements and confidentiality

7.1. Save as provided herein, none of the parties hereto shall disclose any information concerning this Agreement or the transactions contemplated herein or any other arrangement involving the Company and the Investor without the prior written consent of the other parties hereto. Notwithstanding the foregoing, this Agreement may be disclosed:

7.1.1. to the legal and financial advisers and employees of the parties hereto, provided that such advisers are under an obligation of confidentiality at least similar to that provided hereunder; and

7.1.2. otherwise by or on behalf of any party hereto as may be required by any law, regulatory authority, or stock exchange rules.

8. Notices

8.1. All notices delivered hereunder shall be in writing in the English language and shall be communicated to the following addresses:

If to the Company:	[company address, telephone and telefax] Attention: addressee
If to the Investor:	[company address, telephone and telefax] Attention: addressee
If to FB:	[company address, telephone and telefax] Attention: addressee
If to SB:	[company address, telephone and telefax] Attention: addressee

8.2. Any such notice shall be delivered by hand or sent by facsimile or by pre-paid post. Any notice shall be deemed to have been delivered, if delivered by hand, when delivered and if sent by facsimile, on receipt of confirmation of transmission and if sent by pre-paid post (in the absence of evidence of earlier receipt), [48] hours after it was posted (or [six] days if sent by air mail). Any notice received on a day that is not a business day shall be deemed received on the next following business day.

9. General

9.1. Each of the parties confirms and represents that this Agreement has been duly authorized, executed, and delivered by it and constitutes its legal, valid, and binding obligations and that, except for such consents, approvals and authorizations as may be required by the Company to implement the Initial Public Offering, no corporate, shareholder or other consents, approvals or authorizations are required by such party for the performance of its obligations under this Agreement and each of the parties further confirms that it can perform its obligations described hereunder.

9.2. Save for manifest error, calculations, and determinations made in good faith by the Company and the Joint Global Coordinators shall be conclusive with respect to the number of Investor Shares and the Placement price for the purposes of this Agreement.

9.3. No alteration to, or variation of, this Agreement shall be effective unless it is in writing and signed by or on behalf of all the parties hereto.

9.4. This Agreement will be executed in the English language only.

9.5. Each of the Company and the Investor shall bear its own legal and professional fees, costs, and expenses incurred in connection with this Agreement, save that stamp duty arising in respect of this Agreement shall be borne by the Investor.

9.6. All provisions of this Agreement shall, so far as they are capable of being performed or observed, continue in full force and effect notwithstanding completion of the acquisition of the Investor Shares by the Investor in accordance with Clause 4 except in respect of those matters then already performed.

9.7. This Agreement constitutes the entire agreement and understanding between the parties in connection with the investment in the Company by the Investor. This Agreement supersedes all prior communications, understandings, and agreements relating to the subject matter hereof, whether written or oral.

9.8. Each Joint Bookrunner has the power and is authorized to delegate all or any of its relevant rights, duties, powers, and discretions in such manner and on such terms as it thinks fit (with or without formality and without prior notice of any such delegation being required to be given to the Company) to any one or more of its affiliates. Each Joint Bookrunner shall remain liable for all acts and omissions of any of its affiliates to which it delegates relevant rights, duties, powers, and/or discretions pursuant to this Clause 9.8 notwithstanding any such delegation.

9.9. No delay or failure by a party to exercise or enforce (in whole or in part) any right provided by this Agreement or by law shall operate as a release or waiver, or in any way limit that party's ability to further exercise or enforce that, or any other, right. A waiver of any breach of any provision of this Agreement shall not be effective, or implied, unless that waiver is in writing and is signed by the party against whom that waiver is claimed.

9.10. Each of the acknowledgements, agreements, representations, warranties, and undertakings given by the Investor under Clauses 6.1 and 6.2 shall be assigned as a separate representation, warranty, or undertaking and shall be deemed to be repeated on the Delivery Date.

10. Governing law and jurisdiction

10.1. This Agreement and any non-contractual obligations arising out of or in connection with it shall be governed by, and construed in accordance with, English law.

10.2. Each party submits to the non-exclusive jurisdiction of the courts of England.

11. Process agent

The Investor irrevocably appoints [agent] of [address] to receive, for it and on its behalf, service of process in the proceedings in England. Such service shall be deemed completed on delivery, to the process agent (whether or not it is forwarded to and received by the Investor). If for any reason the process agent ceases to be able to act as such or no longer has an address in England, the Investor irrevocably agrees to appoint a substitute process agent acceptable to the Joint Bookrunners, and to deliver to the Company and each of the Joint Bookrunners a copy of the new process agent's acceptance of that appointment, within 15 days thereof.

12. Contracts (Rights of Third Parties) Act 1999

A person who is not a party to this Agreement has no right under the Contracts (Rights of Third Parties) Act 1999 to enforce any term of this Agreement.

13. Counterparts

This Agreement may be executed in any number of counterparts and by the parties to it on separate counterparts, each of which is an original but all of which together constitute one and the same instrument.

Schedule 1: Investor Shares

The number of Investor Shares shall be equal to: (1) [amount subscribed for] (excluding Brokerage) divided by (2) the Placement price, rounded down to the nearest whole board lot of [board lot] Shares.

Schedule 2: Particulars of Investor

Place of incorporation: [ ]

Company number: [ ]

Certificate of incorporation number: [ ]

Principal activities: [ ]

Ultimate controlling shareholder: [ ]

Interest in [industry] business: [ ]

Description of the Investor for insertion in the offer documents: [ ]

In witness whereof each of the parties has executed this Agreement by its duly authorized signatory/signatories on the date set out at the beginning.

SIGNED by [ ]

for and on behalf of
[Company]

SIGNED by [ ]

for and on behalf of
[Investor]

SIGNED by [ ]
for and on behalf of

[Joint Bookrunner]

SIGNED by [ ]
for and on behalf of

[Joint Bookrunner]

Appendix 8
Selected profiles of cornerstone investors

Important disclaimer: The following, selected profiles of cornerstone investors in IPOs in Hong Kong, Malaysia, and Singapore have generally been extracted from IPO prospectuses that are or were readily available on the websites of the relevant stock exchanges or regulators or, in some cases, on the corporate websites of listed companies or the investor firm themselves. These profiles have in some cases been updated, or slightly amended, for the purpose of inclusion in this book. No responsibility whatsoever will be accepted by the author or the publisher for any mistakes or omissions therein.

Aberdeen Asset Management Asia Limited: Established in Singapore since 1992, Aberdeen Asia, a wholly owned subsidiary of the Aberdeen Group, has been investing in Asia for over 20 years. Aberdeen Asia is a pure asset management company and only manages assets for third parties. Aberdeen Asia's clients access its investment expertise drawn from three main asset classes: equities, fixed income, and property, as well as tailored solutions. As at April 2012, Aberdeen Asia had more than 170 staff in Singapore, and managed more than US$100 billion across the region, of which US$80 billion was in equities. Aberdeen has made cornerstone investments in its capacity as fund manager and agent for and on behalf of its clients. At the time of writing, the Aberdeen Group was reportedly in discussions with Standard Life over a possible £11 billion merger, to form a combined group that would control £660 billion worth of assets.[1] (Source: Prospectus for the Singapore IPO of Far East Hospitality Trust, 16 August 2012.)

---

1. Sam Dean, 'Standard Life and Aberdeen Asset Management in £11 billion merger discussion', *Daily Telegraph*, 4 March 2017.

Abu Dhabi Investment Authority (ADIA): Since 1976, the Abu Dhabi Investment Authority has been investing funds on behalf of the government of Abu Dhabi, with a focus on long-term value creation. ADIA manages a global investment portfolio that is diversified across more than two dozen asset classes and sub-categories across North America, Europe, developed Asia, and emerging markets. (Source: Company website.)

Advance Data Services Limited (Mr Ma Huateng/Tencent): Advance Data is an investment holding company incorporated in the British Virgin Islands. It is wholly owned by Mr Ma Huateng, who is the chairman and founder of Tencent Holdings Limited, a company listed on the Stock Exchange of Hong Kong. Tencent Holdings Limited, together with its subsidiaries, is principally engaged in the provision of Internet and mobile value-added services, online advertising services and e-Commerce transactions services to users in the PRC. (Source: Prospectus for the Hong Kong IPO of China Merchants Securities Co. Ltd., 27 September 2016.)

AEW Asia Pte Ltd: AEW and its affiliates actively manage direct and listed property in North America, Europe, and Asia, with primary offices in Boston, Los Angeles, London, Paris, Singapore, and Hong Kong. AEW has entered into cornerstone subscription agreements on behalf of various clients in its capacity as investment advisor. (Source: Prospectus for the Singapore IPO of Keppel DC REIT, 5 December 2014.)

AIA Group Limited: AIA is a life insurance-based financial services provider operating in 15 jurisdictions throughout the Asia-Pacific region. Its principal activity and that of its subsidiaries is the writing of life insurance business, providing life, pensions, and accident and health insurance throughout Asia, and distributing related investment and other financial services products to its customers. AIA has made cornerstone investments through its subsidiaries AIA Singapore Private Limited, American International Assurance Bhd, and American International Assurance Company (Bermuda) Limited. (Source: Prospectus for the Malaysia and Singapore IPO of IHH Healthcare Berhad, 2 July 2012.)

Alipay (Hong Kong) Investment Limited: Alipay (Hong Kong) is a limited company incorporated in Hong Kong, with investment as its principal business. It is indirectly and wholly owned by Zhejiang Ant Small and Micro Financial Services Group Ltd. which focuses on serving small and micro enterprises and ordinary customers, and owns businesses, mainly including Alipay, Yuebao, Zhaocaibao, Zhima Credit, and Ant Check Later. (Source: Prospectus for the Hong Kong IPO of China Zheshang Bank Co. Ltd., 16 March 2016.)

Anbang Investment Holdings Co. Limited: Anbang Investment is incorporated in Hong Kong. It is principally engaged in investment businesses and is indirectly wholly owned by Anbang Life Insurance Co. Ltd. The holding company for Anbang Life is Anbang Insurance Group Co. Ltd. Anbang Insurance is one of the largest insurance groups in China. Its businesses include life insurance, property and casualty insurance, health insurance, pension insurance, banking, and asset management. (Source: Prospectus for the Hong Kong IPO of China Logistics Property Holdings Co. Ltd., 30 June 2016.)

APG Strategic Real Estate Pool: APG Pool is a collective investment fund established under Dutch law in 2009 in the form of a fund for joint account (*fonds voor gemene rekening*). APG Pool is a contractual arrangement between APG Algemene Pensioen Group N.V. in its capacity as manager of APG Pool, Stichting Depositary APG Strategic Real Estate Pool as depository of APG Pool, and each of the participants in APG Pool. The purpose of APG Pool is to build a diversified portfolio in listed and private real estate investments. (Source: Prospectus for the Singapore IPO of Far East Hospitality Trust, 16 August 2012.)

Archer-Daniels-Midland Company (ADM): ADM is a corporation incorporated in Delaware, United States, whose common stock is listed and traded on the New York Stock Exchange. ADM is one of the world's largest processors of oilseeds, corn, wheat, cocoa, and other feedstuffs, and is a leading manufacturer of vegetable oil and protein meal, corn sweeteners, flour, biodiesel, ethanol, and other value-added food and feed ingredients. It operates an extensive grain elevator and transportation network to procure, store, clean, and transport agricultural commodities. (Source: Prospectus for the Hong Kong IPO of Agricultural Bank of China Limited, 30 June 2010.)

Bank of China Group Investment Limited: BOCGI is the principal vehicle and platform for the direct investment and fund management business of Bank of China Limited, which is listed on the Stock Exchange of Hong Kong and the Shanghai Stock Exchange. It is also an integral part of Bank of China in pursuit of internationalization and diversification of its business. Over the years, it has invested extensively in major infrastructure and key projects in the real estate, industry, energy, transportation, media, hotel, and financial services industries. (Source: Prospectus for the Hong Kong IPO of China Development Bank Financial Leasing Co. Ltd., 24 June 2016.)

BlackRock Inc.: BlackRock is a Delaware corporation listed on the New York Stock Exchange. It is one of the world's preeminent asset management firms and a provider of global investment management, risk management, and advisory services to institutional, intermediary, and individual investors around the world. BlackRock makes cornerstone investments through a wide variety of funds or accounts under management through direct or indirect subsidiaries, including Blackrock Investment Management, LLC. (Source: Prospectus for the Malaysia and Singapore IPO of IHH Healthcare Berhad, 2 July 2012.)

BOCOM International Global Investment Limited: BOCOM Investment is an indirect wholly owned subsidiary of Bank of Communications Co. Ltd. Its principal business is investment holding. Headquartered in Shanghai, Bank of Communications Co. Ltd. is the first nationwide, state-owned joint-stock commercial bank in China, with both national and global coverage. The Asset Management Business Center (BankComm AMBC) is a department under Bank of Communications Co. Ltd. mainly responsible for the overall investment operations of asset management businesses, research and development of relevant products and service systems, business risk management, system development and maintenance and business operations support within the Bank of Communications Co. Ltd. group. BOCOM Investment, as a cornerstone investor, holds H shares for and on behalf of independent third-party clients of BankComm AMBC (as a discretionary investment advisor). (Source: Prospectus for the Hong Kong IPO of Everbright Securities Company Limited, 8 August 2016.)

The Boeing Company: Boeing is the world's largest aerospace company and leading manufacturer of commercial airplanes and defence, space, and security systems. It was incorporated in 1916 and is listed on the New York Stock Exchange. Boeing supports airlines and government customers in more than 150 countries, with products and tailored services including commercial and military aircraft, satellites, electronic and defence systems, launch systems, advanced information and communication systems, and performance-based logistics and training. It employs approximately 160,000 people across more than 65 countries. (Source: Prospectus for the Hong Kong IPO of BOC Aviation Limited, 19 May 2016.)

Caiyun International Investment Limited (Yunnan Metropolitan Construction Investment Group): Caiyun International, incorporated in Hong Kong in 2015, is a wholly owned subsidiary of Yunnan Metropolitan Construction Investment Group Co. Ltd. (YMCI). It was established for YMCI's investments in overseas projects and transactions. YMCI, founded in 2005, is an investment and financing platform for urban development under the Yunnan SASAC (State-owned Asset Supervision and Administration Commission) and is wholly owned by the Yunnan SASAC. YMCI focuses on urban development as well as urban environment, and has played an important role in implementing the Yunnan provincial government's blueprint for urban planning and municipal construction. Over the years, YMCI has diversified its business portfolio to include leisure and tourism, healthcare, and other businesses. (Source: Prospectus for the Hong Kong IPO of China Merchants Securities Co. Ltd., 27 September 2016.)

Capital Group Inc.: Capital Group is a major global institutional investor. It makes cornerstone investments on behalf of a variety of funds and subsidiaries, including Capital Guardian Trust Company, Capital International, Inc. and Capital International Sarl. (Source: Prospectus for the Malaysia and Singapore IPO of IHH Healthcare Berhad, 2 July 2012.)

Capital Research Global Investors: Capital Research is a division of Capital Research and Management Company. It manages EuroPacific Growth Fund, New World Fund, Inc. and American Funds Insurance Series—International Fund, which are mutual funds located in the United States. (Source: Prospectus for the Malaysia and Singapore IPO of IHH Healthcare Berhad, 2 July 2012.)

CCCC International Holding Limited: CCCC International is a company incorporated in Hong Kong and a subsidiary and the overseas investment platform of China Communications Construction Company Limited (CCCC). CCCC was established in 2006 under the approval of China's State Council. It is a listed company on the Stock Exchange of Hong Kong and Shanghai Stock Exchange. According to its 2015 annual report, CCCC and its subsidiaries are a leading transportation infrastructure group in the PRC and an industry leader in each of the group's four core business, namely, infrastructure construction, infrastructure design, dredging, and heavy machinery manufacturing. CCCC is also China's largest port design and construction company, China's leading highway and bridge construction and design company, China's leading railway construction enterprise, China's largest international engineering contractor, and China's largest engineering design company, as well as the world's largest dredging company and container crane manufacturer. (Source: Prospectus for the Hong Kong IPO of China Development Bank Financial Leasing Co. Ltd., 24 June 2016.)

CES Global Holdings (Hong Kong) Limited (China Eastern): CES Global is incorporated in Hong Kong as a wholly owned subsidiary under China Eastern Air Holding Company, with a share capital of HK$34.14 billion. It mainly serves as China Eastern's vehicle for various investment assignments and proprietary businesses.

China Eastern itself is a large state-owned aerial transportation group. (Source: Prospectus for the Hong Kong IPO of DFZQ, 22 June 2016.)

Mrs Chen Huaidan (SingHaiyi Group): Mrs Chen is the group managing director of SGX-Catalist-listed SingHaiyi Group Limited, which specializes in property development and investment. She is the wife of Mr Gordon Tang (see that name). (Source: Prospectus for the Singapore IPO of OUE Commercial Real Estate Investment Trust, 17 January 2014.)

Cheung Kong (Holdings) Limited (Mr Li Ka-shing): Cheung Kong is a company listed on the Main Board of the Stock Exchange of Hong Kong and is controlled by Mr Li Ka-shing [Note: Hong Kong's richest person]. Its principal business activities are investment holding and project management. Its subsidiaries are active in the field of property development and investment, hotel and serviced suite operation, property and project management, and investment in securities. It has also entered into cornerstone subscriptions through Ruperta Limited, a limited liability company incorporated in the British Virgin Islands, and an indirectly wholly owned subsidiary, as well as through Issamed Investments Limited, an indirect wholly owned subsidiary. See also Hutchison Whampoa Limited. (Source: Prospectus for the Hong Kong IPO of Agricultural Bank of China Limited, 30 June 2010.)

China Chengtong Holdings Group Limited: China Chengtong is a large enterprise group under the supervision of the State-owned Asset Supervision and Administration Commission (SASAC) of the State Council of China with total assets of approximately RMB100 billion, and belongs to the first batch of standard board-of-director enterprises in the transformation of central enterprises authenticated by the SASAC of the State Council. It serves as a significant operating platform, contributing to structural and distributional adjustments and strategic recombination of central enterprises. The main businesses of China Chengtong are shareholding management, asset management, capital operation, financial service, equity investment, initiating the establishment of fund and fund management companies, etc. It has been recognized as a state-owned capital operating company pilot since 2016. China Chengtong owns more than a hundred subsidiaries in China, which include: (i) three companies listed on the Shanghai Stock Exchange, namely CMST Development Co. Ltd., Guangdong Guanhao High-Tech Co. Ltd., and Yueyang Forest & Paper Co. Ltd.; (ii) one company listed on the Main Board of the Stock Exchange of Hong Kong, namely China Chengtong Development Group Co. Ltd.; and (iii) two companies listed on the Shenzhen Stock Exchange, namely Foshan Huaxin Packaging Co. Ltd. and MCC Meili Paper Industry

Co. Ltd. (Source: Prospectus for the Hong Kong IPO of Postal Savings Bank of China, Co. Ltd., 14 September 2016.)

China Development Bank International Holdings Limited: China Development Bank International is a wholly owned subsidiary and the overseas strategic investment platform of China Development Bank Corporation (CDB). It mainly engages in equity investment and asset management business. As at 31 December 2015, CDB had total assets of more than RMB12.3 trillion. (Source: Prospectus for the Hong Kong IPO of BOC Aviation Limited, 19 May 2016.)

China Fintech Investment Company: China Fintech is a wholly owned subsidiary of China Fintech Fund Management Company Limited (CFF) and is incorporated in the Cayman Islands. It targets investments in global high-tech companies, especially those at an expanding or mature stage of development in the fields of financial technology, e-commerce, e-supply chain management and logistics services in greater China, Europe, and North America. CFF was founded by CM International Capital Limited, one of the international investment platforms of China Minsheng Investment Group, one of the leading private investment companies in China; GF Investments (Cayman) Company Limited, a wholly owned subsidiary of GF Securities Limited (listed on the Stock Exchange of Hong Kong) and one of the leading non-state-owned securities companies in China; and LR Capital Management Company (Cayman) Limited, a leading global investment company. CFF is dedicated to the advancement of Internet finance through broadening and deepening the scope of Internet technology in the industry. (Source: Prospectus for the Hong Kong IPO of China Logistics Property Holdings Co. Ltd., 30 June 2016.)

China Investment Corporation (CIC): Headquartered in Beijing, CIC was founded in 2007 as a wholly state-owned company incorporated in accordance with the Company Law of the PRC and is also known as China's sovereign wealth fund. CIC invests on a commercial basis, with an objective to seek long-term, risk-adjusted financial returns. CIC has also subscribed for cornerstone investments in IPOs through Beijing Hanguang Investment Corporation, which is a wholly owned subsidiary of its wholly owned subsidiary CIC Capital Corporation. (Source: Prospectus for the Hong Kong IPO of BOC Aviation Limited, 19 May 2016.)

China Life Franklin Asset Management Co. Limited: China Life Franklin is incorporated in Hong Kong and is a joint venture between China Life Asset Management Company Limited, China Life Insurance (Overseas) Company Limited and Franklin Templeton Investments. China Life Franklin holds licences granted by the Hong Kong Securities and Futures Commission (SFC) to carry out Type 9 (asset management) and Type 4 (advising on securities) regulated activities. (Source: Prospectus for the Hong Kong IPO of BOC Aviation Limited, 19 May 2016.)

China Life Insurance (Group) Company: China Life is a large state-owned financial and insurance company headquartered in Beijing. Its businesses cover life insurance, property and casualty insurance, pension plans (corporate annuity), asset management, alternative investments, and overseas operations. It has invested in various banks, securities companies, and other financial and non-financial institutions through its capital operations. China Life and its subsidiaries constitute the largest business insurance group in the PRC with assets exceeding RMB3 trillion and are one of the largest institutional investors in the PRC capital markets. (Source: Prospectus for the Hong Kong IPO of Everbright Securities Company Limited, 8 August 2016.)

China Orient Asset Management (International) Holding Limited: China Orient, also known as COAMI, is a company incorporated in Hong Kong with limited liability and is principally engaged in investment management. COAMI is a subsidiary of China Orient Asset Management Corporation, a state-owned enterprise and one of the state-owned asset management companies in the PRC. COAMI is the primary overseas platform for the latter. As an asset management company, COAMI's main investment strategies involve investing in non-performing assets, equities, fixed income, and properties. (Source: Prospectus for the Hong Kong IPO of Greentown Service Group Co. Ltd., 28 June 2016.)

China Reinsurance (Group) Corporation: China Re was jointly incorporated by China's Ministry of Finance (12.72 per cent) and Central Huijin (71.56 per cent). China Re provides comprehensive products and services including reinsurance, primary insurance, asset management, and insurance brokerage, etc. China Re was listed on the Main Board of the Stock Exchange of Hong Kong in 2015. (Source: Prospectus for the Hong Kong IPO of China Development Bank Financial Leasing Co. Ltd., 24 June 2016.)

China Resources (Holdings) Company Limited: The principal business of China Resources is investment holding. The company, together with its subsidiaries, is a diversified conglomerate in Hong Kong and the PRC, with its core businesses in consumer products (retail, beverage, and food), power, real estate, cement, gas, medications, and financial services. It has also entered into cornerstone subscriptions through Commotra Company Limited, a limited liability company and a wholly owned subsidiary incorporated in Hong Kong, with its principal business activities in securities investment holding. (Source: Prospectus for the Hong Kong IPO of Agricultural Bank of China Limited, 30 June 2010.)

China Shipbuilding Capital Limited: China Shipbuilding Capital, also known as CSCL, is a wholly owned subsidiary of China Shipbuilding Industry Corporation (CSIC), and is registered in Hong Kong. CSIC is a very large state-owned enterprise in China, authorized by the PRC central government to engage in investment and capital management and was a Fortune Global 500 company for six consecutive years. CSIC owns a group of competitive enterprises specialized in manufacturing and the repair of marine equipment and research and development institutions in China. China Shipbuilding Capital, as the overseas financing and investment platform of CSIC, mainly engages in industrial investment, investment consulting, financial leasing and advisory business for the aforesaid businesses. CSIC has also made a cornerstone investment through CSIC Investment One Limited, a 60 per cent British Virgin Island subsidiary, with the remaining 40 per cent owned by China Shipbuilding & Offshore International (H.K.) Co. Limited. (Source: Prospectus for the Hong Kong IPO of Everbright Securities Company Limited, 8 August 2016.)

China South Industries Assets Management Co. Ltd.: China South Industries is a company incorporated in the PRC in 2001 with a registered capital of RMB2 billion. Its principal businesses are investment and information consulting. As a wholly owned subsidiary of China South Industries Group Co. Ltd., it is the integrated platform for capital operation and financial asset integration of the group. As one of the Fortune Global 500 Companies, its principal businesses include manufacturing of vehicles and equipment manufacturing. (Source: Prospectus for the Hong Kong IPO of BOC Aviation Limited, 19 May 2016.)

China Travel Service (Holdings) Hong Kong Limited: The principal business activities of CTS Holdings encompass a diversified business portfolio, including travel agency and its related operations, tourist hospitality, logistics operations, industrial investment in steel production, and property development in the PRC. CTS Holdings is also a controlling shareholder of China Travel International Investment Hong Kong Limited, whose shares are listed and traded on the Main Board of the Stock Exchange of Hong Kong. It has also entered into cornerstone subscriptions through China Travel Finance & Investment (H.K.) Limited, a limited liability company incorporated in Hong Kong and a wholly owned subsidiary. (Source: Prospectus for the Hong Kong IPO of Agricultural Bank of China Limited, 30 June 2010.)

Chow Tai Fook Nominee Limited (Mr Cheng Yu-tung): Chow Tai Fook is a company incorporated in Hong Kong and was wholly beneficially owned by Mr Cheng Yu-tung, a businessman (deceased in 2016) and one of the richest persons in Hong Kong (see also NWS Financial Management Services Limited). Chow Tai Fook has also made cornerstone investments through Well Ease Limited, a wholly owned subsidiary incorporated in the British Virgin Islands. (Source: Prospectuses for the Hong Kong IPOs of Industrial and Commercial Bank of China Limited, 16 October 2006, and China Merchant Securities Co. Ltd., 27 September 2016, respectively.)

CIMB-Principal Asset Management Berhad: CIMB-Principal is an asset management company with regional investment capabilities. Established in 1995, it is one of the largest asset management companies in Malaysia, with regional footprint covering Singapore, Indonesia, and Thailand. (Source: Prospectus for the Malaysia and Singapore IPO of IHH Healthcare Berhad, 2 July 2012.)

CITIC Pacific Limited: CITIC Pacific Limited is listed on the Stock Exchange of Hong Kong. Its main businesses include special steel manufacturing, property development and investment, power generation, aviation, tunnels, communications, and distribution of motor vehicles and consumer products throughout China. Its former chairman was Mr Yung Chi-kin. CITIC Pacific and its former chairman have also made cornerstone subscriptions through Allied Stars Enterprises Inc. and Kingswell International Holdings Ltd., both companies incorporated in the British Virgin Islands. Allied Stars Enterprises Inc. is a wholly owned subsidiary of CITIC Pacific Limited. Kingswell International Holdings Ltd. is wholly beneficially owned by Mr Yung Chi-kin. (Source: Prospectus for the Hong Kong IPO of Industrial and Commercial Bank of China Limited, 16 October 2006.)

CM Securities Investment Limited (China Minsheng): CMSI is a limited liability company incorporated in the British Virgin Islands and a wholly owned subsidiary of China Minsheng Financial Holding Corporation Limited, or CMF Group. Its main business is investment. CMF is an investment holding company whose shares are listed on the Main Board of the Stock Exchange of Hong Kong. CMF is an important strategic component of China Minsheng Investment Corporation Limited, a large private investment group in China, whose focus is on investment and investment banking, and which provides comprehensive financial services for PRC and global enterprises. The market capitalization of CMF was approximately HK$22.9 billion as at the end of May 2016. (Source: Prospectus for the Hong Kong IPO of DFZQ, 22 June 2016.)

CMY Capital Markets Sdn Bhd (Mr Chua Ma-yu): CMY Capital is incorporated in Malaysia and is an active global investor privately owned by Mr Chua Ma-yu. (Source: Prospectus for the Malaysia and Singapore IPO of IHH Healthcare Berhad, 2 July 2012.)

CSCEC Capital (Hong Kong) Limited (China State Construction Engineering): CSCEC Capital (Hong Kong) was incorporated in Hong Kong and is a wholly owned subsidiary of China State Construction Engineering Corporation Limited (CSCECL). CSCEC Capital (Hong Kong) is primarily engaged in financing, lease and restructuring transactions and other related management services. CSCECL is one of the largest construction and real estate conglomerates in the PRC. It was established in 2007 and has been listed on the Shanghai Stock Exchange since 2009. CSCECL is principally engaged in housing construction, infrastructure construction and investment, real estate development and investment, design and prospecting. (Source: Prospectus for the Hong Kong IPO of Everbright Securities Company Limited, 8 August 2016.)

Dazhong Transportation (Hong Kong) Limited: Dazhong was incorporated in Hong Kong and is a wholly owned subsidiary of Dazhong Transportation (Group) Co. Ltd. The latter is primarily engaged in urban transportation, modern logistics, tourist services, real estate, and self-operated financial services. The principal businesses of Dazhong include taxi and automobile rental and management of car parks, modern logistics, and transportation. (Source: Prospectus for the Hong Kong IPO of Everbright Securities Company Limited, 8 August 2016.)

DBS Bank Ltd.: DBS is a leading financial services group in Asia, with over 250 branches across 17 markets. The bank's capital position is among the highest in Asia-Pacific. DBS was recognized as 'Asia's Best Bank' by *The Banker*, a member of the *Financial Times* group, and 'Best Managed Bank in Asia-Pacific' by *The Asian Banker*. The bank was also named 'Safest Bank in Asia' by *Global Finance* for six consecutive years from 2009 to 2014. DBS has taken cornerstone positions both on behalf of itself and for private banking clients. As at 30 September 2014, its private banking business in particular had total assets under management of approximately S$89 billion. (Source: Prospectus for the Singapore IPO of Keppel DC REIT, 5 December 2014.)

East Pacific (Holdings) Limited: East Pacific is a company incorporated in Hong Kong. Its principal business is investment holding and it mainly invests in real estate, aviation, luxury hotels, and property management. (Source: Prospectus for the Hong Kong IPO of China Merchants Securities Co. Ltd., 27 September 2016.)

Eastspring Investments Berhad: Eastspring Investments is part of Prudential plc. It was incorporated in 2000 and is a wholly owned subsidiary of a Malaysian resident holding company, which in turn is related to the Prudential group. It has a comprehensive family of funds designed to accommodate most investment objectives, investment horizons, and risk tolerance levels. The ultimate parent company of the Prudential group is Prudential plc, which is headquartered in London and is listed on the stock exchanges in both London and New York. See also Eastspring Investments (Singapore) Limited. (Source: Prospectus for the Malaysia and Singapore IPO of IHH Healthcare Berhad, 2 July 2012.)

Eastspring Investments (Singapore) Limited: Eastspring Investments (Singapore) is a wholly owned subsidiary of UK-based Prudential plc. It serves as the hub of its regional asset management business and manages a wide range of funds across various asset classes to service both retail and institutional clients. In Singapore, it is one of the largest fund management companies with approximately S$86 billion in funds under management, of which approximately S$62 billion are discretionary funds managed in Singapore (as at the end of March 2014), and it offers a wide range of retail unit trusts to meet the diverse needs of its investors in Singapore. See also Eastspring Investments Berhad. (Source: Prospectus for the Singapore IPO of Keppel DC REIT, 5 December 2014.)

Elion International Investment Limited: Elion International Investment Limited is a wholly owned subsidiary of Elion Resources Group Limited. It is also the group's only investment platform in Hong Kong. Its main businesses include desert ecosystem restoration, efficient and clean use of coal, natural gas, ecological photovoltaic development, and utilization of mineral resources, investment into research and development, ecological construction and tourism development. Its assets amounted to approximately RMB90 billion as at 31 December 2015. The group has effective control over Elion Clean Energy Co. Ltd., an A-share company listed on the Shanghai Stock Exchange. (Source: Prospectus for the Hong Kong IPO of BOC Aviation Limited, 19 May 2016.)

Employees Provident Fund Board (EPF): EPF is a social security institution in Malaysia formed under the Employees Provident Fund Act 1991 (Act 452). It provides retirement benefits for members through management of their savings. (Source: Prospectus for the Malaysia and Singapore IPO of IHH Healthcare Berhad, 2 July 2012.)

Fast Retailing (UNIQLO): Fast Retailing, which was established in 1963, is a Japanese retail holding company listed on the Tokyo Stock Exchange and Stock Exchange of

Hong Kong. It is a leading retailer of quality clothing for men, women, children, and infants under its mainstay brand UNIQLO and other global brands, which comprise GU, Theory, Comptoir des Cotonniers, Princesse tam.tam, and J Brand. (Source: Prospectus for the Hong Kong IPO of Nameson Holdings Limited, 30 March 2016.)

Fidelity International and FIL Investment Management (Hong Kong) Limited: Fidelity International offers world-class investment solutions and retirement expertise and is one of the largest asset managers in the world. As a privately independent company, investment is its only business. FIL Investment Management (Hong Kong) Limited was established in Hong Kong in 1981 and is a subsidiary of Fidelity International. It has been managing Hongkongers' retirement assets since 1989. Fidelity is the largest manager in the ORSO employee choice market and the largest pure investment manager to offer a Mandatory Provident Fund (MPF) scheme in Hong Kong. (Source: Company website and other publicly available information.)

Fortress Capital Asset Management (M) Sdn Bhd: Fortress Capital is an established, independent asset management and private investment group that was formed in 2003. It is a licensed fund manager under the Capital Markets and Services Act 2007 of Malaysia. It manages investment portfolios for institutional investors and the high net worth segment, providing its clients with independent access to public and private equity opportunities across the Asia-Pacific region. (Source: Prospectus for the Singapore IPO of Keppel DC REIT, 5 December 2014.)

Fortune Eris Holding Company Limited (CSSC Shipping): Fortune Eris, a company incorporated in the British Virgin Islands, is a special investment vehicle directly and wholly owned by CSSC (Hong Kong) Shipping Company Limited (CSSC Shipping). CSSC Shipping was established by China State Shipbuilding Corporation in Hong Kong. CSSC Shipping is one of the leading financial services institutions in the field of shipping finance, focusing on financial leasing, asset management, consultancy, investment, and financing for ship, offshore and marine engineering, among other services. (Source: Prospectus for the Hong Kong IPO of China Development Bank Financial Leasing Co. Ltd., 24 June 2016.)

Fosun International Limited: Fosun is a leading investment group taking roots in China, and with a global foothold. Fosun is listed on the Stock Exchange of Hong Kong. Fosun has also made cornerstone investments through its subsidiaries Peak Reinsurance Company Limited (see that name), Fosun Hani Securities Limited, and Century Surety Company. Fosun Hani Securities is a registered securities broker with licences in Hong Kong to deal in securities on behalf of retail customers and corporate customers. It is also an important Hong Kong–based integrated finance platform of Fosun. A wholly owned subsidiary of Fosun, Meadowbrook Insurance Group, Inc. is a professional property and casualty insurer and an insurance administration services company focusing on niche markets. Meadowbrook is registered in Michigan, in the US. Meadowbrook markets and underwrites specialty property and casualty insurance programs and products on both an admitted and non-admitted basis through a broad and diverse network of independent retail agents, wholesalers, program administrators, and general agencies that value service and have specialized knowledge and focused expertise. Century Surety is a wholly owned subsidiary of Meadowbrook and is principally engaged in insurance business. (Source: Prospectus for the Hong Kong IPO of China Merchants Securities Co. Ltd., 27 September 2016.)

Fujifilm Corporation: Fujifilm is a corporation incorporated under the laws of Japan whose businesses include the development, production, sales, and service of its products in the imaging solutions business, such as colour films, digital cameras, photofinishing equipment and colour paper, chemicals and services for photofinishing, and those in the information solutions business, such as equipment and materials for medical diagnostics and life science, graphic arts, flat panel display materials, recording media, optical devices, electronic materials and inkjet materials. It is a wholly owned subsidiary of FUJIFILM Holdings Corporation, which is a company listed on the Tokyo Stock Exchange. (Source: Prospectus for the Hong Kong IPO of China Resources Pharmaceutical Group Limited, 17 October 2016.)

Fullerton Fund Management Company Ltd. (Temasek Holdings): Fullerton is an Asian and emerging market specialist, with investment capabilities that span equities, fixed income, multi-assets and alternatives. It was incorporated in Singapore in 2003 and it is a wholly owned subsidiary of Singapore sovereign wealth fund Temasek Holdings (Private) Limited (see that name). With more than 20 years of experience in Asian financial markets, Fullerton provides its clients investment solutions that are long term, research based and conviction led. Its clients include government agencies, pension plans, insurance companies, endowments, sovereign wealth, and private wealth. Fullerton is licensed under the Securities and Futures Act in Singapore and regulated by the Monetary Authority of Singapore. (Source: Prospectus for the Hong Kong IPO of BOC Aviation Limited, 19 May 2016.)

GIC Direct Investments Pte. Ltd.: Incorporated in Singapore, this company is an investment holding company managed by GIC Special Investments Pte. Ltd., the private equity investment arm of Government of Singapore Investment Corporation

Pte. Ltd., a sovereign wealth fund in Singapore, with a portfolio size of more than US$100 billion. GIC is one of the largest fund management companies in the world. (Source: Prospectuses for the Malaysia and Singapore IPO of IHH Healthcare, 2 July 2012, and the Hong Kong IPO of Industrial and Commercial Bank of China Limited, 16 October 2006, respectively.)

Great Boom Group Limited (Mr Yu Yusheng): Great Boom is an investment vehicle incorporated in the British Virgin Islands. It engages in global financial investments including foreign exchange products, stocks and structured products. Its sole director, Mr Yu Yusheng, also engages in property development in China and Australia. (Source: Prospectus for the Hong Kong IPO of DFZQ, 22 June 2016.)

Great Eastern (OCBC): Founded in 1908 and now a member of the OCBC group, Great Eastern is the oldest and most established life insurance group in Singapore and Malaysia. With over S$60 billion in assets and around 4.7 million policyholders, it has three distribution channels—a tied agency force, bancassurance, and a financial advisory firm. (Source: Company website.)

Great Wall Pan Asia International Investment Co. Limited: Great Wall is a wholly owned subsidiary of China Great Wall Asset Management Corporation (CGW) (which was restructured as a joint-stock company in December 2016) and serves as an investment platform for its parent. Great Wall is a company registered in Hong Kong. CGW mainly conducts asset management, investment, credit, and investment banking businesses. (Source: Prospectus for the Hong Kong IPO of Postal Savings Bank of China, Co. Ltd., 14 September 2016.)

Greentown China: Greentown China is a Cayman Islands–incorporated real estate developer listed on the Stock Exchange of Hong Kong. China Communications Construction Group (Limited) and The Wharf (Holdings) Limited (listed on the Stock Exchange of Hong Kong) are the two largest shareholders of the company and interested in 29 per cent and 25 per cent of the issued share capital of Greentown China, respectively. See also CCC International Holding Limited and Mr Woo Kwong-ching. (Source: Prospectus for the Hong Kong IPO of Greentown Service Group Co. Ltd., 28 June 2016.)

Guoco Management Co. Ltd.: Guoco is an investment and management company incorporated in Hong Kong and wholly owned by Guoco Group Limited (listed on the Main Board of the Stock Exchange of Hong Kong), which in turn is an indirect subsidiary of Hong Leong Company (Malaysia) Berhad (see Hong Leong Assurance

Berhad). Guoco Group Limited has four core businesses: principal investments, property development and investment, hospitality and leisure business and financial services. (Source: Prospectus for the Hong Kong IPO of AIA Group Limited, 18 October 2010.)

GuoLine Capital Limited (Hong Leong Assurance): GuoLine is an investment holding company incorporated in Bermuda and is an indirect subsidiary of Hong Leong Assurance Berhad (see that name). (Source: Prospectus for the Hong Kong IPO of AIA Group Limited, 18 October 2010.)

Haier Group (HK) Financial Holdings Limited (Haier Group Corporation): Incorporated in Hong Kong, Haier Group (HK) is a wholly owned subsidiary of Haier Financial Holdings Limited (Haier Financial Holdings). Haier Financial Holdings is one of the major subsidiaries established by its group (the Haier Group) for its network strategies across China. Haier Group established a complete service chain throughout the financial industry after more than ten years of development. The financial subsidiaries under Haier Group are engaged in various financial services such as finance lease, small loans, consumer financing, financial factoring, third-party payment, a financial supermarkets platform, and settlement and asset transaction platforms. Haier Group also owns venture investment firms specialized in equity investment and funds management. The ultimate beneficial shareholder of both Haier Group (HK) and Haier Financial Holdings is Haier Group Corporation. (Source: prospectus for the Hong Kong IPO of COFCO Meat Holdings Limited, 19 October 2016.)

Havenport Asset Management Pte. Ltd.: Havenport is a company incorporated and headquartered in Singapore. It is an Asia-Pacific equity specialist and manages assets for sovereign wealth funds, corporate pension plans, endowment schemes, and retail unit trusts, with clients spread across the globe and in the region. (Source: Prospectus for the Singapore IPO of Far East Hospitality Trust, 16 August 2012.)

Hengjian International Investment Holding (Hong Kong) Limited: Hengjian International was incorporated in Hong Kong and its principal business is investment holding. Hengjian International is wholly owned by Guangdong Hengjian Investment Holding Co. Ltd. and is its only overseas investment vehicle. Guangdong Hengjian is a wholly state-owned investment holding company incorporated in the PRC through which the State-owned Assets Supervision and Administration Commission (SASAC) of the People's Government of Guangdong Province performs the responsibilities of an investor. It is the only provincial-level state-owned capital operating company in

Guangdong Province and has the support of the People's Government of Guangdong Province. (Source: Prospectus for the Hong Kong IPO of Everbright Securities Company Limited, 8 August 2016.)

High Action Limited (Mr Thomas Lau Luen-hung/Lifestyle China): High Action is a company incorporated in the British Virgin Islands and is wholly and beneficially owned by Mr Thomas Lau Luen-hung. High Action is principally engaged in the business of investments. Mr Lau is the chairman, chief executive officer and executive director of Lifestyle China Group Limited and the chairman and non-executive director of Lifestyle International Holdings Limited, both companies listed on the Stock Exchange of Hong Kong since July 2016 and April 2004 respectively. Mr Lau is also a member of the Chinese People's Political Consultative Conference Shanghai Committee and a member of the board of directors of Shanghai Jiao Tong University. (Source: Prospectus for the Hong Kong IPO of China Resources Pharmaceutical Group Limited, 17 October 2016.)

HNA Group Co. Ltd.: See Victory Global Group Limited.

Hong Kong Kunsheng Investment Limited (Mr Xie Zhikun): Kunsheng Investment is an investment holding company incorporated in Hong Kong and is principally engaged in investment holding activities. Kunsheng Investment is ultimately controlled by Mr Xie Zhikun (see also Keenway International Investment Limited). (Source: Prospectus for the Hong Kong IPO of Yadea Group Holdings Ltd., 9 May 2016.)

Hong Leong Assurance Berhad: Hong Leong is a company incorporated in Malaysia principally engaged in the underwriting of life insurance business in Malaysia and is an indirect subsidiary of Hong Leong Financial Group Berhad, a company listed on the Kuala Lumpur Stock Exchange, which, in turn, is an indirect subsidiary (non-wholly owned) of Hong Leong Company (Malaysia) Berhad. The group has also made cornerstone investments through Wing Trade Investments Limited, an investment holding company incorporated in the British Virgin Islands and a subsidiary of Hong Leong Financial Group Berhad, and Asia Fountain Investment Company Limited, an indirect wholly owned subsidiary of Guoco Group Limited and GuoLine Capital Limited and an indirect, wholly owned subsidiary of Hong Leong Company (Malaysia) Berhad. See also GuoLine Capital Limited and Guoco Management Co. Ltd. (Source: Prospectus for the Hong Kong IPO of AIA Group Limited, 18 October 2010.)

Hony Capital Group, L.P.: Hony Capital is an exempted limited partnership established under the laws of the Cayman Islands as an investment vehicle and is managed by Hony Group Management Limited (as sole general partner), 80 per cent of which is held by Hony Managing Partners Limited, which in turn is wholly owned by Exponential Fortune Group Limited. The series of private equity investment funds, together with their respective management companies/general partners was founded in the early 2000s to capture investment opportunities as a private equity platform. Through more than a decade, Hony Capital has become one of the most successful and reputable Chinese private equity firms, especially in the restructuring and reorganization of China's state-owned enterprises. Hony Capital also invests through its wholly owned subsidiary Colour Wish Limited. (Source: Prospectus for the Hong Kong IPO of BOC Aviation Limited, 19 May 2016.)

HPL Investers Pte Ltd and Como Holdings Inc. (HPL/Mr Ong Beng Seng): HPL Investers is a wholly owned subsidiary of Hotel Properties Limited (HPL), which is listed on the Singapore Stock Exchange. The principal business activities of HPL and its subsidiaries are those of hotel ownership, management and operation, property development and investment holding. Como Holdings Inc., a company beneficially owned by Mr Ong Beng Seng (the husband of fashion icon Christina Ong), has investments in hotel, property, and retail operations worldwide. (Source: Prospectus for the Malaysia and Singapore IPO of IHH Healthcare Berhad, 2 July 2012.)

Hui Ding Holdings Limited (China Huiyuan Juice/Mr Zhu Xinli): Hui Ding Holdings is an investment holding company incorporated in the British Virgin Islands. Its controlling shareholder is Huiyuan International Holding Limited, which is wholly owned by Mr Zhu Xinli. Huiyuan International Holding Limited is also the parent holding company of China Huiyuan Juice Holding Limited, a major beverage company listed on the Stock Exchange of Hong Kong. (Source: Prospectus for the Hong Kong IPO of Bank of Tianjin Co. Ltd., 15 March 2016.)

Hung Jia Finance Limited (Mr Zhu Lijia and Mrs Sun Hongyan): Hung Jia is an investment company incorporated in the British Virgin Islands owned by Mr Zhu Lijia and his spouse Mrs Sun Hongyan as to 50 per cent each. They also collectively hold 85 per cent of Yingkou Hong Jia Investments Limited, a company incorporated in the PRC and principally engaged in managing real estate, industrial and commercial projects, as well as in providing business and financial consultancy services. In addition, Mr Zhu is an executive director of Enviro Energy International Holdings Limited, a company incorporated in the Cayman Islands and listed on the Stock Exchange of Hong Kong. (Source: Prospectus for the Hong Kong IPO of DFZQ, 22 June 2016.)

Hutchison Whampoa Limited (Mr Li Ka-shing): Hutchison Whampoa is a Hong Kong–based multinational conglomerate controlled by Mr Li Ka-shing [Note: Hong Kong's richest person]. Its shares are listed on the Main Board of the Stock Exchange of Hong Kong. It has also made cornerstone subscriptions through Turbo Top Limited, an indirect wholly owned subsidiary. See also Cheung Kong (Holdings) Limited. (Source: Prospectus for the Hong Kong IPO of Industrial and Commercial Bank of China Limited, 16 October 2006.)

Hwang Investment Management Berhad (Hwang-DBS/Nikko): Hwang Investment, formerly known as HwangDBS Investment Management Berhad, was incorporated in Malaysia in 1997 and began operations in 2001. It is supported by one of Malaysia's leading integrated financial services groups, Hwang-DBS (M) Berhad, whose principal subsidiaries include HwangDBS Investment Bank Berhad, with several decades of experience in the securities industry, and Nikko Asset Management Asia Limited (formerly known as DBS Asset Management Ltd.), an independent Asian investment management franchise, with its parent company Nikko Asset Management Group headquartered in Tokyo. (Source: Prospectus for the Malaysia and Singapore IPO of IHH Healthcare Berhad, 2 July 2012.)

Indus Capital Partners, LLC: Indus is registered as an investment adviser with the US Securities and Exchange Commission (SEC). It has made cornerstone investments through Indus Pacific Opportunities Master Fund Ltd. and Indus Asia-Pacific Master Fund Ltd., which are both private investment vehicles and exempted companies incorporated and validly existing under the laws of the Cayman Islands. Indus Capital Partners, LLC is the investment manager of these funds. (Source: Prospectus for the Singapore IPO of Far East Hospitality Trust, 16 August 2012.)

International Finance Corporation (IFC): IFC is a member of the World Bank Group and fosters sustainable economic growth in developing countries by financing private sector investment, mobilizing capital in the international financial markets, and providing advisory services to businesses and governments. See also Peak Reinsurance Company Limited. (Source: Prospectus for the Malaysia and Singapore IPO of IHH Healthcare Berhad, 2 July 2012.)

JF Asset Management Limited: JF Asset Management Limited is the Asia-Pacific equity investment arm of J.P. Morgan Asset Management and has a network of investment professionals based in the region. In 2012, it managed US$78 billion for investors around the globe. (Source: Prospectus for the Malaysia and Singapore IPO of IHH Healthcare Berhad, 2 July 2012.)

Joy Orient Investments Limited (Sino-Ocean Group): Joy Orient is a company incorporated in the British Virgin Islands with limited liability and an investment vehicle indirectly wholly owned by Sino-Ocean Group Holding Limited. Sino-Ocean is incorporated in Hong Kong with limited liability and its shares have been listed on the Main Board of the Stock Exchange of Hong Kong since 2007. Sino-Ocean and its subsidiaries have over 60 development projects in 19 high-growth cities in the Beijing-Tianjin-Hebei region, the Northeast region, the Central region, and the Southern region of the PRC. As at 31 December 2015, projects located in first- and second-tier cities of the PRC accounted for about 93 per cent of Sino-Ocean's total landbank. (Source: Prospectus for the Hong Kong IPO of China Logistics Property Holdings Co. Ltd., 30 June 2016.)

Keck Seng (Malaysia) Berhad and Keck Seng Investments (Hong Kong) Limited: Keck Seng (Malaysia) is a company listed on the Kuala Lumpur Stock Exchange. Its business consists of the cultivation of oil palm, processing and marketing of refined palm oil products, property development, property investment and share investment. Keck Seng Investments (Hong Kong) is a company listed on the Stock Exchange of Hong Kong. Its principal activities and those of its subsidiaries are hotel and club operations, property investment and development, and the provision of management services. (Source: Prospectus for the Malaysia and Singapore IPO of IHH Healthcare Berhad, 2 July 2012.)

Keenway International Investment Limited (Mrs Xie Rutong): Keenway International is an investment holding company incorporated in the British Virgin Islands and is principally engaged in investment holding activities. Keenway International is ultimately controlled by Mrs Xie Rutong, the daughter of Mr Xie Zhikun (see Hong Kong Kunsheng Investment Limited). (Source: Prospectus for the Hong Kong IPO of Yadea Group Holdings Ltd., 9 May 2016.)

Kencana Capital Sdn Bhd: Kencana is an investment holding company. Through its related companies, it has a diversified investment portfolio ranging from oil and gas (being one of the top five global Engineering, Procurement, Installation and Commissioning (EPIC) players), engineering and construction, information technology services, education and training, as well as real estate. (Source: Prospectus for the Malaysia and Singapore IPO of IHH Healthcare Berhad, 2 July 2012.)

Khazanah Nasional Berhad: Khazanah is a sovereign wealth fund and the investment arm of the government of Malaysia. Khazanah holds and manages selected commercial assets of the government and undertakes strategic investments on behalf of the nation.

It has interests in over 80 companies across multiple sectors and industries, in Asia and the Middle East. (Source: Company website and other publicly available information.)

Kumpulan Wang Persaraan (Diperbadankan) (KWAP): KWAP manages the pension contributions of Malaysian civil servants and employees of statutory bodies and local authorities authorized by Minister of Finance of Malaysia. KWAP is a statutory body incorporated under the Retirement Fund Incorporated Act 2007. (Source: Prospectus for the Hong Kong IPO of AIA Group Limited, 18 October 2010.)

Kuok Group: The Kuok Group was founded by Malaysian tycoon Mr Robert Kuok Hock-nien. Apart from a multitude of businesses in Malaysia, his companies have investments in many countries throughout Asia. His business interests include sugarcane plantations, sugar refineries, flour milling, animal feed, oil, mining, finance, hotels (Shangri-La), properties (Kerry Properties), trading, freight and publishing. He also owns a stake in Wilmar International, the world's largest listed palm oil company. The Kuok Group has also made cornerstone investments through Silver Pebble Holdings Limited, a private company limited by shares and incorporated in Hong Kong. (Source: Prospectus for the Hong Kong IPO of Industrial and Commercial Bank of China Limited, 16 October 2006.)

Kuwait Investment Authority (KIA): KIA is an autonomous government body of Kuwait responsible for the management and administration of funds and assets entrusted to it by the Ministry of Finance of Kuwait, for and on behalf of the State of Kuwait. KIA invests across various asset classes and markets around the globe, with its main office located in Kuwait City and a branch office in London. (Source: Prospectuses for the Hong Kong IPOs of AIA Group Limited and Agricultural Bank of China Limited, 18 October and 30 June 2010, respectively.)

Mr Lee Shau-kee (Henderson Land): Mr Lee Shau-kee is a Hong Kong–based real estate tycoon and majority owner of Henderson Land Development, a property conglomerate with interests in properties, hotels, restaurants, and Internet services. He has taken cornerstone participations through Chinfit Limited, a private company incorporated in the British Virgin Islands, indirectly wholly owned by Shau Kee Financial Enterprises Limited, which in turn is wholly owned by Lee Financial (Cayman) Limited, of which Mr Lee is a substantial shareholder. (Source: Prospectus for the Hong Kong IPO of Industrial and Commercial Bank of China Limited, 16 October 2006.)

Legit Value Limited (Leshi/China Bridge Capital): Legit Value, a company registered in the British Virgin Islands, is wholly owned by Shenzhen Letv-China Bridge Capital Buyout Fund & Investment Management (Limited Partnership) (Letv-China Bridge Capital). Letv-China Bridge Capital is a joint venture established by Beijing Leshi Streaming Media Advertising Co. Ltd. (a wholly owned subsidiary of Leshi Internet Information & Technology Corp., Beijing ('Leshi', a company listed on the Shenzhen Stock Exchange) and Shenzhen China Bridge Investment Fund Management Co. Ltd. (China Bridge Capital). Leshi is a leading Internet company in China, with operations encompassing, among others, Internet videos, films and television programs production and distribution, intelligent terminals, application market, e-commerce and cloud computing. China Bridge Capital is a capital management corporation in China focusing on the provision of integrated merger and acquisition financial services, with a particular emphasis on global investment in emerging industries, fund management, transnational mergers and acquisitions, and corporate restructuring. (Source: Prospectus for the Hong Kong IPO of China Merchants Securities Co. Ltd., 27 September 2016.)

Lembaga Tabung Angkatan Tentera (LTAT): LTAT is the armed forces fund board of Malaysia. One of its objectives is to provide retirement and other benefits to officers and members of the other ranks in the Malaysian armed forces and a saving scheme for mobilized members of the volunteer forces. (Source: Company website.)

Lembaga Tabung Haji (LTH): LTH is a statutory body incorporated in Malaysia under the Lembaga Tabung Haji Act 1995 (Act 535). Its functions are to administer the depositors' fund and all matters concerning the welfare of pilgrims (to Mecca) and to formulate policies in connection with the welfare of pilgrims. (Source: Prospectus for the Malaysia and Singapore IPO of IHH Healthcare Berhad, 2 July 2012.)

Mr Lim Chap Huat (Soilbuild Group): Mr Lim is the owner and executive chairman of Soilbuild Group Holdings Ltd. Soilbuild Group is an integrated property group with a track record of more than 38 years in constructing, developing, and managing residential and business space properties. Soilbuild has completed a multitude of purpose-built business spaces and manages close to four million square feet of business space for lease. The group further developed a range of residential properties from high-end luxury condominiums to townhouses and conservation terraces. In 2013, Soilbuild Construction Group Ltd., a member of Soilbuild Group, was listed in Singapore to provide the group greater visibility and a funding platform to expand its construction capabilities and reach overseas markets. In the same year, Soilbuild

Business Space REIT, which is sponsored by Soilbuild Group, was also listed there. (Source: Prospectus for the Singapore IPO of Keppel DC REIT, 5 December 2014.)

Lion Global Investors Limited (OCBC): Lion Global Investors, a member of Oversea-Chinese Banking Corporation Limited Group (OCBC), is one of the largest asset management companies in Southeast Asia, with total assets under management of S$28.4 billion (US$22.6 billion) as at 31 March 2012. Established as an Asian asset specialist since 1986, Lion Global offers equities and fixed income funds to institutional and retail investors globally. It has one of the largest and most experienced investment teams dedicated to regional and global equities and fixed income markets. The company's commitment to investment excellence begins with a team-based and research-intensive approach, combining in-depth market insights with comprehensive sector knowledge. Lion Global Investors Limited is 70 per cent owned by Great Eastern Holdings Limited and 30 per cent owned by Orient Holdings Private Limited, a wholly owned subsidiary of Oversea-Chinese Banking Corporation Limited. (Source: Prospectus for the Singapore IPO of Far East Hospitality Trust, 16 August 2012.)

London International Trading (Asia) Limited (Reckitt Benckiser): London International Trading is a Hong Kong–incorporated company and a wholly owned subsidiary of Reckitt Benckiser Group plc (Reckitt Benckiser). It is a regional group holding company, whose focus is on health-related activities in China. Reckitt Benckiser, headquartered in Slough, United Kingdom, is a world-leading consumer health and hygiene company and is listed on the London Stock Exchange. It has operations in over 60 countries and sales in most countries across the globe. (Source: Prospectus for the Hong Kong IPO of China Resources Pharmaceutical Group Limited, 17 October 2016.)

LRC. Belt and Road Investment Limited: LRC. Belt and Road is incorporated in the Cayman Islands and is a joint venture between Strategic Global Investment Corporation Limited and Mr Soul Htite. LRC. Belt and Road is the principal investment entity of Strategic Global, with a focus on investment opportunities in companies serving 'Belt and Road' initiatives issued by the National Development and Reform Commission, the Ministry of Foreign Affairs, and the Ministry of Commerce of the PRC in March 2015. Strategic Global is a global investment house with expertise in global family office investment and alternative investment products. Mr Htite is a financial technology expert, as well as the co-founder of Lending Club (listed on the New York Stock Exchange), a network-based loan platform, and the founder and CEO of Dianrong.com, an Internet finance and technology solutions company in China.

(Source: Prospectus for the Hong Kong IPO of China Logistics Property Holdings Co. Ltd., 30 June 2016.)

Maybank Asset Management: Maybank Asset Management has entities across three key ASEAN markets, namely Malaysia, Singapore, and Indonesia, and provides a diverse range of Asia-focused investment solutions for conventional and Islamic assets as well as private equity. It possesses vast capabilities in managing local and Asia-focused portfolios, ranging from equity, fixed income to money market instruments for corporations, institutions, pension funds, insurance and *Takaful* companies and individual clients through direct mandates, unit trust, and wholesale funds. As of July 2016, Maybank Asset Management had approximately US$5.7 billion in total asset management, of which 46 per cent was conventional and 54 per cent Shariah-compliant. (Source: Company website.)

Mercuries Life Insurance Company Limited: Mercuries Life was incorporated in Taiwan and is listed on the Taiwan Stock Exchange. It is principally engaged in the life insurance business and primarily provides individual life insurance services, individual health insurance services, individual accident insurance services, individual annuities insurance services, individual universal insurance services and group insurance services, as well as investment insurance products. Mercuries Life's controlling shareholder, Mercuries & Associates Holding Ltd., also a company listed on the Taiwan Stock Exchange, owns extensive businesses in general merchandise, dining, department stores, shoe retail business, retail business, financial services, biochemical technology, recreation and charity, etc. (Source: Prospectus for the Hong Kong IPO of Everbright Securities Company Limited, 8 August 2016.)

Myriad Asset Management Limited: Myriad is a Hong Kong–based independent asset management company that has grown rapidly since being established in 2011. The Myriad Opportunities Fund is an Asia-Pacific integrated multi-strategy investment fund investing a focused portfolio across the corporate capital structure with a focus on equities, but also convertible bonds, and credit. Myriad is managed by the CIO and founder, Carl Huttenlocher, who has over 15 years of experience managing hedge fund strategies. (Source: Prospectus for the Singapore IPO of Far East Hospitality Trust, 16 August 2012.)

Nan Fung Group: Nan Fung Group is an established property developer in Hong Kong with global interests in property markets, financial investments, shipping, hotel investment and a diverse range of business partnerships. The group was founded by the late Mr Chen Din-hwa. He previously made cornerstone investments together with his wife, Mrs Vivien Chen Wai-wai, through Gavast Estates Limited and Gentfull Investment Limited, both companies incorporated in Hong Kong. (Source: Prospectus for the Hong Kong IPO of Industrial and Commercial Bank of China Limited, 16 October 2006.)

Newton Investment Management Limited: Newton is a company incorporated in England and Wales and a global investment manager. (Source: Prospectus for the Malaysia and Singapore IPO of IHH Healthcare Berhad, 2 July 2012.)

Nordea Investment Management AB: Nordea Investment is incorporated in Sweden. It is one of the largest asset managers in Europe and had EUR189 billion under management as of 31 December 2015. In its management of the funds, Nordea Investment works to deliver superior financial performance to the funds' investors. (Source: Prospectus for the Hong Kong IPO of China Resources Pharmaceutical Group Limited, 17 October 2016.)

Norges Bank Investment Management: Norges runs the Norwegian government's pension fund, saving for future generations in Norway. The fund's market value is approximately NOK7,246 billion and is invested across 78 countries, 9,050 companies representing 1.3 per cent of listed companies worldwide and 2.3 per cent of listed companies in Europe. The fund generated an annual return of 5.6 per cent from its inception in 1998 to the end of 2015, measured in the fund's currency basket. After management costs and inflation, the return was 3.7 per cent. The return in US dollars was 5.8 per cent. (Source: Company website.)

NTUC Income Co-operative Limited: NTUC Income was established in 1970 to provide affordable insurance for workers in Singapore. As a social enterprise, it was made different from the start with a mission to provide value for customers and not to maximize profits for shareholders. Since 2007, NTUC Income has been transforming into a modern financial institution to meet the needs of an increasingly sophisticated and affluent generation. NTUC Income had over two million customers and S$27.6 billion of assets under management as at 31 December 2011. It is a major force in the industry, having attained leadership positions in life, health, annuity, and motor insurance. (Source: Prospectus for the Singapore IPO of Far East Hospitality Trust, 16 August 2012.)

NWS Financial Management Services Limited (New World/Mr Cheng Yu-tung): NWS is an indirect wholly owned subsidiary of NWS Holdings Limited, a company incorporated in Bermuda with limited liability and whose shares are listed on the

Main Board of the Stock Exchange of Hong Kong. It was controlled by the late Mr Cheng Yu-tung. NWS Holdings Limited is the infrastructure and service flagship of New World Development Company Limited (also listed in Hong Kong) and embraces a diversified range of businesses in Hong Kong, mainland China, and Macau. Its infrastructure portfolio includes roads, energy, water, and ports and logistics projects while its services division comprises facilities management (e.g., management of the Hong Kong Convention and Exhibition Centre and Free Duty), contracting and transport (e.g., Hip Hing Construction and bus and ferry services) (see also Chow Tai Fook Nominee Limited). (Source: Prospectus for the Hong Kong IPO of AIA Group Limited, 18 October 2010.)

Och-Ziff Capital Management Group: Och-Ziff is an American hedge fund manager and global alternative asset management firm. As of August 2016, the firm had more than US$39 billion in assets under management. Och-Ziff makes cornerstone investments through a variety of affiliated investment funds. (Source: Prospectus for the Malaysia and Singapore IPO of IHH Healthcare Berhad, 2 July 2012 and other publicly available information.)

Oman Investment Fund: Oman Investment Fund is a sovereign wealth fund of the government of Oman responsible for investment in public equity, private equity, and real estate globally. (Source: Prospectus for the Hong Kong IPO of BOC Aviation Limited, 19 May 2016.)

Peak Reinsurance Company Limited (Fosun International/IFC): Based in Hong Kong and authorized by the Office of the Commissioner of Insurance of Hong Kong, Peak Re was licensed in 2012. With shareholder funds of US$717 million as of 31 December 2015, Peak Re offers treaty reinsurance services across the Asia-Pacific and Europe, Middle East and Africa (EMEA) regions and the Americas, tailor-made risk transfer, and capital management solutions. Peak Re is backed by Fosun International Limited (see that name), a leading investment group taking roots in China with a global foothold, and the International Finance Corporation (see that name), a member of the World Bank Group focusing on private sector development. The two shareholders have respectively invested 85.1 per cent and 14.9 per cent in Peak Re. Fosun is listed on the Stock Exchange of Hong Kong. (Source: Prospectus for the Hong Kong IPO of BOC Aviation Limited, 19 May 2016.)

Permodalan Nasional Berhad (PNB): PNB was incorporated in 1978. It was conceived as an instrument of the government of Malaysia's New Economic Policy to promote share ownership in the corporate sector among *Bumiputera* (ethnic Malays) and develop opportunities for suitable Bumiputera professionals to participate in the creation and management of wealth. The PNB Group is now Malaysia's leading investment institution, with a diverse portfolio of activities that includes unit trust funds, property trust funds, property management, and asset management. In 2012, PNB managed over RM 200 million in assets. (Source: Prospectus for the Malaysia and Singapore IPO of IHH Healthcare Berhad, 2 July 2012.)

Pertubuhan Keselamatan Social: Also known as Malaysia's social security organization (SOSCO), Pertubuhan Keselamatan Social was established in 1971 under the Ministry of Human Resources to implement and administer the social security schemes under the Employees Social Security Act 1969, namely the Employment Injury Scheme and the Invalidity Scheme. It now provides social security protection to all employees and their dependents in Malaysia. (Source: Company website.)

PICC Life Insurance Company Limited: PICC Life is a life insurance company approved by China's State Council and the China Insurance Regulatory Commission. PICC Life was founded in 2005 and is headquartered in Beijing. It is a subsidiary of The People's Insurance Company (Group) of China Limited (listed on the Stock Exchange of Hong Kong). PICC Life is principally engaged in life insurance, accident insurance, and other insurance business. Its total assets as of 31 December 2015 amounted to RMB358 billion. (Source: Prospectus for the Hong Kong IPO of China Merchants Securities Co. Ltd., 27 September 2016.)

Pinpoint Asset Management Limited: Pinpoint is the investment manager of Pinpoint China Fund and Pinpoint Multi-Strategy Fund, both of which are Cayman Island exempted companies. Pinpoint is a limited liability company incorporated in Hong Kong in 2010. It is an independent research and management company that provides active asset management services to institutional investors, pension funds, private banking, funds of funds, family offices, and high net worth individuals. It is licensed to conduct asset management business in Hong Kong. (Source: Prospectus for the Hong Kong IPO of DFZQ, 22 June 2016.)

Prestigious Leader Limited (China Everbright): Prestigious Leader is an investment holding company established in the British Virgin Islands and is principally engaged in investment holding activities. Prestigious Leader is a wholly owned subsidiary of China Everbright Limited, which is listed on the Stock Exchange of Hong Kong. China Everbright, through its subsidiaries and associates, is principally engaged in the provision of financial services and persistently pursues a cross-border macro asset management strategy, with specific focuses on fund management and investment business, namely primary market investment, secondary market investment, structured financing and investment, and aircraft leasing. (Source: Prospectus for the Hong Kong IPO of Sinco Pharmaceuticals Holdings Limited, 29 February 2016.)

The Prudential Insurance Company of America: PICA (sometimes also known as PRICOA) is a New Jersey stock life insurance company, owned by Prudential Financial, Inc. (unrelated to Prudential plc, which is listed on the London Stock Exchange). PICA's primary businesses are offering non-participating individual life insurance, annuities, group insurance, and retirement services. (Source: Prospectus for the Hong Kong IPO of Everbright Securities Company Limited, 8 August 2016.)

Qatar Investment Authority (QIA) and Qatar Holding LLC: Qatar Holding is the strategic and direct investment arm of QIA, the sovereign wealth fund of the Kingdom of Qatar. Key investment assets of Qatar Holding include or have included Barclays Plc., Credit Suisse Group, Harrods, Hassad Food Company, J. Sainsbury Plc, the London Stock Exchange, Lagardère SCA, Porsche SE, Qatar Exchange, Qatar Telecom, Qatar National Bank, and Volkswagen AG. (Source: Prospectus for the Hong Kong IPO of Agricultural Bank of China Limited, 30 June 2010.)

Rabobank International Holding B.V.: Rabobank International is incorporated in the Netherlands and is a direct wholly owned subsidiary of Coöperatieve Centrale Raiffeisen-Boerenleenbank B.A., also known as Rabobank Nederland. Rabobank Nederland is an international financial services provider based in the Netherlands operating on the basis of cooperative principles. The Rabobank group operates in around 50 countries. Its operations include domestic retail banking, wholesale and international retail banking, asset management and investment, leasing, and real estate. In the Netherlands, its focus is on all-finance services and, internationally, on food and agriculture as the largest food and agribusiness bank in the world. (Source: Prospectus for the Hong Kong IPO of Agricultural Bank of China Limited, 30 June 2010.)

RHB Asset Management Sdn Bhd: RHB Asset Management is a wholly owned subsidiary of RHB Investment Bank, under the Corporate and Investment Banking arm of the RHB Banking Group. Established in 1989, it manages a full range of investment instruments, customized according to client risk profile, including conventional and Shariah-compliant instruments. The investments and mandates managed include equity, fixed income, hybrid structures, structured deposits, cash management, investment-linked and unit trust products. It also distributes a full array of domestic and global unit trust funds, encompassing conventional and *Shariah*-compliant funds.

The funds distributed include equity, mixed assets, fixed income, money market, structured, capital guaranteed, and funds of funds. (Source: Company website and other publicly available information.)

Seven Group Holdings Limited: Seven Group is an Australian diversified operating and investment company listed on the Australian Securities Exchange (ASX). The company has a market-leading presence in Australian broadcast television, magazines publishing and online media through Seven Media Group. It has major shareholdings in publicly listed companies, including West Australian Newspapers Holdings, publisher of the leading newspapers in Western Australia, and Consolidated Media Holdings, which has interests in subscription television in Australia. It also operates in the industrial equipment industry in Australia and China through the wholly owned WesTrac Group, which is the Caterpillar dealer for Western Australia, New South Wales, the Australian Capital Territory, and six provinces in Northeast China. (Source: Prospectus for the Hong Kong IPO of Agricultural Bank of China Limited, 30 June 2010.)

Shandong Tianye Real Estate Development Group Co. Ltd. and Ruifuxiang Investment Limited: Shandong Tianye is a company in Jinan, China, and its principal businesses include real estate, clean energy, mining, financial investment and the cultural industry. Ruifuxiang is a company incorporated in Hong Kong and is a wholly owned special purpose overseas investment vehicle of Shandong Tianye. (Source: Prospectus for the Hong Kong IPO of Bank of Tianjin Co. Ltd., 15 March 2016.)

Shanghai Electric Group Hongkong Company Limited: Shanghai Electric is a wholly owned subsidiary of Shanghai Electric (Group) Corporation, incorporated in Hong Kong. The latter is an equipment-manufacturing industry group registered in Shanghai. Its main businesses cover high-efficiency clean energy, new energy and environmental protection, industrial equipment and modern service industry. Shanghai Electric is the overseas investment and financing platform of the group, with its main businesses in general contracting, industrial investment, business consulting, import and export of machinery, and electronic products. (Source: Prospectus for the Hong Kong IPO of DFZQ, 22 June 2016.)

Shanghai International Port Group (HK) Co. Limited: Shanghai International Port Group (HK) is a company incorporated in Hong Kong and wholly owned by Shanghai International Port (Group) Co. Ltd. (SIPG). It is principally engaged in port services, online shopping centre and investment holding in the PRC. SIPG is a company incorporated under the laws of the PRC and listed on the Shanghai Stock Exchange and is the operator of the public terminals in the Port of Shanghai in the PRC. SIPG is principally engaged in port-related businesses, the main business segments of which include container, bulk cargo, port logistics, and port services. As of 31 December 2015, SIPG was, directly and indirectly, held as to approximately 61.07 per cent by the State-owned Assets Supervision and Administration Commission (SASAC) of the Shanghai Municipal Government. (Source: Prospectus for the Hong Kong IPO of Postal Savings Bank of China, Co. Ltd., 14 September 2016.)

Shaoxing Lingyan Equity Investment Fund Partnerships (Limited Partnership): Lingyan Fund is a limited partnership incorporated in the PRC. Its managing partner is Zhejiang Lingyan Capital Management Co. Ltd. and its principal business is equity investment. The investors of Lingyan Fund mainly include Shenzhen Pingan Dahua Huitong Wealth Management Co. Ltd., Hangzhou Hangfeng Holding Co. Ltd., Medium, Micro and Small Enterprises Investment Group Co. Ltd., and Shaoxin Binhai Concrete Co. Ltd. (Source: Prospectus for the Hong Kong IPO of China Zheshang Bank Co. Ltd., 16 March 2016.)

Shenwan Hongyuan Group Co. Ltd.: Shenwan Hongyuan is a company incorporated in the PRC and listed on the Shenzhen Stock Exchange. The principal business activities of Shenwan Hongyuan include investment management, industrial investment, equity investment and investment consulting. Shenwan Hongyuan also carries out securities business through its wholly owned subsidiary, Shenwan Hongyuan Securities Co. Ltd., which was established in 2015 with a registered capital of RMB33 billion and about 8,000 employees. It has 18 branches and 309 business units, as well as overseas branches in Hong Kong, Tokyo, Singapore, and Seoul, among other cities. (Source: Prospectus for the Hong Kong IPO of China Zheshang Bank Co. Ltd., 16 March 2016.)

Shima Seiki MFG. Ltd.: Shima Seiki was established in 1962 and has been publicly listed on the Tokyo Stock Exchange since 1996. Beginning with the full automation of the glove-knitting machine, it has grown into a leading company in the computerized flat knitting industry with a high global market share. It has a wholly owned subsidiary in Hong Kong. (Source: Prospectus for the Hong Kong IPO of Nameson Holdings Limited, 30 March 2016.)

Sichuan Huifeng Investment Development Co. Ltd. (Kelun Pharmaceuticals): Sichuan Huifeng is an investment holding company established in the PRC in June 2003 and is principally engaged in investment and assets management. Sichuan Huifeng is owned by 15 individuals and is also a shareholder of Kelun Pharmaceuticals as to

68.2 per cent. (Source: Prospectus for the Hong Kong IPO of Sinco Pharmaceuticals Holdings Limited, 29 February 2016.)

SIIC Treasury (B.V.I.) Limited (Shanghai Industrial Investment): SIIC Treasury is a company incorporated in the British Virgin Islands and is the investment platform of, and is wholly owned by Shanghai Industrial Investment (Holdings) Company Limited (SIIC). SIIC is a conglomerate enterprise under the Shanghai Municipal Government and is principally engaged in financial investment, pharmaceutical, infrastructure, real estate, consumer products, and emerging industries. (Source: Prospectus for the Hong Kong IPO of DFZQ, 22 June 2016.)

Silk Road Fund Co. Ltd.: Silk Road Fund is a medium- to long-term development and investment fund. It was established in 2014 with its initial capital contributed by the State Administration of Foreign Exchange (SAFE), China Investment Corporation (CIC—see that name), Export-Import Bank of China and China Development Bank (see also China Development Bank International Holdings Limited). It invests in a broad spectrum of sectors, including infrastructure, resources and energy, industry cooperation and financial cooperation. Silk Road Fund also invests through its wholly owned subsidiary CIZJ Limited. (Source: Prospectus for the Hong Kong IPO of BOC Aviation Limited, 19 May 2016.)

Sinotak Limited (Mr Zhang Wei): Sinotak was incorporated in 2011 in the British Virgin Islands with limited liability. It is wholly owned by Mr Zhang Wei and is principally engaged in investment activities. (Source: Prospectus for the Hong Kong IPO of Bank of Tianjin Co. Ltd., 15 March 2016.)

Standard Chartered Bank: Standard Chartered Bank (SCB) is a company incorporated in England with limited liability by Royal Charter in 1853. It is a wholly owned subsidiary of Standard Chartered PLC, whose shares are listed on the stock exchanges in both London and Hong Kong. Standard Chartered PLC operates through a number of subsidiaries, including SCB, and is a leading international banking and financial services company that focuses on the markets of Asia, Africa, and the Middle East. (Source: Prospectus for the Hong Kong IPO of Agricultural Bank of China Limited, 30 June 2010.)

State Grid Overseas Investment Limited: State Grid Overseas Investment is a wholly owned subsidiary of State Grid Corporation of China (SGCC) and serves as its comprehensive platform of overseas investment and financing. SGCC is the largest grid company in China and the biggest utility company in the world. SGCC focuses on the construction and operation of power grids, covering 26 provinces, autonomous regions, and municipalities. SGCC has in turn also made cornerstone investments through Yingda International Trust Co. Ltd. Yingda Trust has grown into an established trust company with RMB236 billion in asset under management at the end of 2015 and maintains a zero-default rate. It is dedicated to clean energy financial services and strives to be a leader in the industry. (Source: Prospectuses for the Hong Kong IPOs of Postal Savings Bank of China Co. Ltd., 14 September 2016, and China Merchants Securities Co. Ltd., 27 September 2016, respectively.)

Summit SPV (Mr Tong Jinquan): Summit SPV, an investment holding company incorporated in the British Virgin Islands, is wholly owned by Mr Tong Jinquan, the founder of the Summit Group. Mr Tong also wholly owns Shanghai Summit Pte. Ltd. Mr Tong has over 20 years of experience in property investment, property development, and property management and he founded the Summit Group in 1994. The Summit Group's areas of business encompass industrial investment, investment management, trading, property development, hotel management, property management, business consultancy, convention and exhibition services, goods export and technology import, software services, and maintenance of office equipment. The total assets of the Summit Group as at 31 December 2012 amounted to more than RMB22 billion. (Source: Prospectus for the Singapore IPO of OUE Commercial Real Estate Investment Trust, 17 January 2014.)

Sun Hung Kai Properties Group (Kwok family): Sun Hung Kai is controlled by the Kwok family and is one of the largest property companies in Hong Kong. It is listed on the Stock Exchange of Hong Kong. It has made cornerstone investments through Joylight Limited and Rupert International Limited, both companies incorporated in the British Virgin Islands. Joylight is wholly owned by Winlead Limited, which in turn is wholly and ultimately owned by Sun Hung Kai Properties Limited. Rupert International is wholly owned by Kerrisdale Company Limited, which in turn is wholly and ultimately owned by a family trust established for the benefit of the Kwok family. (Source: Prospectus for the Hong Kong IPO of Industrial and Commercial Bank of China Limited, 16 October 2006.)

Talent Charm Limited (K-Boxing): Talent Charm, a company incorporated in the British Virgin Islands, is a wholly owned subsidiary of K-Boxing Investment Holdings Co. Ltd., which is the holding company of K-Boxing Men's Wear (Shanghai) Co. Ltd. K-Boxing is considered one of the most valuable menswear brands in the PRC. As an overseas platform, Talent Charm is principally engaged in overseas investment management. (Source: Prospectus for the Hong Kong IPO of Nameson Holdings Limited, 30 March 2016.)

Mr Gordon Tang (SingHaiyi Group): Mr Tang is a non-executive director of SGX-Catalist-listed, SingHaiyi Group Limited, which specializes in property development, real estate investment, real estate co-investing, property trading, and real estate management service. He is the husband of Mrs Chen Huaidan (see that name). (Source: Prospectus for the Singapore IPO of Keppel DC REIT, 5 December 2014.)

Teda HK: Teda HK is a company incorporated in Hong Kong. It is a special investment vehicle directly and wholly owned by Tianjin Teda Investment Holding Co. Ltd. Tianjin Teda Investment Holding invests in the following industries: industrial manufacturing, agriculture, infrastructure development and construction, finance, insurance, securities, real estate, transportation, electricity, gas, construction, warehousing, and tourism. (Source: Prospectus for the Hong Kong IPO of Bank of Tianjin Co. Ltd., 15 March 2016.)

Temasek Holdings (Private) Limited: Incorporated in 1974, Temasek (the name for Singapore before the fourteenth century) is an Asian investment company and one of the principal sovereign wealth funds in Singapore. Supported by international offices in Asia and Latin America, Temasek owns a diversified investment portfolio concentrated principally in Singapore, Asia, and the emerging economies. It has also made cornerstone subscriptions through Cairnhill Investments (Mauritius) Pte Ltd, a wholly owned subsidiary. (Source: Prospectus for the Hong Kong IPO of Agricultural Bank of China Limited, 30 June 2010.)

Tewoo Investment Co. Limited (Tianjin SASAC): Tewoo Investment is a company incorporated in Hong Kong with limited liability. Tewoo Investment is a wholly owned subsidiary of Tewoo Group Co. Ltd. Its principal activity is investment, while Tewoo Group is a state-owned enterprise of Tianjin engaged in the distribution of manufacturing materials. Tewoo Group's principal activities include the import and export of metals, energy resources, minerals, chemicals and automotive and electro-mechanical products, and other products falling within the five categories of commodities, as well as modern logistics, real estate development and financial services. Tewoo Group is wholly owned by the State-owned Assets Supervision and Administration Commission (SASAC) of Tianjin. (Source: Prospectus for the Hong Kong IPO of Bank of Tianjin Co. Ltd., 15 March 2016.)

Three Gorges Capital Holdings Co. Ltd.: Three Gorges Capital is a wholly owned subsidiary directly held by China Three Gorges Corporation. As its capital operation service platform, financial investment platform and new business incubator platform, Three Gorges Capital primarily engages in businesses including industrial investment, equity investment, securities investment, asset management, and investment consultancy. (Source: Prospectus for the Hong Kong IPO of China Development Bank Financial Leasing Co. Ltd., 24 June 2016.)

Tianfang Jincheng (Tianjin Government): Tianfang Jincheng is a company incorporated in Hong Kong. It is principally engaged in trading and investment activities and is directly and wholly owned by Tianjin Real Estate Group Co. Ltd., which is also the single largest shareholder of Tianjin Realty Development (Group) Co. Ltd. Tianjin Real Estate is wholly owned by the Tianjin government and is a large state-owned real estate enterprise in Tianjin. (Source: Prospectus for the Hong Kong IPO of Bank of Tianjin Co. Ltd., 15 March 2016.)

United Overseas Bank Limited (UOB): UOB is a leading bank in Asia. It provides a wide range of financial services through its global network of over 500 offices in 19 countries and territories in the Asia-Pacific region, Western Europe and North America, including banking subsidiaries in Singapore, Malaysia, Indonesia, Thailand, and China. (Source: Prospectus for the Hong Kong IPO of Agricultural Bank of China Limited, 30 June 2010.)

Usaha Tegas Sdn Bhd: Usaha Tegas (also known as the UT Group) is a Malaysia-based investment holding company. It has also made cornerstone investments through Mezzanine Equities N.V., which is an indirect subsidiary. (Source: Prospectus for the Malaysia and Singapore IPO of IHH Healthcare Berhad, 2 July 2012.)

Value Partners Hong Kong Limited: Value Partners was established in 1999. It acts as an investment manager or investment advisor to certain investment funds and is a wholly owned subsidiary of Value Partners Group, which is listed on the Stock Exchange of Hong Kong. Value Partners Group is one of Asia's largest independent asset management firms and is headquartered in Hong Kong. It manages absolute return long-biased funds, long-short hedge funds, exchange traded funds, quantitative funds, as well as fixed-income products for institutional and individual clients in the Asia-Pacific region, Europe, and the United States. (Source: Prospectus for the Hong Kong IPO of DFZQ, 22 June 2016.)

Victory Global Group Limited (HNA Group): Victory Global is a wholly owned subsidiary of HNA Capital Group Co. Ltd. and serves as an investment platform for its parent. It is a business company registered in the British Virgin Islands and its ultimate parent is HNA Group Co. Ltd. Victory Global's principal business is investment and consulting. HNA Group is a Chinese conglomerate founded in 2000 and headquartered in Haikou, Hainan, and involved in the aviation, real estate, financial services, tourism, logistics, as well as other industries. At the time of writing, it owned, among other investments, a 9.9 per cent stake in Deutsche Bank. (Source: Prospectus for the Hong Kong IPO of Postal Savings Bank of China, Co. Ltd., 14 September 2016.)

Wellington Management Company, LLP: Wellington Management is an investment adviser registered under the US Investment Advisers Act of 1940, as amended, and is organized as a Massachusetts limited liability partnership. It has made cornerstone investments on behalf of various investment advisory clients. (Source: Prospectus for the Singapore IPO of Keppel DC REIT, 5 December 2014.)

Mr Peter Woo Kwong-ching: Mr Woo is a Hong Kong businessman. He is the chairman of Wheelock and Company Limited and The Wharf Holdings Limited. He has made cornerstone investments through Bright Palace Investments Limited, East Advance Investments Limited, Hero Honour Investments Limited, Lorita Investments Limited, and United Develop Investments Limited, all companies incorporated in the British Virgin Islands and ultimately controlled by him. See also Greentown China. (Source: Prospectuses for the Hong Kong IPOs of AIA Group Limited, 18 October 2010, and Industrial and Commercial Bank of China Limited, 16 October 2006, respectively.)

Yancoal International (Holding) Company Limited (Yankuang Group): Yancoal International is a wholly owned Hong Kong subsidiary of Yanzhou Coal Mining Company Limited, with project management, mining and sales of coal as its principal businesses. Yanzhou Coal Mining is a company listed on the New York Stock Exchange, the Stock Exchange of Hong Kong, and the Shanghai Stock Exchange. Its principal businesses include mining, washing, and processing and sales of coal, coal chemicals, manufacturing of machinery and electrical equipment, and power and heat generation. Yanzhou Coal Mining's ultimate controlling shareholder is Yankuang Group Company Limited, the principal business of which is coal production and sales, coal chemicals, coal-electrolytic aluminium, manufacturing of a whole set of machinery and electrical equipment, and finance investment. (Source: Prospectus for the Hong Kong IPO of China Zheshang Bank Co. Ltd., 16 March 2016.)

Mr Yang Dehe (Hai Run Group): Mr Yang is the head of the Hai Run Group of companies, which is involved in trading and investment holding activities and includes Singapore-based subsidiary Hai Run Pte. Ltd. He has also been the general manager and director of Guang Dong Hai Run Development since 1995. (Source: Prospectus for the Singapore IPO of OUE Commercial Real Estate Investment Trust, 17 January 2014.)

Yunnan Energy Investment (H K) Co. Limited: Yunnan Energy is a Hong Kong incorporated, wholly owned subsidiary of Yunnan Provincial Energy Investment Group Co. Ltd. and serves as its offshore platform for its overseas investment, financing and capital management activities. Its main businesses include equity investment and project investment and management. Yunnan Energy Investment Group is a state-owned enterprise supervised by the State-owned Asset Supervision and Administration Commission (SASAC) of the Yunnan Provincial People's Government. Its main businesses include investment and management for energy, including electric power, natural gas and coal; investment and management of electric power-related businesses and products, including environmental protection; and new energy and investment in petroleum, gas, and pipeline project networks. (Source: Prospectus for the Hong Kong IPO of DFZQ, 22 June 2016.)

Zhejiang Provincial Seaport Investment & Operation Group Co. Ltd.: Zhejiang Seaport Group is a state-owned company incorporated in the PRC, the business of which includes the development and utilization of marine resources, marine industry investment, sea- and port-related resource management and capital operation, investment, construction and operation of ports, shipping services, reserve, trading and processing of bulk commodities (excluding hazardous chemicals), marine construction, port engineering design and supervision. (Source: Prospectus for the Hong Kong IPO of China Zheshang Bank Co. Ltd., 16 March 2016.)

Zhejiang Silicon Paradise Asset Management Group Co. Ltd.: Zhejiang Silicon Paradise, also known as TTGG, is a company established in the PRC with limited liability and is principally engaged in asset management. Its ultimate controlling shareholder, HEAVEN-SENT Capital Management Group Co. Ltd., has been listed on the new over-the-counter Bulletin Board in the PRC since July 2015. (Source: Prospectus for the Hong Kong IPO of Greentown Service Group Co. Ltd., 28 June 2016.)

Appendix 9

Target list of potential cornerstone investors (by jurisdiction)

Brunei

Brunei Investment Agency (BIA)

France

Amundi

Carmignac

Crédit Agricole

Germany

DWS

Munich Re

Hong Kong and China

AIA Group

Anbang Investment

Bank of China Group Investment (BOCGI)

BOCOM International Global Investment

CCB International

CCCC International

Cheung Kong (Holdings) (Mr Li Ka-shing)

China Asset Management (China AMC)

China Chentong Holdings

China Development Bank

China Eastern Air

China Fintech Investment

China Great Wall Asset Management

China Investment Corporation (CIC)

China Life Franklin Asset Management

China Life Insurance

China Merchants Securities

China Minsheng/CM Securities Investment
China Orient Asset Management International (COAMI)
China Re
China Resources
China Shipbuilding Industry Corporation
China South Industries
China State Construction Engineering (CSCE)
China Travel Service
Chinese Estates (Mr Joseph Lau's family)
Chow Tai Fook (the late Mr Cheng Yu-tung)
CITIC Pacific
CSSC Shipping
East Pacific Holdings
Elion Resources group
FIL (Fidelity)
Fosun International/Peak Re
Great Boom (Mr Yu Yusheng)
Greentown China (China Communications Construction/The Wharf)
Guoco Management
Haier Group
Harvest Global
Henderson Land (Mr Lee Shau-kee)
Hengjian International (Guangdong Hengjian Investment Holding)
Hillhouse
Hony Capital
HNA Group
HSBC Asset Management
Huiyuan International (Mr Zhu Xinli)
Hutchison Whampoa (Mr Li Ka-shing)
JF Asset Management (J.P. Morgan Asset Management)
Lifestyle Group (Mr Thomas Lau Luen-hung)
Matthews Asia
Mirae Asset
Myriad Asset Management
Nan Fung Group
National Social Security Fund (NSSF)
New China Life

New World China (Cheng family)
PICC Life
Pinpoint Asset Management
SAFE Investment Company
Segantii Capital
Shanghai Electric
Shanghai International Port
Shui On Land (Mr Vincent Lo)
SIIC Treasury (Shanghai Municipal Government)
Silk Road Fund
Sino Group (Mr Robert Ng)
Sino-Ocean Group
State Grid Corp. of China
Summit Group (Mr Tong Jinquan)
Sun Hung Kai Properties (Kwok family)
Tencent Holdings (Mr Ma Huateng)
Three Gorges Capital
Value Partners
The Wharf Holdings (Woo family)
Wheelock and Company (Woo family)

Indonesia

Lippo (Riady family)

Jordan

Capital Investment

Kuwait

Kuwait Investment Authority (KIA)

Malaysia

Am Investment
CIMB Principal
CMY Capital (Mr Chua Ma-yu)
Eastspring Investments Berhad
Employees Provident Fund Board (EPF)
Fortress Capital
GE Life
Genting Group
Hong Leong Assurance
Hwang Investment Management

Keck Seng
Kenanga
Kencana Capital
Khazanah Nasional Berhad
Kumpulan Wang Persaraan (Diperbadankan) (KWAP)
Kuok Group/Kerry Properties/Shangri-La
Lembaga Tabung Angkatan Tentera (LTAT)
Lembaga Tabung Haji (LTH)
Libra Invest
Maybank Asset Management
Permodalan Nasional Berhad (PNB)
Pertubuhan Keselamatan Social (SOSCO)
Public Mutual
RHB Asset Management
Usaha Tegas (UT) Group

The Netherlands

APG Strategic Real Estate Pool
PGGM
Rabobank
Robeco

Norway

Norges Bank Investment Management

Oman

Oman Investment Fund

Qatar

Qatar Holding LLC and Qatar Investment Authority (QIA)

Singapore

Aberdeen Asset Management
AEW Asia
BroadPeak
DBS Asset Management
DBS Bank
Eastspring Investments Singapore
Fullerton Fund Management
GIC
G.K. Goh
Mr Gordon Tang/Mrs Chen Huaidan

Great Eastern
Havenport Asset Management
Hotel Properties Limited (HPL) (Mr Ong Beng Seng)
Lion Global
Mr Peter Lim
New Silk Road
NTUC Income
OCBC
Pavilion
Pioneer
Pinebridge
Seatown
Temasek Holdings
UOB Asset Management

South Korea

Korea Investment Corporation (KIC)

Sweden

Nordea Investment Management

Switzerland

Jabre Capital

Taiwan

Cathay Life
Fubon Life
Mercuries Life Insurance

United Arab Emirates

Abu Dhabi Investment Authority (ADIA)
Abu Dhabi Investment Council (ADIC)
Al Mal Capital
Investment Corporation of Dubai
Istithmar World
Legatum
Mubadala Development Company

United Kingdom

F&C Investments
Gartmore
Genesis Capital
Global Asset Management (GAM)

Henderson Global
Lazard AM
Legal & General
Newton Investment Management
Pictet
Schroders
Threadneedle
UBS Asset Management
Universities Superannuation Scheme (USS)

United States

Baring Asset Management
Berkshire Hathaway
BlackRock
Capital International
Capital Research
Capital World
Citadel
D.E. Shaw
Eton Park
Farallon (Noonday)
Fidelity
General Atlantic
Indus Capital
International Finance Corporation (IFC)
Invesco
J.P. Morgan Asset Management
Moore Capital
Och-Ziff Capital Management
Point72 Asset Management (SAC Capital)
Prudential Insurance (PRICOA)
Putnam
RCM
Soros
State Street
T. Rowe Price
Templeton Emerging Markets
Templeton Global Advisors

TIAA (ex-TIAA-CREF)
Vanguard
Wellington Management Company

Notes:
1. When an investor is located in more than one location, generally only the main office or place of incorporation has been shown.
2. Some of the above investors specialize in investments in certain industry sectors only.
3. A target list of cornerstone investors for an IPO would include only a subset of the above and/or other investors and, in any event, probably not more than 50 names, depending on the size of the transaction.

Glossary

'A' shares: In mainland China, shares that are listed and traded on the Shanghai or Shenzhen stock exchanges. 'A' shares are quoted in renminbi.

accredited investor: A type of investor in the US to which sales of securities may be made pursuant to an exemption from registration requirements. Accredited investors represent a wider universe of investors than the Qualified Institutional Buyers (QIBs) which can be accessed through a Rule 144A private placement. See also **Qualified Institutional Buyer (QIB)**.

adjustments to cornerstone subscriptions: After the pricing of an IPO, the number of shares subscribed for by a cornerstone investor may be slightly revised, taking into account considerations such as the board lot and foreign exchange rates.

admission to listing: The process whereby a stock exchange accepts for listing the securities of a company. In order for this to happen, the company must satisfy the initial listing requirements and its offer document must have been positively vetted by the exchange itself or the securities regulator (depending on the jurisdiction).

aftermarket: The market once the securities of a newly listed company have started to trade.

agent: A manager that invests moneys on behalf of other investors, rather than for his or her own account.

allocation: The amount of stock that a retail investor, an institutional investor, and/or a cornerstone investor receives in an IPO.

alternative investment fund: A term often used to designate a hedge fund. See also **hedge fund**.

anchor investor: An institutional investor that places a large order at an early stage in the book of demand for an IPO. Accordingly, anchor investors expect to be 'well treated' by the bookrunners when it comes to their allocations but, unlike cornerstone investors, do not benefit from guaranteed allocations. This is an informal, rather than an official or regulated role or title.

anti-dilution rights: Preferential rights to purchase additional securities to be issued by a company in an IPO, so as to maintain a certain percentage of shareholding in the company. For pre-IPO investors, such rights must usually be terminated upon listing.

application to listing: Communication to a stock exchange, usually by way of a draft prospectus and other documents, pursuant to which an issuer makes an application to list securities on that exchange. The application to listing is often primarily drafted by legal advisers, with the help of investment banks.

asset manager: A generic term for an institutional investor. Through their portfolio managers (PMs), asset managers often manage collective investment schemes and invest across a spectrum of assets (equities or fixed income securities, foreign exchange, commodities or real estate). When asset managers have a mandate to make investment decisions on behalf of their clients, they manage funds on a discretionary basis.

average daily trading volume (ADTV): The average trading volume per day in the securities of a company, as measured over a period of time (typically 20, 30, or 60 days).

balloting: A mechanism through which securities are allocated to retail investors by a share registrar after the closing of the public offer in an IPO.

best efforts underwriting: See **'soft' underwriting**.

board lot: The minimum number of shares (or multiple thereof) in which a company can be traded on a stock exchange.

bookbuilding: The process through which securities are marketed to, and orders taken from, institutional investors in an equity capital markets transaction. In an IPO, bookbuilding is usually conducted simultaneously with the investor roadshow and follows pre-deal investor education (PDIE, also known as pre-marketing) and the determination of the price range.

bookrunner: One of the most important levels among underwriting banks in a syndicate. A bookrunner manages the book of demand and, importantly, determines allocations made to institutional investors. There can be more than one bookrunner in an IPO and a bank can also be appointed in other roles simultaneously with that of bookrunner, most commonly as a sponsor (or its equivalent, depending on the jurisdiction), global coordinator and/or lead manager. In the US and some other markets, a distinction is sometimes made between 'active' bookrunners (who actively manage an offering) and passive bookrunners (who, in practice, leave much of the work to the active bookrunners).

brokerage fee (or commission): A fee paid to a bank by an institutional, cornerstone, or retail investor when buying securities issued or sold in an IPO or other equity capital markets transaction. Some IPOs and equity capital markets transactions do not carry any brokerage fee.

bulge-bracket investment banks: The name given to those large investment banks with global reach that typically dominate the league tables.

Bursa Malaysia: The Malaysian Stock Exchange, based in Kuala Lumpur.

business due diligence: The due diligence conducted by investment banks and legal advisers, usually by way of interviews with management into the affairs of a company preparing for listing. Business due diligence focuses on the business of the company and serves to accurately describe it in the offering circular. Business due diligence also includes site visits and third-party interviews, and is supplemented by documentary and financial due diligence. See also **documentary due diligence** and **financial due diligence**.

business trust: A type of transaction structure whereby assets can be monetized through an IPO. A business trust broadly follows the same format as a real estate investment trust (REIT), but is not limited to the real estate sector. Typically, it involves investments in infrastructure assets, such as toll roads, ships, aircraft, telecoms assets, airports, tank farms (dedicated sites with large tanks for the bulk storage of oil), bridges, turnpikes or wind farms in lieu of (or in addition to) property. This can also extend to 'social' infrastructure, such as retirement homes, student accommodation and even prisons that are run by private sector operators. As with REITs, investors in a business trust own units (rather than shares) in a vehicle that is publicly listed and traded on a stock exchange. A trustee-manager holds, manages, and operates the assets in which the trust invests for the benefit of all unitholders. A key difference is that business trusts enable the distribution (typically of 90 per cent and up to

100 per cent) of free cash flow, rather than limiting distributions to accounting profits. In addition, business trusts have greater flexibility to acquire and own assets as compared to other trusts. Business trusts have mainly been listed in Singapore and, to a lesser extent, in Hong Kong. They are also allowed in Malaysia. See also **real estate investment trust (REIT)**.

buy-side: Another term for (generally) institutional investors.

capital structure: The proportion between equity and debt capital (minus cash and cash equivalent securities) on the balance sheet of a company. The capital structure is sometimes adjusted prior to listing by increasing gearing to enable the payment of a special dividend to the issuer's pre-listing shareholders.

'Chinese Wall': A barrier established between the advisory and financing, securities and other departments of an investment bank. Chinese walls are set up to prevent and resolve conflicts of interest between the various activities carried out by an investment bank and are enforced by compliance departments. See also **compliance** and **crossing**.

clawback: The process through which securities initially allocated to the placement (or institutional) tranche of an IPO are reallocated to the retail (or public offer) tranche. Such clawback can either be at the discretion of the bookrunners or made automatically, depending on the rules laid out by the stock exchange. Automatic clawback triggers are a feature of IPOs in Hong Kong.

closing: The final step in the IPO process, when securities are delivered to investors versus payment. Closing is usually subject to a number of conditions precedent, including the delivery of a number of documents.

comfort letters: Letters issued by a firm of accountants to a company and the lead underwriters of an IPO in relation to the financial information included in a prospectus and/or offering circular. Comfort letters usually include negative assurance language. See also **negative assurance**.

Companies Registry: A place where official documents of a company are filed, must be kept, and may be displayed or viewed by members of the public.

compensation provisions: Contractual obligations whereby compensation may be paid to a pre-IPO investor in the event that a company does not get admitted to listing within a specified period of time (these are generally allowed if the amount to be compensated is set out in the investment agreement, or can be derived from the compensation provisions under the agreement).

compliance: A department in an investment bank, investment manager or corporate tasked with ensuring that internal and external laws and regulations are followed and also with avoiding and resolving conflicts of interest that may occur between its divisions. See also **'Chinese Wall'**.

concurrent retail offering: A retail offering which takes place concurrently with an institutional placement, generally during the last few days of bookbuilding. A concurrent retail offering is conducted at a maximum price, effectively equivalent to the top end of the institutional bookbuilding range, and subject to refund in the event that the offer price for retail investors is determined to be below the top end of the range. There is also a refund to account for the difference between the number of securities applied for (and paid) by the retail investor and the number actually received by that investor as an allocation.

conditions precedent: Conditions required for the closing or underwriting of an IPO, or for a cornerstone investor subscription to be enforced. Generally, these include, among other things, pricing, the signing of agreements, and the delivery of various documents such as legal opinions and comfort letters.

confidentiality agreement: In the context of cornerstone investors in IPOs, an agreement signed by a prospective cornerstone investor pursuant to which it agrees to keep confidential certain advanced information given to it. The term non-disclosure agreement (NDA) is also often used.

conflict of interest: In the context of an IPO, a conflict arising between the corporate finance and securities departments of an investment bank, or a conflict arising between the principal investment side of the bank and other departments. This may also apply to transactions entered into between shareholders and directors of a company and the company itself. See also **related-party transactions**.

connected-party transactions: See **related-party transactions**.

conversion premium: The premium to the share price at which a bond may be converted into the ordinary shares of a company pursuant to certain conditions, including the performance of the company's share price over a period of time.

conversion rate: The ratio between one-on-one meetings held with, or calls made by a bank to, investors during an institutional roadshow or cornerstone investor process, and the number of orders actually placed by those same investors in the book of demand (or cornerstone book). It can be computed on an overall basis, by bank, by region, or by investor type. This information is commonly included in case studies of past transactions for IPO pitches. Sometimes also called hit rate.

convertible bond: A bond issued by a company and convertible into ordinary shares of that company, usually at a premium and pursuant to certain conditions, including the performance of the company's share price over a period of time. An exchangeable bond is issued by a company but is exchangeable into shares of another company, owned by the former, or exchangeable into Treasury stock owned by the issuer. Pre-IPO (but not cornerstone) investments are often made using convertible bonds. See also **conversion premium**.

cornerstone investor: Generally, a high-quality institutional investor, hedge fund, or tycoon that is allocated on a guaranteed basis prior to the start of bookbuilding a significant amount of stock at the offer price, so as to provide momentum and leadership for the IPO. The names of, and allocations made to, cornerstone investors are disclosed in the offering circular(s) and prospectus and, in some (but not all) jurisdictions, they have to abide by a lock-up. In Hong Kong, cornerstone investors increasingly take the form of Chinese corporates and state-owned enterprises in particular.

crossing: The action of bringing a portfolio manager (or a research analyst, salesperson or trader) over the Chinese Wall, to make him or her an insider for compliance purposes. See also **'Chinese Wall'**.

delivery versus payment (DVP): A procedure whereby the delivery of the securities to investors (by the, or a bookrunner) is simultaneous with payment for the shares (by investors) to that bookrunner, for onward payment to the issuer, net of fees. IPOs in most developed markets are now settled on a DVP basis.

director nomination rights: Contractual obligations pursuant to which a pre-IPO investor may be allowed to choose one or more directors on the board of directors of a company. Any directors that may be nominated in this way are normally subject to retirement and reappointment requirements under the company's articles of association after listing.

disclaimer: In the context of cornerstone investors in an IPO, a statement included at the outset of a draft offer document to bring investors' attention to the fact that it cannot legally cannot be relied upon to purchase securities in the IPO.

discount to offer price: In some IPOs, the discount to which retail investors are sometimes entitled over the institutional offer price. See also **retail discount**. Cornerstone investors do not benefit from a discount and pay the same price as institutional and, usually, retail investors, that is, the IPO or offer price.

dividend policy: The manner in which a company intends to pay dividends to investors after its shares have been listed in an IPO, usually expressed as a payout ratio.

dividend yield: The dividend per share divided by the price per share, expressed as a percentage.

documentary due diligence: A component of the overall due diligence process whereby legal advisers review contracts, agreements, and other relevant documents relating to the issuer and its shareholders to ascertain their enforceability and authenticity. See also **due diligence**.

'double dipping': The practice whereby a cornerstone investor in an IPO also places a separate order in the institutional book of demand. This is not allowed in Hong Kong.

dual listing: A listing by a company on two separate stock exchanges, where the initial listing on the home market is usually referred to as the primary listing, home market, or anchor market, while the other is referred to as the secondary listing.

due diligence: The process through which the parties involved in the execution of an IPO investigate the affairs of a company, so as to satisfy themselves with the accuracy of disclosure, adequacy of the business, financial and legal aspects of the issuer and to ensure that all the necessary material information required by a reasonable investor to invest in the IPO has not only been accurately included in the prospectus, but also not been omitted, and that it is also not misleading. Due diligence usually takes the form of business due diligence (including site visits, where appropriate, as well as third-party interviews), financial due diligence, and documentary due diligence. Conducting appropriate due diligence provides the basis for due diligence defence against prospectus liability. See also **business due diligence**, **documentary due diligence**, and **financial due diligence**. Cornerstone investors also conduct due diligence into the business of the issuers in whose securities they may invest.

equity capital markets (ECM): A generic term for financing transactions involving the issue or sale of equity capital. ECM transactions include IPOs; primary and secondary offerings; placements; public offerings; follow-on transactions; the issue of American depositary receipts (ADRs), global depositary receipts (GDRs), and their derivatives in other countries; accelerated bookbuildings (ABBs); block trades; convertible and exchangeable bonds; special purpose acquisition companies (SPACs); private investments in public equity (PIPEs); the issue of preferred shares; real estate investment trusts (REITs), business trusts, and other property funds and infrastructure funds.

equity capital markets (ECM) team: A specialist team within an investment bank, tasked with the origination and execution of equity capital markets transactions (including IPOs). ECM teams are often set up as a joint venture between both sides of the Chinese Wall for revenue and cost allocation purposes. Cornerstone investor marketing is primarily conducted by ECM teams and, specifically within them, by the equity syndicate desk. See also **equity syndicate**.

equity story: Similar to an investment case. The key attributes of a company, as marketed to investors in an IPO.

equity syndicate: A desk within an equity capital markets (ECM) team tasked with liaising with other banks and sales teams to coordinate the marketing of ECM transactions (including IPOs). Syndicate desks are particularly involved in coordinating pre-deal investor education (PDIE), roadshow schedules, and bookbuilding, as well as pricing, allocations, and stabilization. They are also generally in charge of any cornerstone investor process.

exclusivity rights: Rights to the effect that a company is not allowed to issue or offer any shares, options, warrants, and rights to any direct competitor of a pre-IPO investor or to other investors on terms more favourable than the terms on which the securities are issued to that pre-IPO investor. Such rights are usually only allowed where the investment agreement includes an explicit 'fiduciary out' clause, so that directors are allowed to ignore the terms if complying with the terms would constitute a breach of their fiduciary duties, that is, the directors must not be prevented from exercising their judgement to ascertain whether certain corporate actions are in the best interest of the company.

fiduciary: See **agent**.

final offering circular: The version of an offering circular that includes the offer price, statistics based on the offer price, such as gross or net proceeds to be realized in the IPO, and any changes that have occurred and need to be disclosed since the publication of the preliminary offering circular. Nowadays, a simple pricing schedule is often published instead.

financial due diligence: A component of the overall due diligence process for an IPO with a focus on the company's finances. See **due diligence**.

Financial Services Development Council (FSDC): The FSDC was established by the government of the Hong Kong Special Administrative Region in 2013 in response to the financial services industry's call for a high-level government advisory body to support the sustained development of the industry. The FSDC engages the industry and formulates proposals to promote the further development of Hong Kong's financial services industry and map out the strategic direction for the development of Hong Kong as an international financial centre. The 22 council members are appointed by the chief executive of Hong Kong, have different expertise and professional experience, and are broadly representative of various subsectors of the financial services industry.

'firm' shares: The shares issued by a company and/or sold by existing shareholders in an IPO or equity capital markets transaction, excluding shares that are the subject of an overallotment option. See also **Greenshoe**.

fixed price offers: Offers of securities that are conducted at a fixed price, rather than pursuant to an indicative price range. Other than for retail or public offers (which are conducted at the top end of such price range), these are now rare.

follow-on equity offering: An equity capital markets transaction conducted after a company has become listed for the first time in an IPO.

***force majeure* clause**: A clause pursuant to which underwriting arrangements can be rescinded on the occurrence of extraordinary events such as war, terrorism, tsunamis, earthquakes, or other acts of God.

free float: The amount or proportion of the shares of a company in public ownership. The free float also includes investments made by cornerstone investors.

front office: The client-facing side of an investment bank, as opposed to the back office.

global coordinator: A senior level or rank among investment banks in a syndicate of underwriters. A global coordinator is usually tasked with the overall coordination and execution of a transaction. More than one bank may be appointed in this capacity. This role is often combined with that of sponsor, bookrunner, and lead manager.

going-public convertible bond: Sometimes also called pre-IPO convertible bond. A bond issued by a company and convertible into its shares upon listing of that company in an IPO on a stock exchange. Going-public convertible bonds are redeemed at a (usually) significant premium to par, together with accrued interest, in the event of non-conversion. A number of additional privileges are also usually granted to investors in going-public convertible bonds.

governing law: The law under which a contract may be drafted. In the context of cornerstone investments, this will usually be Hong Kong law, Malaysian law, Singapore law, English law, or New York law.

grading (of investors): The process through which investors are ranked by quality in a book of demand prior to allocations being made. The grading of investors is done by the equity syndicate desks and is often extensively discussed between bookrunners when more than one house is appointed in this role.

Greenshoe: Equivalent to overallotment option. A mechanism through which additional shares beyond the 'firm' shares are allocated to institutional investors in order to stabilize the share price during the first 30 days of trading. See also **'firm' shares**.

gross fees: The fees paid by an issuer and/or selling shareholders to a syndicate of underwriters in an equity capital markets transaction.

'H' shares: Shares listed in Hong Kong and issued by, or sold in, a company incorporated in mainland China. H share companies are different from red chips, which have, after a reorganization, transferred their assets and liabilities to an offshore entity, usually a Cayman Islands company. See also **red chips**.

Hang Seng index: A widely used, free float–adjusted, market capitalization–weighted stock market index comprising 45 companies listed on the Main Board of the Stock Exchange of Hong Kong.

'hard' underwriting: The process through which one or more banks commit to buying, on a firm basis and at an agreed price, a number of shares from an issuer or from a shareholder in a company, usually for onward sale to end investors. Hard underwriting is rare for institutional tranches of IPOs (although it is still market practice in countries such as Indonesia) but more common in aftermarket transactions such as block trades. Public offer tranches, however, are usually hard underwritten.

hedge fund: A type of investor managing money on behalf of high net worth or accredited investors (among others), subject to a lock-up, which can be for several years. Hedge funds generally focus on liquid investments across asset classes and can adopt a variety of investment strategies, often (but not always) hedging their investments using short selling or derivatives. See also **alternative investment fund**.

high net worth (HNW) individual: A wealthy person with financial assets generally in excess of US$1 million and sometimes more, depending on the wealth manager.

hit rate: See **conversion rate**.

indemnity clause: A clause in an underwriting, subscription or sale and purchase agreement whereby one party agrees to indemnify another against misstatements in, or omissions from, the offering circular, as well as against breaches of laws and terms of the agreement such as representations, warranties, and undertakings. Indemnity clauses can also be found in non-disclosure agreements.

independent adviser: A bank or boutique adviser or consultant generally not part of the syndicate of underwriters and separately advising the issuer and its shareholders on an IPO. Independent advisers are also often involved in the cornerstone process that is conducted by the senior underwriters.

information rights: Special rights granted to pre-IPO investors whereby they can, from time to time, be made privy to financial or other information about the company. Following an IPO, such rights are usually only allowed when the pre-IPO investor receives published information or information which is at the same time made available to the general public, with a view to avoiding unequal dissemination of information, unless safe harbours apply.

infrastructure fund: A fund consisting of infrastructure assets such as airports, toll roads and the like, either listed on a stock exchange or sold to institutional investors in a wholesale fund. Most common in Australia, in particular as issued by members of the Macquarie and (previously) Babcock & Brown groups, and in Singapore, through the business trust structure. See also **business trust**.

initial public offering (IPO): The action of listing a company's shares for the first time on one or more stock exchanges. One also talks of a 're-IPO' if a listed company gets de-listed and re-listed again at a subsequent time.

institutional investors: Investors that manage money usually on behalf of other parties, for example sovereign wealth funds, asset managers, mutual funds, charities, insurance companies, banks, pension funds, hedge funds, or individuals. In an IPO, institutional investors are distinct from retail or public investors and are accessed through the placement, placing or international tranche.

institutional offering: Also called international offering, institutional tranche, placement, or placing. In an IPO, an offering to institutions and distinct from the retail or public offer. Institutional offerings are generally conducted on a bookbuilt basis and using a price range, whereas public offers are often (but not always) conducted at a fixed price, usually the top end of the indicative price range.

interim accounts: Quarterly or half-yearly financial reports and accounts.

InvestHK: Established in July 2000, InvestHK is an organization whose vision is to strengthen Hong Kong's status as the leading international business location in Asia. Its mission is to attract and retain foreign direct investment, which is of strategic importance to the economic development of Hong Kong. It works with overseas and mainland Chinese entrepreneurs, SMEs, and multinationals that wish to set up an office (or expand their existing business) in Hong Kong.

investment banks: Banks that provide advisory, financing, and securities services to government, corporate, and institutional investor clients. Sometimes the term 'investment bank' may refer only to that part of a bank that provides corporate finance (including advisory, mergers and acquisitions, and financing) services to its clients, excluding sales, research, and trading departments.

investment case: See **equity story**.

investment horizon: The length of time an investor normally holds on to an investment. For example, pension funds normally have a long investment horizon, to match assets with their long-dated liabilities.

investor education: Nowadays often called pre-deal investor education (PDIE). See also **pre-marketing**.

investor undertakings: Undertakings made by an investor in a contract. In the case of cornerstone investors, these would be found in the non-disclosure and subscription agreements.

IPO price: The offer price at which an IPO is allocated to investors, after bookbuilding and the public offering have closed.

IPO timetable: The length of time it takes to bring an IPO to market, from the kick-off meeting following the award of a mandate to investment banks and other parties, to closing and the exercise of the overallotment option (if any).

issue manager: The equivalent of a sponsor bank in Singapore. See also **sponsor**.

joint and several underwriting obligations: Underwriting obligations whereby remaining underwriters are required to pick up the underwriting obligations of a defaulting underwriter in proportion to their initial underwriting amounts. Very rare in equity capital markets transactions, where several underwriting obligations are the norm. See also **several underwriting obligations**.

lead manager: A senior level among investment banks in a syndicate of underwriters, usually combined with the role of bookrunner. However, a lead manager that is not also a bookrunner has little ability to perform in a marketing capacity in an IPO.

liquidity: A measure of the activity in the trading of a listed company. Liquidity is typically expressed as a daily average number of shares or currency amount traded, over a period of time, generally measured over 20, 30, or 60 days. See also **average daily trading volume (ADTV)**.

listing committee: A committee of a stock exchange where decisions are made to admit candidates to listing.

lock-up: A period of time during which the issue of new shares by a company or sell-downs in its shares by one or more of its material shareholders (usually defined as owning more than 5 per cent of the company's outstanding share capital) or cornerstone investors are prohibited. IPO lock-ups are typically for 180 days but can, on occasion, last for a year or more. The global coordinator or bookrunner of an IPO can have the contractual ability (seldom used) to waive a lock-up. In Asia, cornerstone investors are nowadays only locked-up for IPOs that are listed in Hong Kong.

'long only': A type of institutional investor known for its stable, long-term investment horizon and for not using short-position hedging. Often the term 'long only investors' is used to distinguish these from hedge funds.

main board: The main market of a stock exchange on which a company may seek a listing. Some stock exchanges have also established smaller boards or second markets, with less stringent listing requirements and typically for the listing of smaller or emerging growth companies.

management discussion and analysis (MD&A): Also known as management discussion and analysis of financial condition and results of operations. The disclosure of financial information in a prospectus derived from market practice in the US. An MD&A consists of a narrative discussion and explanation of changes in the principal line items in a company's consolidated profit and loss account and cash flow statements for the period under review. A similar analysis is also conducted of the company's capitalization and indebtedness. An MD&A also includes a summary of the company's principal accounting policies.

market positioning: See **equity story**.

material contracts: Contracts whose value represents more than a certain threshold of assets or earnings of a company (usually in the order of 5 per cent).

maximum price: In a concurrent retail offering, the price paid by retail investors, which, in an IPO with no retail discount, is equivalent to the top end of the bookbuilding price range. Retail investors are reimbursed the difference between the maximum price and the offer price in the event that the IPO is not priced at the top end of the range. There is also a refund to account for the difference between the number of securities applied for (and paid) by the retail investor and the number actually received by the investor as an allocation. Cornerstone investors agree to subscribe for securities at any price within a price range, including the maximum price.

minimum number of public shareholders: The minimum number of public shareholders a company must have in order to be admitted to listing on a stock exchange. This varies from one listing platform to another, but is usually in the order of a few hundred shareholders or more.

Monetary Authority of Singapore (MAS): The regulator for the securities market (and the *de facto* central bank) in Singapore.

multi-bookrunner syndicates: Syndicates of underwriters for IPOs that include more than one bookrunner bank. This is generally the case for IPOs greater than US$100 or US$200 million.

naked short: A device used to stabilize an IPO above and beyond an overallotment option. A naked short, where allowed, involves the stabilizing agent shorting shares using its own balance sheet without the 'cover' of a borrowing agreement. This can be a costly strategy if the share price rises in the aftermarket. Naked shorts for stabilization purposes are prohibited in many markets, although not in the US.

narrative: In the context of cornerstone investors, how a cornerstone is described in a prospectus or offering circular. This usually includes a few lines on the nature of the investor's business, perhaps also including several statistics, such as the amount of funds it has under management or, in the case of a listed company, its market capitalization at the most practicable date.

negative assurance: A statement by the accountants working on an IPO that, having performing specified procedures, nothing came to their attention that caused them to believe that specified matters do not meet a specified accounting standard (for example, that nothing came to their attention that caused them to believe that any material modifications should be made to the unaudited financial statements for them to be in conformity with generally accepted accounting principles).

negative pledge: For a pre-IPO investor, this may include provisions not to create or effect any mortgage, charge, pledge, lien, or other security interest on a company's assets and revenues, or not to dispose of any interest in the economic rights or entitlements of a share that the controlling shareholder owns or controls. Any such pledges that remain after listing must usually be in line with normal terms of debt issues.

non-deal roadshow: An investor roadshow that is made by a corporate irrespective of any capital markets transaction, for example, in connection with the announcement of interim results or investor conferences.

non-disclosure agreement (NDA): See **confidentiality agreement**.

no reliance: A disclaimer or undertaking whereby a cornerstone investor may not legally rely on a document or draft of a prospectus or offering circular provided to it in connection with its investment.

noyaux durs: Reference shareholders, first introduced in French privatizations in 1986, to ensure that a significant portion of IPOs—of businesses often essential to the French economy—went to friendly, stable, or long-term investors (that is, generally, French corporates and financial institutions).

obligations of cornerstone investors: These vary from jurisdiction to jurisdiction but generally include the fact that their name (and, possibly, their individual allocation) must be disclosed in a prospectus and offering circular, and that their investment must be locked-up for a period of time after an IPO, among other obligations.

odd lot: A block of securities consisting of a number of securities smaller than, or that is not a multiple of a board lot. Trading in odd lots generates additional costs. See also **board lot**.

offer for sale: See **secondary offering**.

offer for subscription: See **primary offering**.

offer information statement (OIS): The term used for a domestic offering circular in connection with IPOs in Singapore.

offering circular: The document published, registered, and distributed to investors by an issuer in an IPO. Broadly equivalent to prospectus, offer document, offer information statement, offering document, disclosure document or, in the US, registration statement. An offering circular may be produced in different versions and in more than one language and includes all the information necessary for a reasonable investor to make an informed decision about buying the shares. An offering circular includes comprehensive information about the company, its business and its financials, as well as about the structure of the IPO and application procedures for investors. Generally, offering circular is the term used for the listing document produced for institutional investors, while the term prospectus is used for the disclosure document published for retail investors.

offer price: See **IPO price**.

Offers and Prospectuses Electronic Repository and Access (OPERA): An Internet-based, electronic information system established by the Monetary Authority of Singapore to display prospectuses and other information about issuers, IPOs, and other capital markets transactions in Singapore. See also **Monetary Authority of Singapore**.

offer structure: The way in which an IPO is structured between various tranches to access various classes of investors. IPOs most commonly include a placement tranche targeted at institutional investors and a public offer tranche targeted at retail investors but may, on occasion, also include additional tranches or further subdivisions of the placement tranche in particular.

one-on-one meetings: One of the components of an IPO roadshow. It consists of a series of meetings between the senior management of an issuer and individual institutional investors. One-on-one meetings are arranged by the bookrunners and reserved for the largest, highest quality investors only.

outsold: When a bank appointed in the same role and on the same basis as other houses has received a lower overall allocation for its orders from investors, either globally or for a particular region, or for a type of investor. An investment bank having outsold others in a particular deal constitutes a popular marketing argument used in pitches for IPOs and other related transactions. This can refer to demand generated as well as to allocations.

overallotment option: See **Greenshoe**.

overhang: A term used when knowledge in the market that a block of securities owned by an investor that may be available for sale depresses the share price of a company. Securities that are locked-up after an IPO often create an overhang nearer to the expiry of the lock-up.

overpricing: When an IPO or equity offering has been priced above a level that can ensure a positive aftermarket performance.

oversubscription: When investor demand that has been generated for an IPO (or a tranche of an IPO) exceeds the number of shares available for sale or issue.

payout ratio: The percentage of earnings paid as dividends to the shareholders of a company.

pension fund: A type of institutional investor that manages money set aside to pay for retirement liabilities.

permitted disclosure: Disclosure of information an investor is authorized to make under the terms of a non-disclosure agreement. Generally, this includes disclosure to its associates or to people working within companies in the same group, or to its advisers or auditors, provided that they all abide by the same confidentiality undertakings. See also **confidentiality agreement**.

physical due diligence: A component of the due diligence process involving the visit of production sites and other physical facilities.

pilot fishing: In Europe, and in the UK in particular, the process through which the bookrunner banks target certain leadership investors at an early stage in an IPO.

placement tranche: A component of the global offer structure for an IPO. Equivalent to institutional offer tranche, international offer, institutional offering, or placing. Part of an IPO targeted at institutional investors, often across multiple jurisdictions, through private placements and pursuant to selling restrictions. Placement tranches are underwritten separately to public offerings or retail tranches, and usually only after the offer price has been determined. See also **institutional offering**.

placing: Another term for a placement or institutional offering.

placing letter: A letter sent to an institutional investor or a cornerstone investor formally informing it of its final allocation in an IPO. Placing letters include details of relevant reselling restrictions, as well as information on taxes, duties, levies, and brokerage fees payable by the investor. Investors must sign and return to the bookrunners a confirmation included in the placing letter, together with details of their brokerage accounts for the settlement of the securities.

plan of distribution: The section in an offering circular summarizing the key terms and arrangements for the underwriting of an IPO. It sometimes also appears under the heading 'Underwriting'.

post-hearing information pack (PHIP): Specifically in Hong Kong, the posting on the website of the exchange of a near final (but slightly redacted) IPO prospectus after the listing hearing and for the benefit of retail investors, so as to provide them with a level playing field with institutional investors (who receive pre-deal research reports). Fairly similar to the posting of a prospectus on OPERA in Singapore, or on the website of the Securities Commission in Malaysia.

pre-agreed allocation: A term commonly used in connection with cornerstone investors, who commit to buying an agreed allocation of stock at the offer price at an early stage in the IPO process, prior to the start of bookbuilding. See also **cornerstone investor**.

pre-deal investor education (PDIE): See **pre-marketing**.

pre-deal research: A research report produced by an investment bank forming part of a syndicate of underwriters prior to the formal launch of an IPO. The issuance and publication of pre-deal research is generally subject to a number of guidelines and restrictions and is prohibited in certain countries.

pre-IPO investment: An investment at an early stage in a transaction by a strategic or institutional investor in a company that will be listed at a later stage. A pre-IPO investment is distinct from an investment by a cornerstone investor in that it is often made earlier and at a (significant) discount to the offer price for the IPO, and often using a convertible bond.

preliminary offering circular: An early version of the offering circular distributed to institutional investors, subject to completion and amendment and published without a price (or, more rarely, with a price range) at the start of the bookbuilding process. Also called pathfinder (in the UK), red, or red herring.

pre-marketing: The process, also now commonly called pre-deal investor education (PDIE), which follows the publication of pre-deal research (outside the US, Canada, and Japan), whereby sell-side research analysts meet with institutional investors across a variety of jurisdictions to convey the equity story, with a view to obtaining feedback so as to be able to determine a price range for bookbuilding.

presentation to research analysts: A physical presentation made by the senior management of an issuer to brief the sell-side research analysts assigned by banks in the syndicate of underwriters to produce pre-deal research.

price cap: The maximum price that may be paid for securities by an investor.

price discovery process: Another term for bookbuilding. See also **bookbuilding**.

price range: A range of share prices, usually around 15 to 20 per cent wide, determined at the end of investor education by the bookrunners, and used to gather orders from institutional investors in a bookbuilding process.

price sensitivity: The level of demand in a book of demand at various price points. A book of demand where most of the orders are at the top end of the range exhibits no price sensitivity.

price talk: The valuation parameters or approximate valuation discussed among market participants for an IPO.

primary equity markets conditions: An assessment of the IPO and new equity issue market, on a global, regional, country, or industry sector basis, made by an investment bank in connection with a pitch or as part of a briefing to an IPO issuer.

primary offering: Either an equity capital markets transaction in general, or, more specifically, the issue of new capital by a company. Also known as an offer for subscription. Distinct from a secondary offering. See also **secondary offering**.

principal adviser: The equivalent of a sponsor bank in Malaysia. See also **sponsor**.

principal investment: An investment made by an investor for its own account, rather than on behalf of third parties. Distinct from an investment made as an agent or fiduciary.

prior consent clauses: Events that require the prior consent of a pre-IPO investor. For example, these may include the declaration of a dividend by any member of the investee group; the sale, lease, or transfer of a substantial part of the company's business or assets; any amendments to constitutional documents; or any change in executive directors. Such terms must be removed before listing unless the issuer can demonstrate that the relevant terms do not disadvantage other shareholders.

private bank: A division of a, or stand-alone, financial institution specializing in the management of assets, often on a discretionary basis, on behalf of high and ultra-high net worth individuals. See also **high net worth individual** and **ultra-high net worth individual**.

private equity: Investors who invest moneys, usually on behalf of third parties, to effect buyouts of businesses, with a view to selling them in an M&A transaction or IPO at a later stage, usually with an investment horizon of a few years.

private placement: A placement to institutional investors or certain types of institutional investors only, pursuant to an exemption from registration requirements. Institutional offerings are usually conducted across a variety of jurisdictions pursuant to private placements, most notably in compliance with Rule 144A in the US. Cornerstone tranches normally rely on private placement exemptions.

privatization: Either the return of state-owned assets to private ownership through an IPO, another equity capital markets transaction or trade sale; or the process through which listed securities are bought back by one or more major shareholders and de-listed.

proceeds: The amount of money raised by a company in an IPO. Can also be expressed as net proceeds, after deduction of the gross fees and expenses to be borne by the issuer.

professional investors: Accredited investors, institutional investors, or high or ultra-high net worth individuals. Distinct from members of the public.

profit forecast: In the context of an IPO, a forecast made by a company of its net earnings for the reporting period immediately following an IPO. A profit forecast can sometimes be included in a domestic prospectus but more rarely in an offering circular which is given international distribution (and especially not in the US). Can also mean a forecast of earnings made, for one or more reporting periods following an IPO, by a sell-side research analyst and/or published in a pre-deal research report.

profit guarantees: Provisions whereby pre-IPO investors may be entitled to compensation if a company's profit does not meet a certain threshold in the future (compensation linked to the market price or market capitalization of the securities is generally not allowed at, and after an IPO).

***pro forma* accounts**: The accounts of a company, re-computed so as to show the financials as if the company structure today had been in existence in preceding years. It is often necessary to compute *pro forma* accounts when material mergers, acquisitions, or disposals have been conducted in the years immediately preceding an IPO.

project name: A code name given to a corporate finance transaction or an IPO for confidentiality reasons.

proprietary trading desk: Also known as a 'prop desk'. A desk within an investment bank using the bank's balance sheet to trade assets for the account of the bank itself, rather than on behalf of third-party clients. Prop desks of investment banks usually cannot act as cornerstone investors in transactions in which these investment banks are involved (unless a waiver is obtained).

prospectus: See **offering circular**.

prospectus drafting: The writing of a prospectus by legal advisers, investment banks and other parties. Traditionally, the first draft of a prospectus for an international IPO is produced by the legal advisers to the issuer.

public exposure: The publication of a draft IPO prospectus on the website of a stock exchange or regulator for the benefit of members of the public.

public offering: A tranche within the offer structure for an IPO and an offering made to retail investors, usually only in the jurisdiction where the shares are listed. The main purpose of a public offering is often to obtain at least the minimum number of public shareholders to qualify for listing. Also called retail offering.

pulling a deal: The action of discontinuing the execution or marketing process for an IPO or for another related transaction. Deals are often pulled as a result of adverse market conditions, poor reception by investors, or low valuation. They can also be pulled because of poor reception during a cornerstone investor process.

put or exit options: Options granted to pre-IPO investors to put back their investments to the issuer or its controlling shareholder. These are generally only allowed when the terms of a pre-IPO investment clearly state that such put or exit option can only be exercised when the listing does not take place.

Qualified Institutional Buyer (QIB): A type of US institutional investor that can be accessed by a non-US issuer through a Rule 144A private placement. This includes most US institutional investors with discretionary assets under management above US$100 million, smaller banks and savings and loan associations with an audited net worth of at least US$25 million, and registered brokers or dealers managing assets of at least US$10 million on a discretionary basis. There are several thousand QIBs.

real estate investment trust (REIT): A type of transaction structure whereby real estate assets can be monetized through an IPO. Through a REIT, the owner of property assets (also called sponsor) can transfer part of its ownership to institutional and public investors through the listing of a vehicle. The sponsor can then set up a REIT manager, which is paid management fees as a percentage of the value of the deposited properties owned by the REIT, as well as performance fees, either based on the net property income or on the performance of the REIT. Acquisition fees on the value of new property acquired as well as divestment fees on the value of divested property are also charged. REITs are now popular in many countries. As with business trusts, REITs are traded in units, rather than shares. See also **business trust**.

red chips: Companies from mainland China listed in Hong Kong which have, after a reorganization and prior to listing, transferred their assets and liabilities to an offshore entity, usually a Cayman Islands company.

red (or red herring): Another term for a preliminary offering circular.

Regulation D of the Securities Act of 1933 (Reg. D): An exemption from registration for the resale of securities to accredited investors (as defined under Rule 501 of the Securities Act) in the US. In effect, this is a somewhat wider exemption from registration than that permitted under Rule 144A. It is used mainly for follow-on transactions such as block trades. See also **Rule 144A of the Securities Act of 1933 (Rule 144A)**.

Regulation S of the Securities Act of 1933 (Reg. S): An exemption from registration for the resale of securities, enabling the sale of shares by a non-US issuer to offshore US institutional investors. When no listing in the US is being sought, the institutional offering or placement is conducted pursuant to either Regulation S or Rule 144A. See also **Rule 144A of the Securities Act of 1933 (Rule 144A)**.

regulator: A body established in most jurisdictions to regulate the securities or financial industry.

re-IPO: See **initial public offering (IPO)**.

related-party transactions: Transactions with companies or persons connected to an issuer or its directors, sometimes made on preferential terms or not on an arm's length basis. In connection with an IPO, related-party transactions are prohibited or must be disclosed in the prospectus after an exemption or specific waiver has been sought and obtained from the regulator or stock exchange. Also called RPTs or connected-party transactions.

representation and attendance rights: This may include rights to nominate senior management and committee representatives contractually granted to pre-IPO investors. Because such appointments are subject to the decision of the board of the company, the directors are not contractually obligated to approve pre-IPO investor nominations without further review, since they owe fiduciary duties to all shareholders.

representations and warranties: In the context of an IPO, usually contractual representations and warranties on the part of the issuer, and of the selling shareholders, with respect to their ownership of the shares (for example, representations that these have not been pledged to a third party), information disclosed in the offering circular, maintenance of listing and their ability to enter into the various agreements. They also warrant that they will abide by the terms of their respective lock-ups. Cornerstone investors also make representations and warranties in the non-disclosure agreement and subscription agreement.

re-pricing: In an IPO, an adjustment made to the price range (and, ultimately the IPO price) used for bookbuilding, either upwards or downwards, in order to respond to market conditions or to poor (or strong) investor demand for the shares, as the case may be. Infrequent in Asia and Europe but, conversely, quite common in the US.

research analyst: Usually, a sell-side equity research analyst employed by an investment bank, with a regional or country focus, or an industry sector specialty. Research analysts are assigned coverage of, and produce research reports on, companies for the benefit of their institutional investor clients. In the context of an IPO, research analysts produce pre-deal research and conduct investor education. See also **pre-deal research** and **pre-marketing**.

re-set: A term used for a feature of certain convertible or exchangeable bonds (most particularly in Asia) when a downward adjustment to the conversion price is made in certain circumstances. A re-set usually encourages an issuer to refinance the bond or perhaps to force conversion. Also called refix.

retail discount: A discount over the institutional offer price for the benefit of retail investors participating in an IPO. Retail discounts are now uncommon. See also **discount to offer price**.

retail investor: A qualifying individual investor targeted, and participating in a public offering. Equivalent to public investor.

retail offering: See **public offering**.

retail tranche: See **public offering**.

reverse roadshow: The process through which potential investors approach or visit an issuer directly (rather than the other way around), perhaps with a view to making an investment in the shares of a company, often by way of a strategic or cornerstone investment.

right of first refusal: A right granted to a party similar to a call option and giving it the option to enter into a contractual arrangement before such an arrangement is opened to other parties. For example, rights whereby the controlling shareholder of a company may grant a right of first refusal to a pre-IPO investor, so that the controlling shareholder must first offer to sell shares to the pre-IPO investor at the same price and on the same terms and conditions as a proposed sale of shares to a third-party purchaser. If the pre-IPO investor does not exercise its right of first refusal, it is then permitted to include its shares for sale together—that is, to tag along—with the shares of the controlling shareholder as part of the sale to the third-party purchaser. Such rights can normally survive the listing of a company since they are purely contractual rights between two shareholders.

risk factors: A key section of the offering circular, usually located in the first few pages of the document and providing investors with an extensive list of factors which could materially and adversely affect the financial condition or results of operations of the issuer or the performance of the shares if they were to occur. Risk factors, which are included for the protection of the company, include a detailed narrative.

roadshow: A series of meetings between a company and institutional investors set up by one or more investment banks. A roadshow may be organized irrespective of any capital markets transaction (see **non-deal roadshow**) or in connection with an IPO or another related transaction. A roadshow usually comprises large group presentations, small group presentations, and one-on-one meetings. Sometimes, video or audio conferences may also be arranged, as well as an Internet roadshow. See also **one-on-one meetings**.

roadshow presentation: The presentation delivered by the management of a company during a roadshow. The roadshow presentation for an IPO is usually drafted by one or more of the lead investment banks and often includes a short video presentation, slides, and a script, as well as a list of questions and answers, all of which are also vetted by legal advisers.

Rule 144A of the Securities Act of 1933 (Rule 144A): a set of rules enacted in 1991 in the US which enable the marketing of securities issued or sold by foreign companies by way of a private placement to Qualified Institutional Buyers (QIBs) in the US.

safe-harbour rules for stabilization: A set of rules issued by a stock exchange setting out how the stabilization of a new equity issue may be conducted and offering a safe harbour for such stabilization activities from allegations of market manipulation. Most markets have explicit safe-harbour rules with respect to stabilization, although certain emerging markets do not.

sale and purchase agreement: An underwriting agreement for the placement or institutional offer tranche of an IPO.

sales trader: See **trader**.

scaling back: The action of reducing the amount of securities ultimately allocated to an investor, as compared with the order initially placed by that investor.

script: Usually, a one-page document used by the bookrunners to (verbally) pitch potential cornerstone subscriptions to investors. This is normally based on publicly available information. Access to more information will only be given after the signing of a non-disclosure agreement by each of the potential cornerstone investors. See also **confidentiality agreement**.

SEC-registered offering: An equity capital markets transaction registered with the Securities and Exchange Commission (SEC) in the US and therefore targeted at both retail investors and institutional investors in the US (and, often, internationally).

secondary listing: See **dual listing**.

secondary offering: Either the sale of securities by a shareholder in an equity capital markets (ECM) transaction (including an IPO); or a follow-on ECM transaction. Distinct from a primary offering. See also **primary offering**.

Securities and Exchange Commission (SEC): The US regulator for the securities industry, based in Washington.

Securities and Futures Commission (SFC): The regulator for the securities market in Hong Kong.

Securities Commission Malaysia (*Suruhanjaya Sekuriti*): The regulator for the securities market in Malaysia, which reviews and registers prospectuses for IPOs listed on Bursa Malaysia.

sell-down: The sale of securities by one or more investors in an IPO or related transaction.

selling restrictions: Restrictions drafted by legal advisers and included in both the plan of distribution (or underwriting) section of a prospectus and the sale and purchase agreement. Selling restrictions set out the jurisdictions in which the securities on offer may be sold to institutional investors by way of private placements. On occasion, the selling restrictions include specific language or disclosure for the benefit of investors in a particular jurisdiction.

sell-side: The securities side of an investment bank, including research analysts, salespeople, sales-traders, and traders.

sequential retail offering: A retail offering that is conducted at a fixed price and after the offer price has been determined at the end of the institutional offering. This generally implies a somewhat longer settlement timetable for institutional investors.

settlement: The payment of the consideration for the securities by investors to (generally) one of the lead banks, for onward payment, minus fees, to the issuer and/or selling shareholders, against the delivery of the securities, usually on a delivery versus payment (DVP) basis.

several underwriting obligations: The usual underwriting arrangement for equity capital markets transactions (including IPOs) whereby shares underwritten by an investment bank defaulting on its obligations are not taken up by the other underwriters.

shareholding threshold: The number of shares bought (or subsequently sold) by an investor making such shareholding publicly disclosable.

share registrar and transfer agent: Usually, a single institution undertaking both roles and tasked with maintaining a record of shareholders in a listed company to establish authenticity of ownership, ensure the accurate payment of dividends, and offer shareholders the opportunity to take up their rights in the event of a rights issue. It is also the responsibility of the share registrar to process and ballot applications from retail investors and to send share certificates to applicants allocated shares in an IPO.

site visits: Visits or tours made by investment banks, advisers, or investors to a company's premises and/or production facilities.

'soft' underwriting: The usual type of underwriting arrangement for the institutional tranche of an IPO, whereby the securities on offer are underwritten once the book of institutional demand has closed and the offer price has been determined. In effect, a soft (or best efforts) underwriting only underwrites the rather remote risk of one or more institutional investors defaulting on their settlement obligations. A soft underwriting is the opposite of a hard underwriting arrangement. See also **'hard' underwriting**.

sovereign wealth fund (SWF): An investment fund set up by the government of a country. SWFs include revenue stabilization funds, which are designed to temper the impact of volatile revenues (for example, oil and gas revenues), and holding funds, which manage government participations or direct investments in state-owned or other enterprises and savings funds, typically devoted to the funding of future pension liabilities. Some sovereign wealth funds are also set up to manage excess foreign reserves. A variety of investment styles, depending on the purposes of such funds, can be found among SWFs. A number of names are well known as significant, high-quality investors in IPOs.

special purpose vehicle (SPV): A company set up for the purpose of carrying out a financial transaction, generally in a tax-efficient manner, for example, the issue of a Eurobond or convertible bond. In this case, SPVs often benefit from a guarantee by their parent company. Cornerstone investors (and especially corporates) often use SPVs (for example, British Virgin Islands–incorporated companies) to effect the transaction.

special rights: Rights granted by a company to pre-IPO investors. For example, these may include price adjustments; put or exit options; director nomination rights; veto rights; anti-dilution rights; profit guarantees; negative pledges; prior consent for certain corporate actions and changes in the articles of the company; exclusivity rights and no more favourable terms; information rights; representation and attendance rights; rights of first refusal and tag-along rights; or compensation provisions in the event the company does not get admitted to listing within a specified period of time.

spin-off: A financial transaction whereby an entire division or subsidiary of a listed company becomes listed as a stand-alone business.

sponsor: A bank, usually (but not always) an underwriter of an IPO, whose responsibility is to advise the issuer on listing and disclosure matters and to liaise with the relevant regulator or stock exchange on documentation matters, with a view to sponsoring the issuer for listing. This term can also be used to designate a corporate selling part of the ownership of some of its property or other assets into a real estate investment trust (REIT) or business trust.

spread of shareholders: The number of public shareholders of a company. Usually, a minimum spread of shareholders (several hundred to several thousand) is required by a stock exchange for a company to be listed.

stabilization: The process through which a stabilizing agent or manager, appointed among the lead banks in an IPO, can resolve imbalances between short-term buyers and sellers in the first trading days or weeks of an IPO and support the share price when it falls below the offer price. The main tool used to stabilize an IPO is an overallotment option. See also **Greenshoe**, **overallotment option**, and **naked short**.

strategic investor: See **pre-IPO investment**.

subscription agreement: An agreement under which a strategic or cornerstone investor agrees to purchase a specified number of shares in a company at an agreed price.

syndicate: A group of investment banks or brokers formed for the purpose of marketing, selling and, generally, underwriting securities.

syndicate structure: How a syndicate of underwriters is organized, taking into account seniority levels among underwriters, across various tranches or jurisdictions.

target investor: An investor identified by an investment bank or broker as a suitable candidate to invest in size in a particular transaction, usually because of its investment style or track record of investing in securities with a similar profile. See also **pilot fishing**.

termination clause: A clause pursuant to which a subscription or an underwriting obligation might be terminated at the option of the investor or underwriter under certain circumstances, usually as a result of a breach of some of the representations and warranties made by the issuer. *Force majeure* clauses also provide for the termination of underwriting agreements in certain exceptional circumstances. See also ***force majeure* clause**.

trader: Also called market maker. An employee of an investment bank or broker tasked with buying and selling securities in the financial markets either on behalf of clients served by salespeople, or for the account of the bank itself (in the case of a proprietary trader). By contrast, a sales trader talks directly to institutional clients to promote new investment ideas and also provides market execution.

trading: The level of buying and selling by investors in a particular security, as measured over a period of time.

tranche: A defined component of a syndicate of underwriters or offer structure.

transaction team: In an IPO, the parties working on the execution of the transaction. The transaction team for an IPO includes members of the management of the issuer, investment bankers, several firms of legal advisers, accountants and, often, a variety of other advisers.

tycoon: A well-known, wealthy individual often chosen as a cornerstone investor in an IPO to provide early momentum and leadership. Most common in Hong Kong and other Asian IPOs.

UK Listing Authority (UKLA): An authority established under the Financial Conduct Authority (FCA) in the UK, which, among other things, reviews and approves prospectuses for IPOs. It also monitors market disclosure by issuers and operates the UK listing regime.

ultra-high net worth individual: A person with investable assets of at least US$30 million, excluding personal assets and property such as a primary residence, collectibles and other durable consumer goods.

under-subscription: A situation where demand generated from investors is below the number of shares offered in an IPO (or a tranche of an IPO).

underwriting: A contractual arrangement whereby one or more investment banks or brokers commit to purchasing shares in a company at an agreed price. Underwriting may be subject to conditions precedent. See also **'hard' underwriting** and **'soft' underwriting**.

underwriting agreement: An agreement evidencing an underwriting arrangement. Often called a sale and purchase agreement for a placement or institutional offer tranche.

underwriting commission: A component of the gross fees payable by an issuer and/or selling shareholder(s) to a syndicate of underwriters.

underwriting section: See **plan of distribution**.

units: Securities that are the equivalent of shares for business trusts and real estate investment trusts (REITs).

use of proceeds: Disclosure made by a company about the use it will make of moneys raised by it in an IPO of equity (or debt) offering. This may, for example, include acquisitions or the retirement of debt. Material changes to the use of proceeds constitute price-sensitive information and must be disclosed.

US securities laws undertakings: Undertakings made by an investor in an agreement in connection with the issue of securities to certify, among other things, that it is a Qualified Institutional Buyer (QIB) as defined in Rule 144A under the US Securities Act of 1933 (and also a 'qualified purchaser' (as defined in Section 2(a)(51)(A) of the US Investment Company Act of 1940)); or, alternatively, not a US person and located outside the United States (within the meaning of Regulation S [or Reg. S] under the Securities Act). See also **Regulation S of the Securities Act of 1933 (Reg. S)** and **Rule 144A of the Securities Act of 1933 (Rule 144A)**.

valuation: The theoretical or actual value of a company in connection with an IPO, using an appropriate valuation methodology and level for the business.

veto rights: Part of the special rights that may be granted by a company to pre-IPO investors. For example, this may include contractual rights to exercise veto power over some of the major corporate actions to be made by the company, such as the making of any petition or passing of any resolution for winding-up, the carrying on of businesses other than the business being carried on by the company, or the amalgamation or merger by any member of the group with any other company or legal entity, etc. Such rights must be terminated upon listing.

waiver: In the context of an IPO, the permission granted to an issuer by a regulator or stock exchange to undertake certain transactions otherwise prohibited under the listing rules. Also used where a bookrunner waives the lock-up adhering to shares owned by an investor or shareholder.

wealth management: See **private bank**.

About the author

Philippe Espinasse spent almost two decades working as a senior investment banker in the US, Europe, and Asia. He now lives in Hong Kong, where he writes and works as an independent consultant.

He is also an honorary lecturer in the Faculty of Law of the University of Hong Kong and sits on the board of a financial institution listed on the Taiwan Stock Exchange as an independent, non-executive director, chairman of the audit committee, and a member (former chairman) of the remuneration committee.

He has published several books on IPOs and has contributed articles to a variety of newspapers and magazines, including *The Wall Street Journal*, *South China Morning Post*, *Nikkei Asian Review*, *China Economic Review*, and the website of BBC News. He pens the 'Clawback' column on Asian equity capital markets for Euromoney's *GlobalCapital*.

He has also published two novels, *Hard Underwriting* and *The Traveler*, both thrillers set in contemporary Hong Kong.

Philippe may be contacted through his websites, www.ipo-book.com (which includes a blog on equity capital markets news and developments) and www.philippe-espinasse.com.

Index

Note: Page numbers in italics refer to tables.